W9-BRU-408

THE GREAT EMPIRES OF THE ANCIENT WORLD

EDITED BY

Thomas Harrison

The J. Paul Getty Museum
Los Angeles

'Look back over the past, with its changing empires that rose and fell, and you can foresee the future too.'

MARCUS AURELIUS

HALF-TITLE: These colossal statues of Ramesses II, from his temple at Abu Simbel (near the border of modern Egypt and Sudan), are among the most imposing statements of royal power from all of antiquity. Created in the 13th century BC, the temple was dedicated to the most important gods of the New Kingdom, Ptah, Amun-Ra and Ra-Horakhti.

TITLE-PAGE: Detail of the carved reliefs of the monumental staircase to the Apadana, the hall in which the Persian king received visitors at the ceremonial capital of Persepolis. The sculpture was undertaken by teams, including specialists responsible for hair or clothing, to ensure a uniform style.

First published in the United Kingdom in 2009 by
Thames & Hudson Ltd,
181A High Holburn,
London, WC1V 7QX
www.thamesandhudson.com

First published in the United States of America in 2009
by the J. Paul Getty Museum, Los Angeles

Getty Publications
1200 Getty Center Drive, Suite 500
Los Angeles, California 90049-1682
www.getty.edu/publications

Library of Congress Control Number: 2009929902

ISBN 978-0-89236-987-4

Printed and bound in China by SNP Leefung Printers Ltd

Contents

INTRODUCTION
NEW VISIONS OF ANCIENT EMPIRES

The Great Empires of the Ancient World offers accessible and authoritative accounts of all the major early imperial powers, from the empires of the Hittites and New Kingdom Egypt in the 2nd millennium BC through to the early Sasanian Persian empire concluding in around AD 300, from the Mediterranean empire of Rome to the (no less vast) dominions of Qin and Han China.

These empires are united not only by the time period in which broadly they emerged and fell. The relationship between them, geographically and chronologically scattered as they were, is an immensely complex one of rivalry, succession and assimilation. Just as the Han empire of China evolved from the Qin (and indeed itself had more than a single phase), so the Mauryan, Kushan and Gupta empires of South Asia all developed in a complex relationship to their predecessors. The Parthian and Sasanian empires, which grew out of one of the successor states which emerged

from the chaos of Alexander the Great's death, both looked back to the Achaemenid Persian empire of the 6th to 4th centuries BC as a model, terming their rulers (as Indian rulers did) 'king of kings' in imitation of the Achaemenids. Both clashed violently with Rome, just as the Achaemenids had with the Greeks; and in both cases the eastern empire then suffered from having its history written by its rivals.

Why study ancient empires now? With the possible exception of the late 19th and early 20th centuries, the history of ancient empires has perhaps never been so timely or generated so much popular interest. This is evidenced, for example, by more or less successful films focused on Roman, Macedonian or Persian empires (*Gladiator* or *Alexander*), or the enormous success of museum exhibitions reappraising ancient empires such as that of the Qin terracotta warriors or the 'forgotten empire' of the Achaemenid Persians. If we are to seek the reasons for the prominence of ancient

RIGHT: A still from the Ridley Scott film *Gladiator* (2000). Gladiatorial games (often featuring exotic imported animals) took place throughout the empire, commanding vast popular audiences.

OPPOSITE: A terracotta warrior, wrapped in protective foam, waits in the old British Library Reading Room of the British Museum before forming part of the enormously successful exhibition, *The First Emperor: China's Terracotta Army.* The terracotta warriors (estimated to number more than 6,000) were buried in a pit near the unexcavated mausoleum of the first Qin emperor, Shi Huang di, in 210 BC.

EGYPTIAN

HITTITE

ASSYRIAN & BABYLONIAN

FIRST PERSIAN

ATHENIAN

HITTITE
1650–1200 BC

ASSYRIAN AND BABYLONIAN
900–539 BC

1600 BC	1500 BC	1400 BC	1300 BC	1200 BC	1100 BC	1000 BC	900 BC	800 BC	700 BC	600 BC

EGYPTIAN
1539–1069 BC

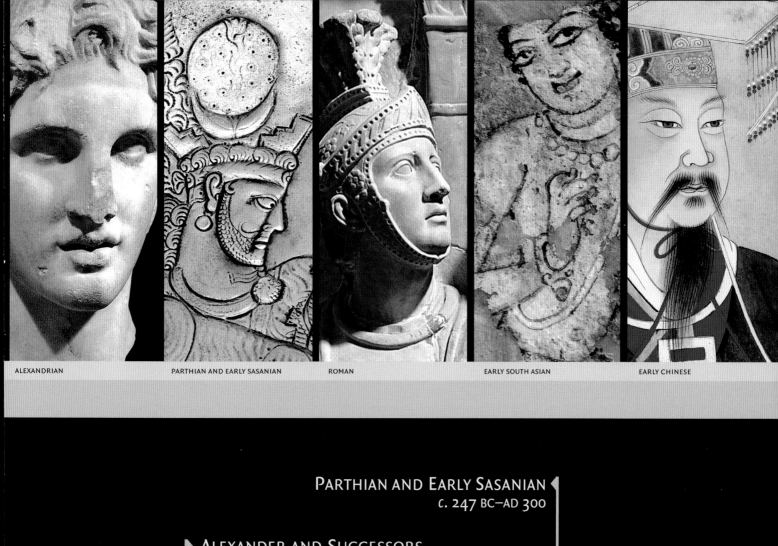

ALEXANDRIAN   PARTHIAN AND EARLY SASANIAN   ROMAN   EARLY SOUTH ASIAN   EARLY CHINESE

PARTHIAN AND EARLY SASANIAN
c. 247 BC–AD 300

ALEXANDER AND SUCCESSORS
338–60 BC

| 500 BC | 400 BC | 300 BC | 200 BC | 100 BC | 0 | AD 100 | AD 200 | AD 300 | AD 400 |

ATHENIAN
478–338 BC

EARLY EMPIRES OF INDIA
323 BC–AD 500

FIRST PERSIAN
550–330 BC

ROMAN
27 BC–AD 476

EARLY EMPIRES OF CHINA

1. The Empire of New Kingdom Egypt 1550–1070 BC
2. The Hittite Empire 1650–1200 BC
3. The Empires of Assyria and Babylonia 900–539 BC
4. The First Persian Empire 550–330 BC
5. The Athenian Empire 478–404 BC, 378–338 BC
6. The Empire of Alexander and his Successors 338–60 BC
7. The Parthian and Early Sasanian Empires c. 247 BC–AD 300
8. The Roman Empire 27 BC–AD 476
9. The Early Empires of South Asia 323 BC–AD 500
10. The Early Empires of China 221 BC–AD 220

empires in the popular consciousness, however, we should look not to Hollywood or the world of museums (both, in any event, perhaps trend-followers rather than leaders), but instead at the jostling for power among modern nations.

On the one hand, the great former imperial powers – the United Kingdom, France, Germany, Russia, among others – have all in different ways been forced to come to new understandings of their imperial pasts, all seeking to accommodate (in strikingly different ways) grand ideas of their national destinies to changed environments. Scholarship on empire has moved on in parallel: in particular, the 'postcolonial' trend in modern writing has encouraged an understanding that empires exist as much in people's minds as in external structures of control. The end of empire is no longer seen as a simple matter of the physical withdrawal from a distant colony; rather, it is now understood, empires shape people's understanding of their position in the world, long after the colonizer's flag has been packed away and the brass band departed. Increasingly, attention has focused on the personal experience of empire, on how – both among the imperial subjects and among 'imperialists' – daily life was imbued with the experience of empire.

This recognition of the indirect and personal ways in which empire may manifest itself has led also to the identification of new empires. Just as previous empires – Russia, Ottoman Turkey, as well as western Europe – have claimed to be the successors of Rome, so now the modern United States has taken its turn. The parallel – real or imagined – between America and Rome has been exploited in numerous different ways, more or less positively and more or less convincingly, by journalists, bloggers, cartoonists, as well as by the employees of neoconservative thinktanks. In a positive assessment, two of the latter, Bill Kristol and Robert Kagan, described the position of the United States in the wake of the first Iraq war as '[holding] a position unmatched since Rome dominated the Mediterranean world'. From a critical perspective, President George W. Bush was compared to (among other Roman emperors) Commodus, Caligula and Nero.

'Nero ... fiddled while Rome burned. George Bush takes yet another vacation', in the words of one blogger.

How should we respond to these parallels? Clearly, the modern appropriation of ancient empires for particular political motives can distort our understanding of ancient empires. All of the chapters in this book reflect and make accessible a vast industry of scholarly reconstruction of ancient empires. Readers can rightly turn to *The Great Empires of the Ancient World* for authoritative accounts independent of passing political currents. On the other hand, there are significant ways in which the history of ancient empires cannot be divorced from modern distortions and appropriations.

The harnessing of ancient history to modern ends is not, first, a new phenomenon. The analogy of ancient and modern empires has been expressed through any number of ways: through imitative architecture, through the heroizing dress of imperial heroes, or (very occasionally) through direct comparison: the conscious search in ancient history for answers to the problems of how to manage an empire in the modern world, how for example to deal with a racially diverse population. Modern empires have looked to a multiplicity of ancient empires for inspiration, rarely just one 'ancestor'. The founders of the American republic (an odd kind of empire admittedly) looked to Carthage as well as to Carthage's historical enemy, Rome. The British found inspiration for their own imperial rule in the Persian empire just as in the Roman. The

OPPOSITE: A detail of the Alexander Mosaic (100 BC), originally from the House of the Faun, Pompeii, but now housed in the National Archaeological Museum in Naples. The mosaic, which is probably a copy of a near-contemporary painting of Alexander, portrays the king in the midst of battle, with his gaze focusing on his bewildered opponent, the Persian Darius III.

BELOW: A bronze equestrian statue of the Roman emperor and philosopher Marcus Aurelius. Now held in a museum, it was previously at the heart of the Piazza del Campidoglio (on the Capitoline Hill in Rome) where it was moved as part of a redesign by Michelangelo.

13

OPPOSITE: Against the imposing classical background of Lutyens' New Delhi, symbol of the British Raj, Indian soldiers of the Border security force march past on their camels. Their Republic Day parade, 26 January 2009, marked the 60th anniversary of the adoption of the constitution of an independent state of India.

BELOW: The art of the Sasanians and Parthians (like the Achaemenid Persians before them) often featured fabulous creatures such as griffins and dragons. This leaded bronze figure, said to have been found near the Helmand river in Afghanistan, is probably dated to around the 2nd or 3rd centuries AD.

Germans, like the British, looked to heroes from the resistance to Roman rule – Arminius/Hermann or Boudicca – as well as to the Romans themselves. Just as with the ancient *translatio imperii*, or succession of empires, the implication is that the latest empire is the summation of its predecessors, taking on their best aspects while tempering or avoiding the worst.

It was in this kind of imperial context, crucially, that the modern understanding of ancient empires was forged. This is true in a number of ways. First, of course, the archaeological excavations which unearthed much of the evidence for the empires discussed in this book were frequently carried out under the auspices, more or less direct, of one or other imperial power. The decipherment of cuneiform – the work of a number of European scholars working simultaneously – opened the floodgates to new ways of looking at the empires of the ancient Near East (Assyrian, Babylonian, Persian among others), and so ultimately led to the undoing of 19th-century narratives, usually derived from classical sources, of decadent eastern powers. But at the same time, these modern empires clearly provided – and arguably still provide – a powerful framework for thinking about the reality of the ancient cultures being uncovered. It is hard, for example, in reflecting on the early empires of South Asia not to be influenced by pervasive images of the British Raj, to be tempted to the conclusion that they were precursors of the British unification of India – itself a much more complex phenomenon – under a single rule.

What anyway is an empire? No single term, in reality, encompasses all the empires discussed in this volume: the Athenians' short-lived naval confederacy-turned-empire was termed *archê* or simply 'rule'; the Latin *imperium*, which has given rise to our term empire (imperialism, significantly, is a modern coinage), was a term used to describe any manner of types of formal authority. Moving beyond this narrow issue of terminology, the modern term 'empire' is used arguably to describe a complete menagerie of different beasts. Some are vast and others small-scale. Some exercised rule over distant colonies, while others simply claimed hegemony over the territory of their neighbours. Some were governed by democratic governments, others by monarchies. Some were heavily bureaucratized, others seem to have possessed scant central control. Some took pains to assimilate their subjects, while others kept those they ruled at arms' length, ruling through an ethnically distinct elite. And all had different means of control at their disposal, dictated not only by technology, but also by the size and terrain of their territory. Whether indeed the term empire should rightly be applied, except by way of analogy, to all those contained in this volume is debatable. If we indeed include the contemporary United States in this list of empires, then this definition is stretched even further. Though recent years have seen some US political commentators use the term 'empire' without embarrassment, Americans have tended to style themselves as anti-imperial. Clearly, we would have to accept that the forms of control by which such an empire is maintained are also ingeniously veiled by comparison with historical empires. But then the Roman empire also was cloaked around in republican language.

One other way in which the modern experience of empire has informed the way we look at the empires of the ancient world concerns the moral judgments we make about them. This is true in two ways. A number of chapters in this volume point to the manner in which the empires in question, those of the ancient Near East, have persistently been characterized as morally flawed or decadent,

The Gate of All Nations, also known as the Xerxes Gate, was the ceremonial entrance of the Persian king's capital of Persepolis. With its doorway flanked by vast figures of winged bulls with human heads, the Gate was clearly intended to awe visitors to the Great King.

while other empires have had a more positive colouring in scholarship. This is explicable partly by the 'orientalist' assumptions of the first narratives, partly by a historical dependence on ancient sources written from other perspectives: our portrayal of the Persian king Xerxes, for example, has been formed by the account of the Greek-Persian wars of (the Greek) Herodotus, just as the Babylonian Nebuchadnezzar's image has been formed through biblical accounts of the Babylonian exile of the Jews that he initiated.

This kind of unthinking moralism inherited from ancient sources is mostly a thing of the past. In broader terms, however, moralism cannot be escaped so easily. It is still tempting in looking at ancient empires (or indeed any empires) to seek to weigh them on moral scales: to deem, for example, that a degree of financial exploitation was comfortably outweighed by the protection afforded to the imperial subjects, or by the 'civilizing mission'

of the imperial power. It is perhaps not an accident, however, that this kind of approach – that of the moral balance-sheet – was one commonly adopted in the context of modern empires, born out of a (more or less) self-conscious desire to vindicate empire. Persisting with these moral scales in mind then might unwittingly reflect the perspective of the imperial power rather than of the subjects of empire – a difference that one can see clearly if one looks at potential modern parallels. One British journalist, Jonathan Freedland, has compared the attractions of togas and central heating in the Roman world with what the US offers the people of the world today: 'It's not togas or gladiatorial games... but Starbucks, Coca-Cola, McDonald's and Disney, all paid for in the contemporary equivalent of Roman coinage ... the dollar.' Ingesting Coca-Cola, however, does not involve ingesting American cultural values, still less a commitment to US foreign policy goals.

Would the subjects of ancient empires have been any less ambivalent in their response to others' attempts to 'civilize' them?

So how in the final analysis should we look at ancient empires? The Greek historian Thucydides, one of the first theorists of empire (more recently described as the 'favourite neoconservative text on foreign affairs'), strikingly made the Athenians say in justification of their rule over their Greek neighbours that 'It has always been a rule that the weak should be subject to the strong.' Empire (broadly defined now to include any attempt by one political organization systematically to dominate others) is simply a fact of life then, and what we can learn from ancient empires is limited by the different conditions in which they operated. Thucydides adds, however, an Athenian afterthought: 'Besides we consider that we are worthy of our power'. What distinguishes one 'empire' from another is partly the means of control

at its disposal, but also perhaps the unique way in which it imagines and seeks to justify itself: brazenly insisting that its rule is justified by past achievements; claiming the mantle (like the Achaemenid Persian empire) of the benign global policeman putting squabbling nations in order, or that the limits of one's empire are the limits of civilization (as with Rome or Qin China); or somehow projecting a sense of timelessness and inevitability, of the universal nature of one set of values (as with the modern USA).

In the Athenians' case also, the inevitability of empire is just another plank of their self-justification. When we focus on this ideological aspect of empires, their ability to recreate themselves endlessly, the differences between ancient and modern empires strip away. It is this complex relationship between past and present, between modern interpreter and ancient empire, that *The Great Empires of the Ancient World* seeks to describe.

Abraham Lincoln sits gazing through the columns of his memorial out onto the National Mall in Washington DC. Dedicated in 1922, the Lincoln Memorial was modelled on the temple of Zeus at Olympia; inscribed on its walls are the texts of both the Gettysburg Address and Lincoln's second inaugural speech as president, both again influenced by classical models.

The civilization of ancient Egypt has probably been the subject of more intense fascination than any other ancient culture. Napoleon's Egyptian campaign at the turn of the 18th to 19th centuries prompted a mass Western 'Egyptomania'. Even ancient writers – most famously, the Greek historian Herodotus – fixated on Egyptian culture and history: on hieroglyphs or on mummification, on the centrality of the Nile, and above all on Egypt's antiquity. The power that Egypt exercised has perhaps been less of a focus of attention, however. For periods in its history – especially during the New Kingdom period (broadly the second half of the 2nd millennium BC) – Egypt's influence stretched in varying degrees south and west through Africa, east across the Levant, and north across the Mediterranean Sea. It was a power which rested on strong trading links and a formidable economy, on vast mineral and agricultural wealth, and on a firmly rooted religious ideology built around the figure of the king.

Pharaohs of the New Kingdom

18TH DYNASTY

1539–1514 BC	Ahmose I
1514–1493 BC	Amenhotep I
1493–1481 BC	Thutmose I
1481–1479 BC	Thutmose II
1479–1425 BC	Thutmose III
(1473–1458 BC	Hatshepsut)
1426–1400 BC	Amenhotep II
1400–1390 BC	Thutmose IV
1390–1353 BC	Amenhotep III
1353–1336 BC	Akhenaten
1336–1332 BC	Smenkhkara
1332–1322 BC	Tutankhamun
1322–1319 BC	Ay
1319–1292 BC	Horemheb

19TH DYNASTY

1292–1290 BC	Ramesses I
1290–1279 BC	Sety I
1279–1213 BC	Ramesses II
1213–1204 BC	Merenptah
1204–1198 BC	Sety II
(1202–1200 BC	Amenmesse)
1198–1193 BC	Siptah
1198–1190 BC	Twosret

20TH DYNASTY

1190–1187 BC	Sethnakhte
1187–1156 BC	Ramesses III
1156–1150 BC	Ramesses IV
1150–1145 BC	Ramesses V
1145–1137 BC	Ramesses VI
1137–1129 BC	Ramesses VII
1129–1126 BC	Ramesses VIII
1126–1108 BC	Ramesses IX
1108–1099 BC	Ramesses X
1099–1069 BC	Ramesses XI

PREVIOUS PAGES: Ramesses III (*c.* 1187–1156 BC) hunting wild bulls in the marshes, as shown on the gateway of his great temple at Medinet Habu. Pharaoh pursuing all forces of disorder to the very edges of the earth, in accordance with the will of the gods, was not only the image but also the idea underlying the expansion of the New Kingdom regime.

LEFT: An African emperor. The innermost of three coffins for Tutankhamun was beaten from more than 100 kg of gold. The king ruled when the New Kingdom's wealth and influence were at their zenith, and his gold identifies him with the glory of the sun-god. Inscribed inside are the words of Thoth, god of wisdom; 'Greetings, O Perfect-of-face, possessor of sun-rays, whom Mortality has completed, whom Burial has exalted.'

HITTITE
EMPIRE

Caspian
Sea

Mycenae

ARZAWA

CILICIA

ASSYRIA

Carchemish

Nineveh

MITANNI

Assur

ALASHIYA

SYRIA

MESOPOTAMIA

LEBANON

Byblos

Qadesh

Euphrates

Mediterranean Sea

GALILEE

Cyrene

Babylon

Tigris

Megiddo

Nippur

Tanis

Gaza

Ur

Avaris
Heliopolis

Persian
Gulf

LIBYA

Memphis

SINAI

FAIYUM

ARABIA

Heracleopolis

Akhtaten

Abydos

Thebes
el-Kab

Aswan

Nile

AKOYTA

Abu Simbel
Buhen
Semna

Red Sea

WAWAT

Sai

KUSH

KAROY

Kerma
Kawa

Napata

AREM

0   400 km

0   300 miles

Area of New Kingdom government ('Black Land')

Maximum extent of New Kingdom control

Timeline

Ahmose defeats
Hyksos kingdom
1530s BC

Hatshepsut's
expedition
to Punt
1470 BC

Tutankhamun's troops
clash with Hittites
1320s BC

Ramesses II
clashes with
Hittites at battle
of Qadesh 1274 BC

Ramesses III drives away Libyan
invaders and 'Sea-peoples'
1180s BC

Troops of (viceroy)
Panehsī occupy Thebes
1088 BC

1500 BC   1400 BC   1300 BC   1200 BC   1100 BC   1000 BC

Thutmose I invades
Kush, then takes army
to Byblos and Mitanni
1480s BC

Thutmose III leads army
at ___ e of Megiddo
1457 BC

Akhenaten suppresses major
rebellion near Nubian goldmines

Merenptah drives
away Libyan
invaders 1209 BC

New dynasty (19th), from
the family of Ramesses I

New dy___ty (20th),
from the family of
Sethnakhte 1190 BC

Campaign of (general)
Piankh against Panehsī
ends in division of Egypt
1082 BC

For a moment in history, which we now call the New Kingdom, Egypt was the richest, most powerful and most influential nation on Earth. The moment lasted for 400 years, from the reign of Thutmose III (*c.* 1479–1425 BC) until the death of the 11th king named Ramesses (*c.* 1099–1069 BC). During those centuries, a nation with a history stretching back, so it

believed, to the very beginning of time, matured to become a populous, multi-ethnic powerhouse of surpassing wealth and intellectual conviction, harnessed to a traditional system of government and a proven military tradition. The gold-mines of Nubia underwrote Egypt's position as the world's richest economy; and far-flung trading networks were founded on brotherhood with nations across northeast Africa, the Near East and the Mediterranean Sea.

The government, religion and art of New Kingdom Egypt were firmly rooted after 1,500 years of rule by god-kings, who from this time would be known as pharaohs. For Thutmose III (54 years as pharaoh) or Ramesses II (67 years), sacred sites such as the Great Sphinx and pyramids at Giza were already ancient and had stood through the ages as proof of the validity of Egypt's most fundamental beliefs. They inspired the pharaohs to rebuild the temples of gods and the monuments of their forefathers, or to 'build anew' and 'increase what was bequeathed to me'. This last sentiment – equating success with family, obligation and expansion – was integral to kingship. Reflecting on his own success as king, in the words of a monument at his southernmost frontier, Thutmose III concedes:

> 'My father, Amun-Ra, was the one who
> did it, it was not an act of man.'

Accordingly, grateful pharaohs rewarded the temples of Amun-Ra and the other gods ever more lavishly with land and labour, with tax revenues and commercial privileges, and with festivals. In so doing, the rulers of the New Kingdom built and bequeathed the Ancient Egypt of our modern imagination.

Belief in Black Land

Historians during the New Kingdom recognized an ebb and flow of power within Egypt. The land, stretching more than 1,000 km (620 miles) along the Nile from the Mediterranean coast to Nubia, had first become a nation with one king and one palace by about 3000 BC. However, in the century preceding the New Kingdom, the land had been carved into three, with kings based at Avaris in the Nile delta, at Thebes in the Nile valley, and at Kerma in Nubia. The kings who ruled Avaris for 108 years styled themselves as Hyksos, 'rulers of foreign lands', a title that has been taken to indicate that they were themselves foreigners, not conquerors of foreign lands. Certainly their towns shared strong cultural, commercial and, presumably, political links with towns in Palestine and Syria as well as with those of the Nile valley. Avaris itself straddled important trade-routes to the Near East and was a major port for the Mediterranean world. In Nubia, a confederation of chiefs recognized at their head a Ruler of Kush, the southern part of Nubia, whose culture, as revealed in archaeology, was distinctly un-Egyptian but whose economic and military clout was considerable. Throughout these two kingdoms a cosmopolitan mix of

OPPOSITE: Statue of Thutmose III from the temple of Amun-Ra at Karnak. In modern accounts of ancient Egypt, Thutmose has been transformed into the 'Napoleon of Egypt', and serves as an icon of the New Kingdom imperial adventure.

23

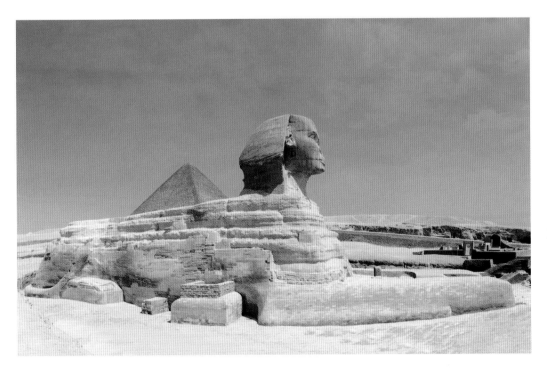

Egypt was already ancient by the New Kingdom, and monuments such as the Great Sphinx at Giza seemed to trace the nation's history to the beginning of time. A complex of temples and royal monuments developed around the Great Sphinx during the New Kingdom.

A pectoral charm of King Ahmose, from the very beginning of the New Kingdom, conforms to Egypt's most ancient images of kingship. The king is shown as the captain of the Sun's boat, whose course is also that of all the activities of this world. Amun and Thoth, the gods of the most secret and profound knowledge, anoint and purify him as he guides the way, and the goddesses, shown as vultures, surround him with the caresses of those who also devour carrion.

ethnic groups and languages had developed over centuries, including ethnic Egyptians living and working in Nubia.

The kings of Thebes, unlike many of their countrymen, saw this state of affairs as a travesty of good order. On one stela erected in the temple of Amun-Ra at Karnak, King Kamose (c. 1541–1539 BC) laments:

> 'Why do I contemplate my might, when there is a Chief in Avaris and another in Kush? I sit joined to an Asiatic and a Nubian, each man holding his slice of this Black Land, dividing the land with me?'

Believing that the rich soil of the Nile-lands formed a single Black Land (kōme), Kamose vowed to 'seek out Asiatics, to crush their places, because east and west are covered with their grease'. So, as the 16th century unfolded, the Theban dynasty was honing its weapons for an orgy of ethnic cleansing.

Kamose's first attack, on Kush, is mentioned only obliquely in sources, but monuments of his at the old fortress of Buhen confirm that he began by taking control of Wawat, the northern part of Nubia. In contrast, the assault on the kingdom of Avaris is described in some detail in the temple of Amun-Ra. First, the population of Nefrusy is slaughtered because it had made 'a nest for Asiatics'. Later his troops intercept a letter from the king of Avaris, Apōp, begging help from Kush. Apōp seems not only afraid but impotent, and soon Kamose has flown with his falcon-fleet to Avaris itself. The city is massively fortified so the Theban marines cannot capture it, but they ravage its estates and orchards, and loot chariot-teams, battle-axes, oils, foreign timber, precious metals and stones from the shipyards. Kamose returns home to streets brimming with excitement and delight, but grim events had been set in motion.

Kamose died suddenly and his successor, Ahmose I (*c.* 1539–1514 BC), was just a child, so a stalemate between Thebes and Avaris prevailed for at least a decade. Nevertheless, the dogma of Black Land held sway within the Theban regime, and Ahmose's eventual campaigns against his Hyksos enemy are well documented in tomb inscriptions, such as those of Ahmose-Saibana and Ahmose-Pennekhbet. Both were marines from the town of el-Kab, keen to record the decorations, slaves and grants of land that they earned from the pharaoh. Ahmose took control of the ancient capital, Memphis; then came as many as five campaigns against Avaris, with savage fighting throughout the rivers and canals of the Nile delta. Ahmose-Saibana relates the outcome starkly:

> 'Avaris was plundered, and I took plunder away from it – one man, three women, i.e. four heads – and the king gave me them for slaves.'

Finally, Theban forces set upon Sharuhen, a fortified town near Gaza in Palestine, at the end of the Horus-roads that crossed the Sinai desert. Once again, Ahmose's marines were hobbled by the need for siege warfare but, after three campaigns, its population also lay slaughtered. Ahmose I had stripped Avaris of its independence, brought the caravans from Palestine under his control and asserted a boundary between Black Land and the lands beyond Sinai that had been obscured in the activities of the Hyksos.

Ahmose's usurpation of control throughout Egypt and Wawat was complete by the end of his reign, although he did face two uprisings against the new order. One was led by 'Aata, probably a Nubian chieftain, 'whose fate hastened his doom', according to Ahmose-Saibana. The second was in Egypt, perhaps in the newly conquered delta. Ahmose's regime was not without opponents but the Theban vision of Black Land prevailed, and in time his son succeeded as Amenhotep I. A generation later, Amenhotep died without a surviving son, but the throne passed unchallenged to a courtier, Thutmose I (*c.* 1493–1481 BC), who fathered a dynasty that ruled Black Land until the death of Tutankhamun, some 175 years later.

SWALLOWING NUBIA

Nubian opposition to Egyptian control was expected. Any expansion, whether along the river or into the surrounding deserts, was bound to be at the expense of Kush, so the annexation of Nubia entailed decades of war. From the reign of Kamose, a new office, 'King's Son', was used to govern the occupied lands; it was never held by an actual son of the king, but his title indicated the elevated status of a viceroy. Kamose had annexed Wawat as far as Buhen, and Amenhotep I as far as the fortified island of Sai, but the troops of Thutmose I campaigned into Kush itself, to Tombos, just 30 km (19 miles) from Kerma. Thutmose also divided Wawat into five districts to negate opposition from within the land's traditional tribal structure. Indigenous chiefs were accorded the status of Egyptian courtiers and encouraged to prosper from the subjugation of their own countrymen. A rebellion instigated by Kush was suppressed by Thutmose II *c.* 1481 BC, once again with great ferocity, at which point the annexation of Wawat was effectively complete.

In broad terms, New Kingdom policy towards Nubia was shaped by two considerations. On the one hand, Wawat and Kush were evidently part of Black Land,

The funerary stela from Buhen in Wawat of an ethnic Egyptian named Sopdhir. Although his name is Egyptian and the text is written in Egyptian, it records his loyal service to the 'Ruler of Kush'.

Stela of the Hyksos, Khyan. As with other Hyksos monuments, the artistic tradition is unequivocally Egyptian and the text, which mentions the 'eldest King's Son', Yanesse, is written in the Egyptian language.

BELOW RIGHT: In balanced scenes at the top of the stela from the temple of Armant, Thutmose III is handed the symbols of power by Montju, the god of war. Behind the king on each side, the goddesses represent Egyptian towns, including Armant herself.

Voices of Empire

In the two centuries since Egyptian hieroglyphs were first deciphered, our basic sources for ancient Egypt have been royal monuments such as temple reliefs and stelae. Yet they were not set up as a witness to history but to the pharaoh's divinity, so alliances and wars are mentioned only in passing or simply overlooked. The battle of Megiddo is prominent on monuments of Thutmose III because it exemplified his supposed authority over every land, but other campaigns are barely visible in the royal record. However, the discovery of the Amarna Archive in 1887, written mostly in Akkadian, the principal diplomatic language of the age, furnished a detailed source for the period c. 1350–1325 BC to complement the rhetoric of the monuments. For the second half of the New Kingdom, a wealth of documents and letters has survived from the village of the royal tomb-builders at Deir el-Medina in Thebes. These occasionally reveal the impact of dynastic affairs on the lives of other Egyptians, albeit Egyptians with high social status and exceptional literacy.

The dawn of the battle of Megiddo is described in the Annals of Thutmose III, a sequence of reliefs around the sanctuary of the temple of Amun-Ra at Karnak

'Year 23, 1st month of Dry-time, day 21; the exact day of the festival of the new moon. His person appeared at dawn. Now, an order was given to the entire army to [move out]. His person set out on a chariot of electrum, clad in his regalia of war like Horus, strong of arm and lord of action, and Montju of Thebes. His father Amun … was the protection of his body in the fighting, and the strength [of Seth] ran through his limbs. Then his person overwhelmed them at the head of his army … They were fleeing headlong to Megiddo with fearful faces, having abandoned their horses and their chariots of gold and silver so they could be pulled by ropes and even their clothes to that town.'

'At a slab of copper [the pharaoh] shot … Afterwards his person placed an example in the house of Amun: a target of wrought copper three-fingers thick with his arrow in it, after he had driven it through leaving a palm-length protruding behind, in order to make those who were in his attendance pray for the strength in might and victory of his arms.'

The supernatural prowess of Thutmose III (c. 1479–1425 BC) from a stela in the temple of Armant

'As for the gold that I wrote to you about: send me however much you have … Then I may finish the work I have started. If … you send the gold that I wrote to you about, then I will let you have my daughter.'

An unnamed correspondent in the Amarna Archive pleads with the pharaoh for this precious commodity, one Egypt had in abundance

Abdiashirta of Amurru pleads his loyalty to the pharaoh, from the Amarna Archive

'Look, Pihanate, my commissioner, is there. Let the king, the sun, ask him whether or not I guard Sumur and Ullassa. When my commissioner is on a mission for the king, the sun, then I am the one who protects the harvest of the grain of Sumur and all the lands for the king, my sun, my lord. Let the king, my lord, recognize me and trust me, in the care of Pihanate, my commissioner.'

The scribe Thutmose, conscripted to Piankh's campaign against Panehsī (see p. 39), writes a letter home to Deir el-Medina

'I have reached my superior. Indeed, I found he had sent a boat to fetch me, and I was met near Edfu. So I reached him at the harbour of Elephantine and he said to me, "You need not come another time." So he said, and gave me bread and beer according to my previous salary. He said, "May the god of war favour you." So now we are moored at Elephantine and he has been saying, "I will go up to attack Panehsī wherever he is." So he is saying. Please ask Amun-of-Karnak, my lord, to bring me back safely.'

One of more than 350 clay tablets in the Amarna Archive, most written in Akkadian, the language of Babylonia, using the cuneiform script of Mesopotamia. These tablets were written as well as read in the Egyptian palace, as witness to the educated, cosmopolitan world of international diplomacy in Bronze-Age Africa and Asia.

and likewise any ruler of Kush was a blatant pretender to pharaoh's hegemony. On the other hand, the vast mineral wealth of Nubia was to become the foundation for a formidable economy. These two considerations had different strategic implications: the conquest of Black Land entailed expansion along the Nile, but the quest for gold required mining-expeditions trekking ever deeper into the deserts. Most mines presented huge difficulties, not least for safety in deserts whose climate and nomadic inhabitants could be equally hostile to Egyptians. Nevertheless, the pharaohs now began to exploit Nubia's mineral wealth on a scale previously unimagined. One inscription of Thutmose I marks the spot where a mining expedition had crossed the desert and found itself back at the Nile, far to the south of Kerma. Its broken words still resound:

'If any Nubian encroaches the mandate that my father, Amun, has given to me, [his head?] shall be lopped off … and he shall have no heirs.'

The reign of Thutmose's grandson, Thutmose III (*c.* 1479–1425 BC), partly shared with the old king's daughter, Hatshepsut

(*c.* 1473–1458 BC), was the decisive moment when Kush, surrounded and crushed, simply capitulated. The government of Black Land was reorganized so that Nubia was swallowed up, and the viceroy (now styled 'King's Son of Kush') was afforded the same powers in Nubia that a pair of viziers held in Upper Egypt and Lower Egypt. A system of control modelled exactly on Egypt's was put in place by founding and developing temple-towns, trading-towns and forts. In Year 32 of Thutmose's reign, more than a century after Kamose's initial attack, Wawat and Kush began to pay 'taxes' (*bāk*) to pharaoh's palace, the same as any district of Black Land.

At the death of Thutmose III, Black Land had attained what would be its essential form for the next four centuries. The remains of the temple of Amun-Ra at Gebel Barkal, near what would become the fortress of Napata, probably represent the southernmost limit of Egyptian control at any period of history. Beyond there, the arid land of Karoy formed a natural frontier. Nubian chiefs now grew wealthy from trade between Black Land and other African nations, such as Ārem, Nmāy and Punt. In Wawat they were typically buried in Egyptian-style tombs,

Nubian officials depicted in attendance at pharaoh's palace, from the tomb of the 'King's Son of Kush', Amenhotep called Hūy, *c.* 1330 BC at Thebes.

and the material culture of the Nubian population took on Egyptian characteristics. Mining expanded so far that expeditions to the gold-laden desert of Akōyta could be supported by ships on the Red Sea. Of course, uprisings against Egyptian control did recur and were not insignificant: an uprising in Akōyta as late as *c.* 1341 BC, in the reign of Akhenaten, required intervention under the command of the King's Son of Kush himself, and some 225 Nubians were slain or impaled as a result. Nevertheless, the area was still being mined by Egyptians 150 years later.

THE EXTENT OF BLACK LAND

Black Land's most exotic trading partner was Punt. Modern historians disagree whether Punt was on the coast of Africa or Arabia, but for the ancients it was simply at the edge of the world.

Here was God's Land, a garden of Amun-Ra's pleasure with the goddess Hathor and an emporium for the gods' own luxuries, especially the heavenly incense called *antō* as well as fragrant woods, spices and exotic hides. Egyptians had first reached Punt a thousand years earlier but contact had long since been lost. So Hatshepsut dispatched a naval expedition 'to open the way', and her temple at Deir el-Bahri in Thebes includes detailed depictions of that fabulous and bizarre land and of ships laden with 'its wonders'. Trade between the nations continued for at least three centuries, and children of Punt's chiefs were among the foreigners raised in the Egyptian palace (see p. 36). However, most wonders from Punt arrived not by sea but with caravans travelling via Ārem and Nmāy in modern Sudan. The edge of the world, in other words, was just a donkey-trip

View of Gebel Barkal in Kush. Here the temples of Amun-Ra, founded by the pharaohs of the late-15th century BC, flourished for more than a millennium, long outlasting Egyptian control in Nubia.

Reliefs in the temple of Hatshepsut at Deir el-Bahri show ships being loaded with exotic goods at Punt, including ebony and ivory, cassia and fragrant woods, perfumes and cosmetics, baboons and monkeys, dogs and leopard-skins.

30

from the frontiers of Black Land, which now spanned 'the four corner-poles of the sky'.

At the far edge of the world, God's Land was discovered in the snow-covered mountains of Lebanon (*Libnān*). Here were terraces of tall, straight timber (the one resource Black Land conspicuously lacked) rising high over the valley of the Euphrates, 'that upside-down water which goes upstream in going downstream'. From the Nile, Lebanon was most easily reached by sea, via Egypt's traditional ally, the magnificent port of Byblos, whose mayor governed a hinterland crisscrossed by trade-routes linking the Levantine ports to great kingdoms in Anatolia and Mesopotamia. Byblos was Egypt's ancient partner in ideas and values as well as trade, and would now be central to a new episode of Egyptian expansion.

MASTERING THE NEAR EAST

No ideology spurred the New Kingdom into conquering lands beyond the Nile: the credo of Black Land involved only Egypt and Nubia. Therefore, the regime's long entanglement with the Near East, one that would sporadically entail war on the grandest scale, was shaped by political self-interest. Moreover, there is no compelling evidence that Egypt's armies were active in neighbouring Palestine until the 22nd Year of Thutmose III, more than 60 years after Ahmose overran Sharuhen and opened up the roads into the Near East. It is no coincidence that Kush's capitulation was by then complete and the southern frontier of Black Land was no longer at war. Our understanding of the subjugation of Nubia is based on Egyptian monuments, in which Nubian voices or dissenting opinions are barely heard. However, for Egypt's activity in the Near East we have not only royal monuments but also diplomatic correspondence – texts both from Egypt and from other nations. The words of friend and foe alike reveal a consistent policy of defending Egypt's interests assertively but with the

Punt, with its characteristic beehive houses raised above a waterway on stilts, was at the edge of the earth, where the realm of gods bordered that of men. The Ruler of Punt, Pirahi, followed by his corpulent wife, is also shown receiving the Egyptian expedition on its shores.

minimum of military intervention. The pharaohs were interested in the ports that handled commerce on the Mediterranean Sea and the towns that managed caravans across the Near East.

On the other hand, the treacherous hills of Palestine were best avoided. Archaeological indications that fortresses from Ashkelon to Jericho were burned or abandoned across several decades at the beginning of the New Kingdom are the calling-cards not of Egyptians but of ruthless local chiefs. Egypt's armies recognized the value of urban communities, and rarely destroyed towns or the lands on which they subsisted. Instead they measured success in terms of plunder fetched for temples or prisoners transported as slaves. To eliminate an important town risked breaking the chain of commerce. Troublesome chiefs were sometimes deposed in favour of more amenable characters but generally the pharaohs left towns in the hands of chiefs with some native wit, albeit after extracting an oath of loyalty. Ironically it takes a stela of Thutmose III to get these quarrelsome chiefs to speak with one voice:

> 'We will not return in our allotted lives to evil-doing against Menkheperra [Thutmose III], our lord, because we have seen his power, and he has allowed us breath only so far as he is pleased to.'

Egypt's policy towards the Near East became discernible during the 1480s BC, when Thutmose I led an army to Nahrān, the 'land of the Twin Rivers', the Orontes and Euphrates. A list of towns in his monumental account suggests that Thutmose avoided Palestine altogether and moved his troops by sea to Byblos, going from there up the coast to Sumur, then through the mountains inland. His purpose is uncertain: perhaps he simply wished to reassert Egypt's presence in the port and its hinterland, and highlight the premium he attached to the timber-terraces. However, he also had a stela carved on the far bank of the Euphrates, marking his boundary on the doorstep of the kingdom of Mitanni. No doubt the king of Mitanni had viewed Nahrān as his own business until then, but his reaction is not recorded.

Three decades later, freed from the exhausting war in Nubia, his grandson, Thutmose III, undertook 17 campaigns in Palestine and Syria in just 21 years. The first of these c. 1458 BC was decisive: he marched his armies from the port of Gaza to besiege the port of Joppa and then fall on the town of Megiddo, which controlled the main trade-routes in the north of Palestine. There he found 'the leaders of all lands standing on their chariots in their tens and hundreds, each one there bringing his own army'. It not clear whether there had been a specific provocation that precipitated the war, but it was a singular event for so many erstwhile rivals to unite on a battlefield. However, Thutmose's armies had long experience of how to wage war proficiently, and soon 'made them as those who had never been, those who wallow in their own blood'. The town was surrounded and taken after seven months. A glimpse of the human cost of this long-ago campaign may be the terracotta cones discovered near Gaza, stamped with the names of Thutmose III and Hatshepsut. Perhaps they formed part of a mass grave for fallen Egyptians, whose individual identities were too numerous to be recorded.

Thutmose III presented his victory at Megiddo as proof that all humanity gathered together would fall before pharaoh, if Amun-Ra so willed. The chiefs of the region had certainly learned what his regime could achieve. In subsequent campaigns, he established bases at Gaza and Byblos, and led armies into the Orontes valley, which was a Syrian highway, and southwards into Galilee to ravage the lands of the chief of Qadesh, who had led the enemy at Megiddo. Qadesh too was a commercial hub, where highways through the mountains of Lebanon met the Orontes valley, so its chief had to be won over for Egyptian ambitions to flourish. Thutmose III also forded the Euphrates to uproot orchards in Mitanni and cut a stela beside that of his grandfather. By the pharaoh's fourth decade, military activity was ongoing but on at least four campaigns his armies contented themselves with displays of arms rather than fighting, while Lebanon, like Wawat and Kush, began paying taxes to the palace. Monuments

Amenhotep IV, who changed his named to Akhenaten ('Spirit of the Sun'), was sometimes shown in this transcendent image of divine kingship: masculine and feminine, human and animalistic, figurative and abstract (OPPOSITE). His Great Wife, Nefertiti, and their six young daughters form a holy family around him in official scenes from homes as well as temples and palaces (BELOW). The artists' determination to show the holy family in the midst of human life has left behind some of the most charming images from Ancient Egypt (RIGHT).

32

Sunshine on the Pharaoh

Across North Africa and the Near East, the pharaoh's power and influence seemed unrivalled in the reigns of Amenhotep III and Amenhotep IV. Their 'span of living' on earth was enshrined in the colossal reinvention of Egypt's oldest temples and the foundation of magnificent new temples and temple-towns. In and around Thebes and across Nubia, Amenhotep III built by far the largest complex of palaces and temples ever created for the adoration of one pharaoh, until his son founded a whole city at Akhtaten – including festival avenues, highways, government offices, farms and factories, and sprawling suburbs – for the same purpose. Throughout Black Land, but above all in Thebes, gilded monuments exalted the gods and their earthly son. The pharaoh was the 'perfect (or entire) god': god and man, heaven and earth. Artists wrestled with new, authentic ways of revealing this truth in art and architecture. Early in his reign, especially at Karnak, Amenhotep IV was represented in an enigmatic form: masculine and feminine, human and supernatural, familiar and disturbing. In other images, especially at Akhtaten, he relaxed with his wife and daughters, each of them caressed by the radiant fingers of the ancient sun-god, Ra-Horakhtī. The artists' inspiration was deeply conservative, but the resultant imagery distanced the pharaoh from the expectations of his people. Traditionally people had turned for spiritual comfort to familiar images from mythology, but now they were instructed to accept the royal family as their sole inspiration in this life and the next.

of Thutmose's son, Amenhotep II (*c.* 1426–1400 BC), also record the ostentatious display of violence. He had seven 'rebellious' chiefs abducted from Syria, slaughtered them himself, and had their impaled bodies hung from the walls of Thebes and Napata. Six years later he sailed from Memphis to depose Qaqa, a chief based near Megiddo, on a campaign characterized in his monumental account by the immolation of the population of a village called Atōrīn.

MANAGING PALESTINE

After the early years of Amenhotep II, military intervention in the Near East was needed only to punish dissent. The towns of Palestine were not subjects and did not pay taxes, but their chiefs were mindful of the shadow cast by the pharaoh, whose caravans and troops crossed their lands at will. They did well to send him gifts and write regularly to affirm their goodwill, in case their activities might be misconstrued as hostile. The discovery in 1887 of an archive of such correspondence, in the royal palace at Akhtaten (modern Amarna), furnished a uniquely detailed source for studying the region during the New Kingdom. It comprises some 350 letters between the pharaoh and his ruling contemporaries during the last years of Amenhotep III (*c.* 1390–1353 BC), the reign of his son, Amenhotep IV (*c.* 1353–1336 BC), and the first years of his son, Tutankhamun (*c.* 1332–1322 BC), in all 20 years or so around 1350 BC. Their hackneyed phrases are an affected blend of indifference on the part of great kings and impotence on the part of local chiefs. The pharaohs, it seems, were willing to indulge the local chiefs in interminable disputes so long as they learned what was happening straight from the horses' mouths.

Most letters can be divided into two groups. One involves kings whose status equalled that of the pharaoh, in Mesopotamia (Mitanni, Babylonia, Assyria), Anatolia (Hatti, Arzawa) and Cyprus (Alashiya). These letters are filled with elaborate greetings and effusions on brotherhood:

'Tell Nimmuariya (Amenhotep III), the king of Egypt, my brother. So speaks Tushratta, king of Mitanni, your brother. For me all goes well. For you may all go well. For Gilukhepa may all go well. For your household, your wives, your sons, your chiefs, your warriors, your horses, your chariots, and in your country, may all go well.'

Brotherhood demands gifts and the exchange of royal women as brides, hence Tushratta continues, 'my father loved you and you in turn loved my father, and, in keeping with this love, my father gave you my sister (Gilukhepa)'. Trading in and out of Egypt is a royal prerogative, so diplomatic gifts are the basic mechanism for international commerce: the pharaoh exports ebony, linen, oils and, most of all, gold, in exchange for silver, copper, oils, and especially timber and horses. Little is said about politics but Tushratta's letter ends, 'with this I send my chief minister, Keliya, and Tunipibri', so the politics is sorted out face to face by officials.

The second group of letters involves chiefs whose authority is local and who subordinate themselves before the pharaoh. Their words exaggerate their servility but remind him how useful they may be:

'To the king, my sun, my lord. Message of Abdiashirta, your servant, the dirt under your feet. I fall at the feet of the king, my lord, seven times and seven times. As I am a servant of the king, and a dog of his house, I guard all Amurru for the king, my lord.'

These 'dogs' outdo one another in claims of loyalty and in demands for gold, troops or other indulgences that only a great king can supply. Likewise, they are ever ready to expose the treachery of their peers, so the political situation is recounted in absurdly chaotic terms. Nevertheless self-serving accounts of their own activities reveal that many risk the pharaoh's wrath in order to gain some political advantage over their peers. Their demands of the pharaoh usually go unheeded, but the culture of brinkmanship does not always benefit Egypt and may engender conflicts that threaten safe passage for the all-important caravans. The raiding of one 'rebel', Labayu, so threatens the

The structure of New Kingdom government. Towns in Syria and Palestine, unlike those in Nubia, were not governed directly from Egypt. Officials below the highest levels formed a pool of administrators assigned to a particular job for a fixed term, not on a career-long basis.

roads around Megiddo that Amenhotep IV orders a group of chiefs to set aside their differences and work together to eliminate Labayu in battle.

A quarter of the letters are from Byblos, whose mayor, Ribhadda, is the only lesser chief sufficiently familiar to ask after the pharaoh's health. Ribhadda's concerns are dominated by the aggression of Abdiashirta, chief of the land of Amurru in the mountains of Lebanon:

> 'Anyway, who is Abdiashirta, the dog, that he tries to take all the cities of the king, the sun, for himself?'

After Sumur is taken from Ribhadda and Byblos itself besieged, Amenhotep IV is obliged to summon Abdiashirta's successor, Aziru, to Egypt, where he is detained for at least a year. Yet the pharaoh allows even Aziru to return to his homeland, where he then defects to the one power in the region able and willing to accept his allegiance in defiance of the pharaoh. This is the first intimation in Egyptian sources of the aggression of Suppiluliuma I of Hatti and the gathering clash of empires (see p. 37).

Later tradition treated Amenhotep IV (who changed his name to Akhenaten, 'Spirit of the Sun') and his immediate successors as bogus pharaohs, but the controversy they provoked was a matter of religion not politics, and during their lifetimes their authority was unopposed within Black Land. The richness of their monuments and the insights from the archaeology and texts they left mark this as the moment when the New Kingdom's power and influence were at their zenith, and decisive military and diplomatic interventions in Nubia and the Near East by Amenhotep IV reveal his command of the international stage. All the while manpower and wealth flowed uninterrupted into ever more massive royal foundations from Nubia to the Nile delta. When Tutankhamun passed away without an heir, so did the line that had ruled Black Land for nearly two centuries, but any strife was managed within the ruling group and settled so that the family of Ramesses I (*c.* 1292–1290 BC) became a new dynasty, which, far from breaking with the past, spoke and acted as a bulwark of tradition.

ASSERTING STRENGTH

From 1500 BC to 1300 BC Black Land's population had probably doubled, perhaps to more than four million. The straggling streets of Memphis were swelled in part by immigrants bringing crucial skills: seamen, merchants, horse-trainers, mercenaries, glassworkers and, of course, translators. Ancient texts reveal names from Babylon to Greece to Libya. However, the traditional structures of Egyptian society held firm, from the domestic level to the king and his palace

The Palace

The heart of New Kingdom Egypt was the palace, which should be understood as the gathering of the highest officials rather than simply a building. The palace embodied two principal zones: the *kāp* for the king's family and the *khōne* ('front') for officials. Each zone had its own staff and offices but they were linked at the *wōkhi* ('marshland-hall'), where the king received reports and petitions from across his realm. The authority to govern required privileged access to the king, in person or in writing, so palace officials travelled with his seal about their necks to indicate their delegated status.

To allow the king to lead the major religious festivals in turn, the palace moved around the nation, while its officials trailed back and forth to Memphis, to the regions and to the foreign dominions. Each strand of government was headed by a *wāre* ('important-one'), who swore loyalty to the king, reported directly to him, and could be dismissed by no one else. Foreign rulers subject to pharaoh held the same status

Sety I, shown in his tomb in the Valley of the Kings. This image of pharaoh exemplifies the grace and physical beauty of New Kingdom monumental art, revealing the ageless vigour and serenity of the divine ruler. Sety's traditional regalia includes the royal *uraeus* (or rearing cobra) at his brow, which may spit fiery destruction at his enemies.

and wrote frequently to him (p. 27). Their children might even be raised in the *kāp* to be immersed in the language and culture of Egyptians. However, the men and women who held the king's ear were potentially also the most divisive element in government, and palace officials were implicated in various episodes of dissent. Indeed, around 1160 BC various queens and officials of the *kāp* under Ramesses III were convicted of plotting to kill the king.

Colossus of Ramesses II in the larger temple at Abu Simbel. From the 14th century BC, New Kingdom temples in Nubia were no longer confined within fortresses, so the monumental landscape became recognizably that of pharaonic Egypt. The recognition now, throughout Black Land, was that life, prosperity and health began with the king and the royal institution of the Palace.

at the heart of the nation. The king would make an elaborate show of rewarding officials at home and abroad, while the temples of the gods who sponsored his success grew to unprecedented sizes, and were able to organize land and labour on a grand scale (see p. 40). Most folk identified themselves with a temple or a major estate, which helped to build a sense of belonging to something beyond the local community – a sense of nation. Increasingly this was also true of Wawat and Kush, where temples became the main instrument of government.

However, beyond Black Land international relations were in flux. The kingdom of Mitanni was being squeezed into submission by Hatti in the north and Assyria in the south. Suppiluliuma I led an army provocatively along the borders of territory loyal to the pharaoh and clashed with the chief of Qadesh, so doubts clouded the loyalty of chiefs in Lebanon and the Orontes valley. Accordingly Ramesses' son, Sety I (*c.* 1290–1279 BC), launched a series of campaigns in which disloyal peoples and cities were forced to acknowledge his hegemony, notably the kingdom of Amurru, which had remained defiant since Aziru defected to Suppiluliuma. Sety's success was considerable, and culminated in the defeat of a Hittite army at Qadesh. However, the issue had not been brought to a settlement at his death and became

part of the legacy for his own son, Ramesses II (*c.* 1279–1213 BC).

The new king kept nipping at the fringes of Hittite expansion and then, in his fourth year, led his armies to Byblos and from there into Amurru. The next year he pounced on a Hittite-sponsored coalition at Qadesh, in the most celebrated battle of the ancient world. In the event, the Egyptian army was tricked by spies and strung out approaching the city. Ramesses himself was ambushed and nearly killed leading the vanguard, and credited his survival only to the intervention of Amun-Ra:

'I found that Amun came when I called him, and gave me his hand, and I rejoiced. He called in support, as if next to me, "Forward! I am with you!"'

In the end the king's leadership and the timely arrival of reinforcements let the African army fight out a grim stalemate, in which the Hittite emperor, Muwatalli, lost sons and other key leaders. Ramesses' account of the battle was later set out across the walls

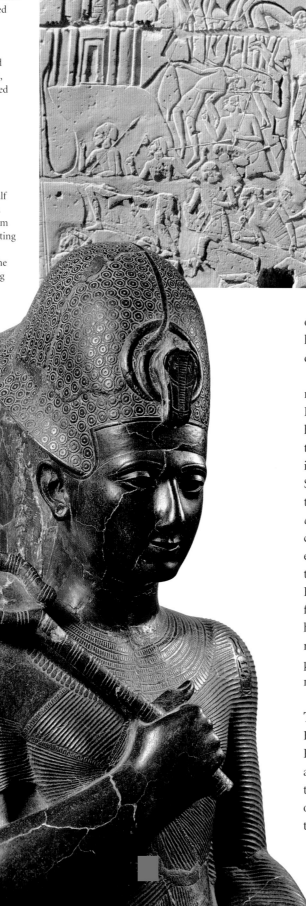

RIGHT: Temples of Sety I and Ramesses II are decorated with scenes from many victories over Hatti and its allies, including the recapture of Qadesh and the conquest of Amurru, but a decisive blow eluded both pharaohs.

BELOW: Ramesses II enthroned: the upper half of a black granite statue. During the New Kingdom a phrase originally denoting the palace – pharaoh or 'great estate' – became the definitive word for a king of Egypt.

of his largest temples, and there is sincere humility in the thanksgiving for his deliverance.

In the inconclusive aftermath, Hatti regained Amurru and conquered Api, but Ramesses then reversed these losses and made his own gains. Both nations came to recognize that the stand-off established at Qadesh was immovable, and indeed that the regime of Shalmaneser I in Assyria now posed a common threat. A diplomatic agreement was desirable, so c. 1258 BC Ramesses agreed a formal division of control over the Near East with the new Hittite emperor, Hattusili III. The Egyptian version of the treaty was also inscribed on a temple-wall at Karnak, and the god-given peace would endure for the rest of the New Kingdom. Thereafter, a handful of campaigns in Palestine, as late as the reign of Ramesses VII (c. 1137–1129 BC), were set-piece displays of arms more than meaningful military ventures.

TENSIONS AND PRESSURES

Inevitably a reign such as the 67 years of Ramesses II, by which he outlived a dozen sons and many more grandsons, generated dynastic tensions. These did not affect the succession of his son, Merenptah (c. 1213–1204 BC), but there were brothers, nephews and others with competing claims to the throne. The succession of Sety II (c. 1204–1198 BC) was usurped, at least in Thebes, by his relative, Amenmesse. The resultant unrest lasted more than a decade and was only ended by a new dynasty, probably from within the royal family, headed by Sethnakhte (*c.* 1190–1187 BC). However, Sethnakhte's son, Ramesses III (*c.* 1187–1156 BC), was the intended (perhaps actual) victim of an assassination plotted within the palace. There is unequivocal evidence that such dynastic crises affected the nation more generally by creating a climate of anxiety. Equally clearly, however, the major institutions of the regime, including the palace, continued to function effectively throughout the events.

A more constant threat to Black Land in the later New Kingdom was invasion from Libya. Both Sety I and Ramesses II sent armies into areas west of Egypt, and Ramesses constructed forts along the fringes of the Nile delta. However, Mashwash and Libu peoples from the west settled frequently in and around Memphis. They had seemingly been accommodated peacefully until suddenly Merenptah used force to drive away a mass incursion, slaying thousands according to his monumental account. Initially famine had brought refugees flocking to be with kinfolk, but among them were non-Libyan peoples, and the incursion threatened to overwhelm the regime's control in the northwest. Mass incursions were driven away twice more, by Ramesses III, but they do seem to have been exceptional events within a long-standing pattern of settlement, from which Egypt gained skilled workers and commercial contacts.

Around 1180 BC Ramesses III also drove away an invasion from the north, by a confederation historians usually call the 'Sea-peoples', although ancient accounts identify only a minority as being 'of the sea'. The fighting by land and in the creek-waters of the Nile delta has been spun by modern writers into a tale of marauders overthrowing mighty empires. In fact, many of the invaders were women and children, and they should probably be recognized as displaced communities, perhaps victims of the break-up of the Hittite empire during the reign of Suppiluliuma II. This invasion made no lasting impression on Egypt

itself, but it seems to have had a lasting impact on the political and cultural make-up of Palestine and, in that sense, held implications for the pharaohs.

The success of Ramesses III in the face of invasions indicates how he still led an effective nation, while the temple-town for Amun-Ra he founded at Medinet Habu remains one of Egypt's greatest monuments. However, the military and building activities of his successors lack lustre. Is this symptomatic of a decline in the pharaohs' authority? In Nubia the infrastructure of government and of gold-mining was long established, so what significant new building was necessary? In the Near East, Hatti's demise left Egypt unchallenged as a superpower. Archaeology has indeed revealed fundamental changes in Palestine's political and cultural landscape following the retreat of Hittite control, but these would have been irrelevant for the pharaohs so long as new rulers accommodated his interests as mindfully as their predecessors. Certainly local chiefs had no other 'great king' to turn to, at least until the re-emergence of Assyria during the 10th century BC. In these circumstances, the absence of military campaigns during the last century of the New Kingdom reflects Black Land's unchallenged mastery. At a local level, there were robberies in the royal cemeteries, especially during the reign of Ramesses IX (*c.* 1126–1108 BC), but palace officials conducted the prosecutions, so anarchy was not seen to erupt.

Nevertheless, two momentous developments at the beginning of the 11th century BC do seem to mark the end of the New Kingdom. One was the emergence of a city within a city at Thebes, where oracles took over the king's role in running the affairs of Amun-Ra's temples and estates. Around 1088 BC, the armies of the King's Son of Kush, Panehsī, occupied Thebes and chased away the high-priest of Amun-Ra. After seven years, the commander of the Egyptian armies, Hrihor, in turn marched into Thebes, was recognized as the new high-priest, and assumed the titles of a king. Another general, Piankh, chased Panehsī's troops back into Nubia. At the other end of the country, a

40

The Temple Economy

Memphis, by the reign of Ramesses II, was an authentic metropolis with a population of hundreds of thousands of souls. Towns from Aswan in the south to Sile on the Mediterranean coast had also swelled in numbers, partly with immigrants attracted by Egypt's undoubted wealth and stability. Larger towns (*nō*) included the administrative centres of the 40 districts, while other large settlements with moorings (*dime*) linked the flow of trade and travel along the Nile. Elsewhere, however, communities might dwindle to mere clusters of farms.

The priorities of government were those of the farmers, whose success was the foundation of the economy, but agricultural production was taxed in kind and redistributed in line with the hierarchies of power. The more powerful you were, the more you received. Legally the earth and all it contains belonged only to pharaoh but, in practice, responsibility for administering much of the land was turned over to the gods' temples in return for the food and other produce needed for vast staffs of priests, administrators, craftsmen and their families. The sheer scale of the temples made them the basic agents for organizing the workforce. Ramesses III, for example, assigned the labour of 86,000 people to various temples of Amun-Ra, over and above the workforces they had accumulated in previous centuries. Some would have been prisoners-of-war or convicts but most were freeborn and tied by contract and tradition to their own land. In exchange for taxes, the farmers' freedom and security of tenure were guaranteed by the palace, and the basics of life were provided for them in times of hardship. In fact, for most Egyptians, the temples typically satisfied physical rather than spiritual needs.

ABOVE: Scenes from the tomb of Pahrī, governor of the town of el-Kab, illustrate harvesting and ploughing, representative of the labour-intensive agriculture that was the main employment for most Egyptians, the principal responsibility for most officials, and the foundation of the economic and social fabric of Black Land.

RIGHT: The mortuary-temple complex of Ramesses II ('The Ramesseum') at Thebes, like all major temples throughout New Kingdom Egypt, comprised not only religious buildings but also the administrative offices and warehouses necessary for collecting and storing agricultural resources on a massive scale.

shadowy figure named Smendes emerged as *de facto* king at Tanis. At face value, this may seem like the collapse of central government but Hrihor, Piankh and Smendes were closely related to one another and also to the pharaoh, Ramesses XI (*c.* 1099–1069 BC). Ramesses' reign remained unqualified outside Thebes, and documents were ascribed not to competing kings but to a special era of 'repeating births', which may refer to the duplication of kings or to a period of renaissance. As a result, it is unclear how far these events stemmed from genuine shifts in power or how far from dynastic squabbling.

BLACK LAND INTERRUPTED

Events in the south had a second, emphatic, outcome. Panehsī, erstwhile King's Son of Kush, used the pharaoh's own armies to put Nubia out of Egyptian rule. After more than four centuries, Black Land, in Kamose's vision, simply ceased to exist. This was the end of the New Kingdom in ideological terms, but the practical effect on the nations of Egypt and Nubia is harder to substantiate. For Egypt there must have been a dramatic reduction in gold and taxes, but Egypt was still rich in natural resources, steeped in the wealth it had garnered for centuries, and there are strong currents of continuity within the regime. At the death of Ramesses XI, a new royal line was headed by Smendes (*c.* 1069–1045 BC), and the royal cemetery was moved to Tanis in the Nile delta, but Tanis was the estate of Amun-Ra in the north and the new kings maintained close links with the high-priests at Karnak, often formalized through marriage. In time the high-priest Psusennes even became king, as Psusennes II (*c.* 950–945 BC). If a major display of arms is sufficient evidence, the New Kingdom outlasted Ramesses XI by 150 years. In the face of Assyrian politicking, Shoshenq I (*c.* 945–925 BC) led a powerful army against Assyria's ally, the kingdom of Israel. Shoshenq's account, inscribed beside his majestic new entrance to the temple of Amun-Ra, is strikingly reminiscent of the campaigns of Thutmose III and Amenhotep II. In other words, the campaign can be understood as an attempt to confirm Egypt's long-standing authority in Palestine, largely unquestioned since the demise of Hatti.

However, despite Shoshenq's success, tensions were at work within Egypt itself that would result in the breakdown of pharaonic authority. For example, Libyan immigration in the Nile delta had created a chiefdom of Libu only loosely bound to the palace. Initially the pharaohs checked such divisions by assigning political offices to their family, and loyal officials were rewarded with the right to hold high offices through inheritance rather than royal favour. The outcome was a regime which owed everything to the pharaoh but which was structurally less coherent than it had been in the New Kingdom. As a result, dynastic rivalries threatened the unity of the nation in a way that seemed impossible during the New Kingdom. An inscription of Osorkon II (*c.* 875–835 BC) bemoans the fact that even his sons were enemies, and another from the temple of Amun-Ra describes the country in terms of 'elemental confusion'. In this sense, the 9th century BC marks the real demise of the New Kingdom.

LEGACY

The story of Nubia after the expulsion of Panehsī's armies from Thebes is notoriously difficult to reconstruct. A loss of centralized control seems to have allowed a number of quasi-pharaonic families to compete for power from places such as Kawa and Semna, once great centres within Black Land. In Wawat, meanwhile, unpredictable patterns of agriculture, perhaps caused partly by political uncertainty, forced most folk to adopt a more nomadic lifestyle on the desert fringes or migrate to more stable areas in Kush. However, Nubia's obscurity ended in a manner as abrupt as it was unforeseen, when a pharaoh from Kush took control of Egypt.

In the middle of the 8th century BC, a line emerged at Napata as the overlords of Kush. Their arts and funerary customs, were essentially those of the New Kingdom, and from the reign of Kashta (*c.* 770–747 BC) they styled themselves as pharaohs. In religion they recognized the pre-eminence of Amun-Ra, and at Gebel Barkal built an enormous new temple on the site founded by Egyptians seven centuries earlier. Kashta's successor, Piye (*c.* 747–715 BC), resolved to celebrate the festivals of Amun-Ra in Thebes itself, and *c.* 728 BC a Nubian army used force to impose his will on Upper Egypt. Within months this Nubian pharaoh had travelled to Memphis and Heliopolis to receive homage from the rulers of Egypt, including no less than four other kings. In victory Piye founded a tradition of kingship in Kush that would be an authority in Africa for a millennium. Yet the well-spring for every aspect of Kush's ruling culture was Black Land and the centuries when Egypt and Nubia had been one nation.

So in Nubia, as in Egypt, the splitting of Black Land was just the latest of many transformations of the kingdoms along the Nile. The pharaohs' monuments still loom large in our imagination, perhaps because their magnificence makes us recognize how shallow the roots of our own culture may be in the scheme of history. Or perhaps we get an inkling that our roots reach into Black Land, as The Bible and the classical historians suggest. A wonderfully comic adventure, *The Tale of Wenamun*, was composed at the end of the reign of Ramesses XI, even as Hrihor, Smendes and Panehsī were playing out the final act of the New Kingdom. In the tale, Egypt's fondest ally, the mayor of Byblos, reflects on history:

> 'So, Amun founded all lands, but he founded them after he had founded the land of Egypt, where you've just come from. Thus, Art started there and has reached where I am, while Learning started there and has reached where I am.'

If so, then it was the New Kingdom which brought the Egyptian, and indeed African, values of Black Land to a wider world. Under the pharaohs, Egypt's gods held sway to the ends of the earth, while their neighbours in Nubia, Libya and Palestine gained affluence and security, at the cost of acknowledging their inferiority. Around the Red Sea and the Mediterranean Sea, through Anatolia and the

Near East, many others grew in wealth and status by embracing, emulating or challenging the pharaohs. Along with gold, ivory and incense, Egyptian caravans and boats transported art, ideas and even poems whose words made their way into the Biblical psalms. Centuries later the land of the pharaohs cast a spell over Cambyses, Alexander, Caesar and Hadrian. There is no reason to suppose that the great civilizing influence of the New Kingdom simply expired one day in the 11th century BC.

Ingres' portrait of the emperor Napoleon, in coronation robes spangled with bees – the ancient Egyptian hieroglyph for 'king'. In 1798, Napoleon had invaded Egypt and commissioned the first scientific survey of its monuments. He was the latest of many European rulers, from Roman emperors onwards, seduced by the quasi-mystical authority of the pharaohs, the ancient *rois-soleil*.

CHAPTER 2
THE HITTITE EMPIRE
1650–1200 BC

The kingdom of the Hittites is perhaps one of the least well known of the empires discussed in this volume. Indeed, whether it qualifies as an empire is itself an open discussion. The Hitttites were at no point a distinct or homogenous group with an ideology of their own dominance or any clear imperial mission. The name 'Hittites' was not their own term, but a name derived from the Hebrew Bible. From their heartland in north-central Anatolia (modern Turkey), however, they established – at least intermittently through the middle centuries of the 2nd millennium BC – a formidable power. Through their network of vassals their sway reached from the Aegean coastline in the west to northern Syria in the southeast. And through a series of striking military successes, not least the sackings of Babylon and Aleppo, their kings established themselves as the equals, and for a brief period even the superiors, of the Great Kings of Babylon and Egypt.

King List

?–1650 BC	LABARNA
1650–1620 BC	Hattusili I
1620–1590 BC	Mursili I
1590–1560 BC	Hantili I
between 1560 and 1525 BC	Zidanta I Ammuna Huzziya
1525–1500 BC	Telipinu
between 1500 and 1400 BC	Alluwamna Tahurwaili Hantili II Zidanta II Huzziya II Muwatalli I
between 1400 and 1350 BC	Tudhaliya I/II Arnuwanda I Hattusili II Tudhaliya III
1350–1322 BC	Suppiluliuma I
1322–1321 BC	Arnuwanda II
1321–1295 BC	Mursili II
1295–1272 BC	Muwatalli II
1272–1267 BC	Urhi-Teshub
1267–1237 BC	Hattusili III
1237–1209 BC	Tudhaliya IV
1209–1207 BC	Arnuwanda III
1207–? BC	Suppiluliuma II

PREVIOUS PAGES: A Late Bronze Age relief of 12 running or marching gods in the Hittite rock sanctuary now called Yazılıkaya. They are believed to be underworld deities.

LEFT: A Late Bronze Age relief carved on the interior of the so-called 'King's Gate', one of Hattusa's three main entrance-ways. Over 2 m (6.5 ft) high, the sculpture probably depicts a god (rather than a king) equipped for battle.

Black Sea

TUMMANNA   KASKA

PALA

UPPER
LAND

WILUSA   Sapinuwa Tapikka

Troy   Hattusa

Lazpa

SEHA R.
LAND   LAND OF
HATTI

Caicus.   *Marassantiya*

Hermus   Salt
Lake

PITASSA   Kussara

ARZAWA-MIRA   Kummanni

Maeander   HAPALLA   Hahhum

LOWER
LAND

Tigris

LUKKA   KIZZUWADNA   Carchemish

TARHUNTASSA

Alalah

UGARIT   *Euphrates*

Mediterranean Sea

AMURRU   SYRIAN
DESERT

ALASHIYA   Qadesh

Sakarya.

Core of Hittite empire

Extent of Hittite control

0 ___ 100 km

0 ___ 100 miles

Foundation of Hittite
kingdom in the early
17th century BC

Beginning of New Kingdom
and development of an empire
1400 BC

Fall of Hattusa and
collapse of kingdom
early 12th century BC

Sack of Babylon
1595 BC

Battle of Nihriya,
fought with Assyrians
1228 BC

1700 BC   1600 BC   1500 BC   1400 BC   1300 BC   1200 BC

King Telipinu establishes
laws of royal succession
1525 BC

Hittite kingdom almost
destroyed in massive invasions
early-mid 14th century BC

Peace Treaty
with Egypt
1258 BC

Destruction of
Carchemish, last
Mitannian stronghold
1327 BC

Battle of Qadesh,
fought with Egypt
1274 BC

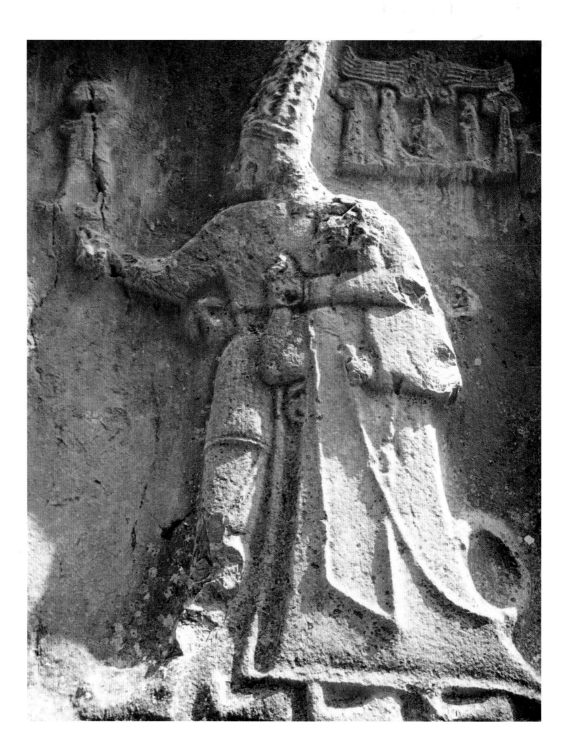

At its greatest extent in the 14th and 13th centuries BC, the kingdom ruled by the Hittites stretched westwards to the Aegean coast of Anatolia and southeastwards across northern Syria to the western fringes of Mesopotamia. How appropriate is it to refer to Hatti, the kingdom of the Hittites, as an empire? There is no doubt that it lacked many of the attributes commonly associated with later empires, like those of Persia, Rome and 19th-century Europe. But if in a broad sense the term 'empire' is applicable to any widespread dominion that contains states and territories subject to a central authority, then Hatti at the peak of its development clearly displayed some of the fundamental characteristics of empire. We shall consider these below, as we investigate the rise of the Hittite kingdom to the status of a major power in the Near Eastern world, and the means which its kings used to maintain its influence in this world through a period of almost 500 years.

THE ORIGINS AND GROWTH OF THE KINGDOM

In the early 17th century BC, an eastern Anatolian king called Labarna went to war against his neighbours. One state after another fell before him, until he had seized control of the entire region extending through Cappadocia southwards to the Mediterranean Sea: 'His country was small. But on whatever campaign he went, he held the enemy lands in subjection by his might. He kept devastating the lands and deprived them of power, and he made them the boundaries of the sea.'

Labarna is generally regarded as the founder of the Hittite ruling dynasty, a line of kings that held power for almost half a millennium until the end of the Late Bronze Age (early 12th century BC), despite several crises in its history that almost destroyed it. The dynasty almost certainly represented one of several Indo-European population groups that arrived in Anatolia some time during the Early Bronze Age (3rd millennium BC). Its ancestral seat was a city called Kussara, probably located in the region near the modern city Sar (classical Comana in Cappadocia). Labarna's reign was marred by rebellions and by power struggles within his own family, until the royal succession passed to his grandson Hattusili (c. 1650 BC). The new king honoured his grandfather's achievements by adding the name Labarna (sometimes written Tabarna) to the royal titulary. But his kingship took a fresh direction when he established a new royal capital on a ruined, abandoned site in north-central Anatolia, in the Land of Hatti. The city was called Hattusa. A century earlier, Hattusa had been destroyed, and its site declared accursed, by a king called Anitta, whose dynasty had also originated in Kussara. The city's re-foundation by Hattusili (though some scholars argue that it had been rebuilt by one of Hattusili's predecessors) effectively marked the beginning of the Late Bronze Age kingdom of Hatti.

OPPOSITE: A Late Bronze Age relief from Yazılıkaya showing the Hittite god Sharrumma extending a protective arm around his protégé, the Hittite king Tudhaliya IV.

49

BELOW: Hattusa's citadel and palace district, now called Büyükkale.

OVERLEAF: The famous Lion Gate, the main entrance into Hattusa.

The clay tablet archives discovered in the Hittite capital Hattusa and some regional centres provide our most valuable source of information on the empire. Military successes were sometimes offset by major crises which threatened the very existence of the kingdom. As we learn from the so-called 'Plague Prayers', the Hittites, fresh from their triumphs over Mitanni and against Egyptian forces in Syria, were afflicted with a plague which raged for 20 years, decimating their population. The archives, in the form of letters and treaties, also tell us much about relations between Hittite kings and their foreign counterparts, in Assyria, Babylon and Egypt. Such exchanges were sometimes cordial, leading to royal marriages between Hatti and Egypt. On other occasions, they were distinctly acrimonious. We also learn much about the ways in which Hittite kings controlled the vast areas of land over which they held sway. Generally, the kings had a policy of non-interference in the internal affairs of a vassal state. But as one of the treaties indicates, incestuous relationships were strictly banned in the vassal states – on pain of death. From a number of documents found in Hattusa, it is clear that a Hittite king often sought to convey the impression of a merciful overlord, prepared to forgive acts of disloyalty by recalcitrant subjects, even when exemplary vengeance was apparently called for.

Luwian hieroglyphic inscription of the Late Bronze Age. Hittite kings sometimes inscribed rock faces with hieroglyphic inscriptions written in the Luwian language (closely related to Hittite) to record their names, titles and exploits.

Then were his sons, his brothers, his relations by marriage, his [blood] relations and his troops united. And the land was small. But on whatever campaign he went, he held the lands of the enemy in subjection by his might. He kept devastating the lands, and he deprived the lands of power; and he made them boundaries of the sea.'

A plague sent by the gods devastates the Hittite kingdom

'What is this, o gods, that you have done? A plague you have let into the land. The Land of Hatti, all of it, is dying; so no one prepares sacrificial loaves and libations for you. The ploughmen who used to work the fields of the god are dead... To mankind, our wisdom has been lost, and whatever we do right comes to nothing. O gods, whatever sin you behold, either let a prophet rise and declare it, or let the Old Women or the priests learn about it, or let ordinary people see it in a dream! O gods, take pity again on the Land of Hatti!'

'I marched against the city Hassuwa, and the men of Hassuwa came against me in battle, reinforced by troops from Aleppo. But I overthrew them. Within a few days I overcame Hassuwa, like a lion with its claws. And when I overthrew it, I heaped dust upon it and seized all its property and filled Hattusa with it.' The Hittite king Hattusili I boasts of one of his conquests in Syria

The Hittite king Mursili II shows mercy to a rebellious vassal ruler in an apparent act of chivalry

'I would certainly have marched against Manapa-Tarhunda and destroyed him utterly, but he sent forth his mother to meet me. She came and fell at my knees and spoke to me as follows: "My Lord, do not destroy us. Take us, my Lord, into subjection." And since a woman came to meet me and fell at my knees, I gave way to the woman and thereupon I did not march against Manapa-Tarhunda's land, but took him and his land into subjection.'

A Hittite king rebukes his generals for failing to engage the enemy during a siege operation

'"Why have you not given battle? You stand on chariots of water, you are almost turned into water yourselves … You had only to kneel before him and you would have killed him or at least frightened him. But as it is you have behaved like women!" Thus they answered him: "Eight times we will give battle. We will confound their schemes and destroy their city." The king answered "Good!"'

The Hittite king Hattusili III sends his daughter to Egypt to wed the pharaoh Ramesses II

'Then he [Hattusili] caused his eldest daughter to be brought, with magnificent tribute going before her, of gold, silver and copper in abundance, slaves, spans of horses without limit, cattle, goats, and sheep by ten-thousands – limitless were the products which they brought to the King of Southern and Northern Egypt, Usimare Setepenre, Son of Re, Ramesses II, given life.'

'For Hatti it is an important custom that a brother does not have sex with his sister or female cousin. It is not permitted. Whoever commits such an act is put to death. But your land is barbaric, for there a man regularly has sex with his sister or cousin … eat, drink, and make merry! But you must not desire to have sex with her.'

The Hittite king Suppiluliuma I warns a vassal ruler against permitting incest in his land

The Hittite king Hattusili III rebukes the king of Babylon for not acknowledging his accession to the Hittite throne

'When I assumed kingship, you did not send a messenger to me. It is the custom that when kings assume kingship, the kings who are his equals in rank send him appropriate greeting-gifts, clothing befitting kingship, and fine oil for his anointing. But you have not yet done this.'

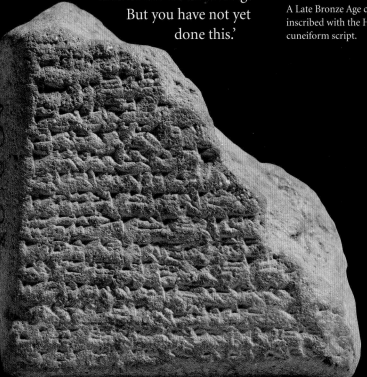

A Late Bronze Age clay tablet inscribed with the Hittite cuneiform script.

54

A Late Bronze Age Hittite cuneiform tablet, impressed with the royal seal.

his successes were tempered by one major failure. Despite repeated attempts, the king never succeeded in breaching the defences of Aleppo, the royal capital of Yamhad. That task was accomplished by his grandson and successor, Mursili I, who captured and sacked the city. Mursili then marched his troops to the Euphrates river, and south along the river to Babylon. This city was also captured, looted and torched by the Hittites, thus bringing to an end the royal line of the Babylonian king Hammurabi.

The assassination of Mursili within a few years of his return from Babylon sparked off a series of power struggles within Hatti between rival branches of the royal family. These continued through the reigns of the first four of Mursili's successors, whose violent occupation of the throne always ended with their forcible removal from it. Mursili's fifth successor, Telipinu, also seized the throne in a coup (*c.* 1525 BC). However, he then sought to stabilize the monarchy by laying down regulations governing the royal succession, and empowering a broadly based council called the *panku* to ensure that these regulations were adhered to. He also attempted to win back some of the subject territories lost to the kingdom during the reigns of his predecessors, whose squabbles had prompted uprisings among his subjects and exposed its core territory to enemy invasion.

THE ERA OF THE NEW KINGDOM

While Telipinu succeeded in both halting his kingdom's slide towards extinction and regaining a number of its lost territories, he failed to restore to it the status and the influence it had achieved in the Near Eastern world during the reigns of Hattusili I and Mursili I. In the century following his death in *c.* 1500 BC, Hatti was ruled by a succession of apparently inconsequential kings, at the same time as Egypt and the Hurrian kingdom of Mitanni were emerging as the dominant powers of the Near Eastern world. Under its 15th-century BC pharaohs Thutmose I and Thutmose III, Egypt had carried out extensive conquests in Syria-Palestine, and established permanent Egyptian sovereignty over many cities and states in the

Hattusili set about asserting his control over a number of eastern Anatolian lands, including those that had rebelled against his grandfather. But his military ambitions extended much further afield. Early in his reign, he embarked on an aggressive new programme of military conquest, taking his forces into northern Syria. Here he attacked the lands subject to the king of Yamhad, and destroyed a number of their cities, such as Alalah on the Amuq plain and Hahhum on the Euphrates. He may also have penetrated deep into northern Mesopotamian territory, in a campaign directed particularly against the kingdom of Tikunani, whose capital likely lay in the region of modern Diyarbakır. Hattusili's eastern campaigns ended mostly in victory. But region. And from its homeland in northern Mesopotamia, Mitanni had extended its sway over large parts of northern Syria and eastern Anatolia. The kingdom of Hatti re-emerged, eventually, as a major player in the international scene when, after many decades of relative insignificance, its fortunes had taken a turn for the better with the accession of a king called Tudhaliya in *c.* 1400 BC. (He is often referred to as Tudhaliya I/II since we cannot be sure whether the events attributed to him belong to one or to two kings so named.) Tudhaliya's occupation of the Hittite throne marks the beginning of a new era in Hittite history, sometimes referred to as the New Kingdom.

Tudhaliya conducted extensive campaigns of conquest both in western Anatolia and in Syria. In the wake of one of his Anatolian campaigns, which resulted in the defeat of an alliance of 22 states called the 'Assuwan Confederacy', he brought back to Hattusa as prisoners of war 10,000 foot-soldiers and an elite chariot contingent, 'lords of the bridle', along with 600 teams of horses. Transportation of conquered populations back to Hatti was to become a regular feature of campaigns conducted by later Hittite kings in enemy and rebel lands. In Syria, Tudhaliya allegedly destroyed the lands of the kings of Aleppo and Mitanni. But this claim, made by a later Hittite king, is probably exaggerated. Mitanni in particular was far from a spent force. Its final showdown with Hatti was yet to come.

For many of his military enterprises, Tudhaliya was partnered by his son-in-law, who was also his adopted son and co-regent Arnuwanda I. From the records of the latter's reign, it is clear that Hittite victories in this early New Kingdom period were offset by instability in a number of the subject territories and ominous developments in enemy territories beyond Hatti's frontiers. These reached their peak in the reign of Arnuwanda's successor (or successor-but-one) Tudhaliya III, during the first half of the 14th century BC. The kingdom suffered its most serious crisis to date when massed enemy forces invaded its homeland territory from all directions, and the Hittite capital was captured and destroyed. Tudhaliya

had before then removed his royal court to a residence-in-exile in the city of Samuha, perhaps located on the upper course of the Marassantiya river (the classical Halys river, known today as the Kızıl Irmak river). From here he planned the recovery of his kingdom, and with the support of his son Suppiluliuma drove the enemies from all his territories. Suppiluliuma, who was very likely the chief architect of the Hittite recovery, succeeded his father on the Hittite throne *c.* 1350 BC, and embarked without delay on the greatest project of his reign – the destruction of the kingdom of Mitanni. This objective was largely achieved in a brilliant one-year campaign in northern Syria and northern Mesopotamia *c.* 1344 BC, but the kingdom lingered on until the siege and capture of its final stronghold, Carchemish on the Euphrates, in 1327 BC.

Suppiluliuma imposed his sovereignty upon many of the northern Syrian states formerly subject to Mitanni, and the yearly military campaigns conducted by his son and (second) successor Mursili (*c.* 1321–1295 BC) re-established and consolidated Hittite rule over many parts of Anatolia. In Syria, mounting tensions between Hatti and Egypt over disputed subject territories culminated in a major military showdown between the Hittite king Muwatalli II and the pharaoh Ramesses II near the city of Qadesh on the Orontes river in 1274 BC. Although the outcome of the battle itself was essentially a stalemate, Hatti was clearly the long-term victor in terms of its territorial acquisitions at Egypt's expense. After Qadesh, a border between Hittite and Egyptian territory just north of Damascus seems to have been tacitly acknowledged by both kings. In 1269 BC, a treaty drawn up between Ramesses and Muwatalli's second successor Hattusili III formalized friendly relations between the two powers; the peace between them, consolidated by two royal marriage alliances, held firm until the fall of the Hittite kingdom early the following century.

Hatti was now entering the final decades of its existence, and by the early regnal years of Hattusili's son and successor Tudhaliya IV (*c.* 1237–1209 BC), there is evidence that the kingdom was already in irreversible decline.

The Royal Seat of Empire

The ruins of Hattusa, capital of the Hittite empire, lie in north-central Turkey, 160 km (100 miles) east of the modern Turkish capital Ankara. Extending over 185 hectares (460 acres), Hattusa was both the religious and the administrative centre of the Hittite world. Thirty-one temples have been discovered there, the largest of which, dedicated to the Storm God, covered more than 20,000 sq. m (215,300 sq. ft). The palace of the king was built on the city's acropolis, walled off from the rest of the city and now known as Büyükkale (Turkish for 'Big Castle'). All those who had business with His Majesty, including vassal rulers and representatives of foreign kings, were escorted by royal attendants through a series of colonnaded courts to a large pillared hall, the focal point of the palace complex, where the king gave audience. Many of the king's family and high-ranking officials lived in private apartments on the acropolis. The city was enclosed within a massive fortification wall, surmounted at 20-m (65-ft) intervals by towers, with a curtain wall in front. Access was provided by a number of gates, the most important of which are now known, from their still surviving sculptures, as the Lion, Sphinx and Warrior-God gates. Excavations carried out at Hattusa for more than 100 years by the German Archaeological Institute are still in progress today. The most recent finds include large granaries, with a storage capacity of tens of thousands of tonnes, and five reservoirs, which for a time provided much of the city's water supply.

Temple of the Storm God, Hattusa. The largest of all known Hittite temples, it had many functions, both religious and secular, and contained one of the most important tablet archives of the Hittite world.

Neo-Hittite relief depicting the weather god Teshub equipped for battle. He brandishes a double-axe in one hand and a thunderbolt in the other. His peaked cap and the winged sun-disk above his head indicate his divine status. He stands upon a bull, the earthly symbol commonly associated with him.

Tudhaliya was not only faced with increasing unrest and uprisings in his subject territories, but also suffered a major military defeat at the hands of the Assyrian king Tukulti-Ninurta I in northern Mesopotamia, and very likely was confronted by plots against him and an open challenge to his authority by members of collateral branches of his own family. Food shortages within Hatti may also have added to the increasing instability of the Hittite kingdom.

In the reign of the last Hittite king Suppiluliuma II (1207–?), Hattusa was abandoned by the royal court, and the city gradually fell into ruin. With its abandonment, or even before it, the kingdom over which it held sway collapsed.

Relics of the culture and civilization of Late Bronze Age Hatti survived in the so-called Neo-Hittite kingdoms which arose in parts of eastern and southern Anatolia and northern Syria during the early centuries of the Iron Age. Indeed there is evidence that in several of the Neo-Hittite kingdoms, descendants of the Late Bronze Age Hittite dynasty survived and continued to hold power for generations after the Late Bronze Age kingdom which the dynasty had ruled came to an end.

THE STRUCTURE OF THE KINGDOM

The core territory of Hatti, commonly referred to by scholars as the Hittite homeland, lay in north-central Anatolia within the region bounded by the Halys river, called the Marassantiya in Hittite texts. By far the largest of its cities was the royal capital Hattusa, the administrative and religious centre of the kingdom. Regional centres within the homeland, such as Sapinuwa (modern Ortaköy) and Tapikka (modern Maşat) where tablet archives have been found, were under the immediate authority of local officials appointed by the king. Of these the most important held the office of BEL MADGALTI (literally 'lord of the watchtower'), which took responsibility for the security of their region, the maintenance of its roads and irrigation channels, the collection of taxes and the administration of justice on the king's behalf. Adjacent to the homeland on its northeastern and southern frontiers were regions known respectively as the Upper and Lower Lands, which served as buffers against enemy incursions. New Kingdom texts refer to the installation of Hittite military governors in them, and the provision of garrisons of Hittite infantry and chariotry. Beyond the homeland and its buffer zones, the kingdom consisted of two viceregal centres, located at Aleppo and Carchemish, and an array of vassal states extending over large parts of Anatolia and northern Syria. Hittite territory in Syria extended to the region north of Damascus, where the frontier with Egypt lay.

The viceregal kingdoms were established at Aleppo and Carchemish by Suppiluliuma I, during the final stages of the king's destruction of Mitanni. The first two viceroys were his sons Telipinu and Piyassili (Sharri-Kushuh). They exercised within their regions all the powers – administrative, military, judicial, religious – of the Great King himself, and sometimes conducted diplomatic negotiations with local Syrian rulers on his behalf. Henceforth, every viceroy until the fall of the kingdom was either the son of the Hittite king or a high-ranking member of his family. The vassal states were ruled by local kings who were bound by oaths of allegiance to the Great King. Their obligations as vassals required them to provide military support to their overlord when called upon, and to act as his local intelligence agents, giving him early warning of anti-Hittite activities in their region. The treaty sometimes stipulated an annual tribute payable by the vassal. A small number of subject-rulers were granted *kuirwana*, or 'protectorate', status. This gave them a few ceremonial privileges, and occasionally the right to annex enemy territory which they had conquered on the Hittite king's behalf. But in practice, their apparently privileged status was little more than a diplomatic fiction. Very much the same obligations, and the same restrictions, were imposed upon the *kuirwana* as upon the vassal rulers. Provided they fulfilled their treaty obligations, both types of rulers were allowed to govern their states as they saw fit. It was only in rare circumstances that a Hittite garrison was imposed upon a subject state, and then only if the state had proved particularly troublesome and a military presence was deemed necessary to restore order and support the Hittite-appointed or endorsed local ruler.

THE KINGDOM IN ITS BROADER CONTEXT

The Near Eastern world was made up of a large array of kingdoms, the majority of which were no more than small city-states, which had an urban centre and a few square kilometres of peripheral territory, normally used for farming or grazing purposes. Many of the Syro-Palestinian kingdoms conquered by the 15th-century BC pharaoh Thutmose III belonged to this category. Larger kingdoms extended over greater expanses of territory and included, in addition to the main urban centre, a number of smaller towns and villages, and sometimes fortified settlements along their frontiers. The five Middle Bronze Age kingdoms of eastern Anatolia, attested as MATU (literally 'lands') in Assyrian colony texts, fell into this category, as did the Late Bronze Age kingdoms of Arzawa in western Anatolia, attested in Hittite texts. Ranking well above both categories, in size, political importance and military might, were the superpowers of the Late Bronze Age Near East. There were four of these – the kingdoms of Hatti, Egypt, Babylon and Mitanni, with Mitanni being replaced after its destruction in the mid-14th century BC by a renascent kingdom of Assyria.

The superior status of these kingdoms was officially recognized in diplomatic texts by the designation of their rulers as 'Great Kings'.

This term (commonly represented by the Sumerogram GAL.LUGAL) was used precisely and exclusively of the four rulers, by themselves in their royal titulary, by their subject rulers and by their foreign counterparts. The Great Kings' acknowledgment of one another as peers is further indicated by their addressing one another as 'My Brother', a form of address used only, in diplomatic protocol, by persons of equal status. One of the Hittite kings, probably Urhi-Teshub, sternly rebuked the 'upstart' Assyrian king Adad-nirari I for addressing him as 'My Brother' before he had been acknowledged, apparently, as a member of the elite group: 'As my grandfather and my father did not write to the King of Assyria about brotherhood, you shall not keep writing to me about brotherhood and Great Kingship. It is not my wish!'

Collectively, the four Great Kings held sway over almost the entire Near Eastern world, incorporating as subject territories within their realms the numerous petty and medium-sized states which constituted the lesser kingdoms of this world. Babylon and Assyria covered between them the whole of Mesopotamia. New Kingdom Egypt's sway extended from Nubia through the land of the Nile into southern Syria and Palestine (Chapter 1). Hatti laid claim at its peak to much of the rest of the Near Eastern world, its authority extending over large parts of northern Syria and Anatolia west of the Euphrates.

We have noted that the core territory of the Hittite kingdom was the region in north-central Anatolia bounded by the Halys/Marassantiya river. This was the essential 'land of Hatti'. Unlike the core populations of many other empires, Hatti's population almost certainly had no strong sense of a common national identity, nor any perception that they had a special status which set them above the peoples of the subject states outside the homeland. In fact, they never used – nor could they have used – a single specific ethnic term to identify themselves. They simply referred to themselves as 'the people of the land of Hatti', adopting a traditional name for the region where they lived which extended back many centuries before Hittite history began. The name 'Hittite' was originally adopted by scholars from the Old Testament, where it is

ABOVE AND RIGHT: Libation vessels in the form of a stag and a bull's protome (an adornment consisting of a frontal view of an animal head or bust of a human), from the 13th century BC.

Sacred Art of the Hittites

Our knowledge of Hittite art is confined largely to figurines and small artefacts, and to reliefs carved on rock faces. The reliefs are devoted almost entirely to religious life, with a king and often his queen depicted as paying homage to a deity, like the storm god or sun goddess, or participating in a religious festival. The king is dressed as a priest. He wears a close-fitting skull cap and a long robe and carries a crook. Libation vessels, or *rhyta*, in which drink offerings are made to the god during a ceremony, are sometimes fashioned into the forepart of an animal, like the bull and stag *rhyta* represented here. They are among the finest examples of Hittite art, in their accurate rendering of detail and in what has been described as their lively and whimsical charm. These qualities are also represented in the figurines of Hittite deities, like the seated goddess and the exquisite miniatures fashioned from gold and lapis lazuli. In their intimate appeal, they contrast strikingly with the more formal and more austere depictions of deities carved on the rock monuments.

ABOVE LEFT: A golden statuette of a Hittite god, *c.* 1300 BC.

ABOVE RIGHT: A seated goddess, in gold, with a child in her lap, from the site now known as Alaca Höyük. *c.* 1300 BC.

LEFT: Statuettes, in gold and lapis lazuli, of various deities worshipped by the Hittites. Dated to the 13th century BC.

used, in the form *hittî*, to refer to a small Canaanite tribe who dwelt in the hills of Palestine in the early 1st millennium BC. There are, however, five biblical passages in which the plural form *hittîm* refers to 'kings of the Hittites' and 'the land of the Hittites'. These Hittites are to be distinguished from the Canaanite group and can confidently be assigned to the Neo-Hittite kingdoms which arose in northern Syria and southern and eastern Anatolia in the late 2nd millennium BC. Many of their inhabitants, particularly their ruling elites, may well have been descendants of the Late Bronze Age 'Hittites'. The latter were a mixed population, made up of a number of different ethnic groups – Hattians, Luwians, Hurrians prominent among them – speaking a range of languages. Though the Indo-European 'Hittite' language (called Nesite by those who wrote and spoke it) remained the official chancellery language of the kingdom throughout its history, it was very likely spoken by only a minority of the homeland's population. And the population mix was constantly changing, particularly during the 14th century BC when tens of thousands of transportees were brought from conquered territories and resettled in the homeland. We have no sense of a culturally or ethnically coherent core population which saw itself as the most important element in an imperial enterprise.

In references to the Hittite kingdom in foreign texts, the term 'Hatti' became virtually synonymous with the kingdom as a whole, including all its subject territories. But it should be emphasized that far from attempting to impose their civilization on the lands which constituted their 'empire', the Hittites were highly receptive to the cultures of these lands, incorporating many elements of them into the fabric of their own society. This was a natural consequence in part of the transportation system, which brought back to the homeland thousands of booty-people each year, constantly enriching and diversifying both the ethnic and the cultural mix of the population. The Hittites also consciously absorbed the foreign cultures, most clearly seen in the Hittites' practice of incorporating the gods of the conquered territories, along with their cults, into their own

pantheon. It was a proud boast of the Hittites that they were the 'people of a thousand gods'. There was no sense in the Hittite kingdom of a core population which saw itself as dominant. The kingdom's ethnic and cultural inclusiveness was one of its most distinctive features. In this respect, it differed from many other political and military powers, both ancient and modern, which have been termed as empires.

THE MILITARY DIMENSION

The driving force behind Hittite imperial enterprises were the Hittite Great Kings, members of a royal dynasty which ruled the kingdom throughout its entire history. The king occupied his throne by right of succession through his family line, and with the endorsement of the gods. He ruled in the gods' name: 'For the land belongs only to the Storm God; Heaven and Earth together with the army belongs only to the Storm God. And he made the Labarna, the king, his deputy and he gave him the whole land of Hattusa.' As the gods' deputy on earth, the king was the chief priest of his realm. He was also the kingdom's supreme judicial authority, and the commander-in-chief of its armies. In both text and sculpture, Hittite kings presented themselves in the image of a lion who pounces without mercy upon its prey. The lions which still today flank the main entrance to the Hittite royal capital symbolize both the might of the Hittite king and the empire over which he held sway. Hittite imperial power was also symbolized by the double-headed eagle, as depicted at the entrance to the Hittite city now called Alaca Höyük, one of the most important cult-cities of the Hittite realm.

Like many of his Bronze Age counterparts, the king regularly led his troops on military campaigns, sometimes on an annual basis. Prowess in the field of battle demonstrated a king's fitness to rule. Indeed, demonstration of such prowess was an important element in the ideology of kingship, and almost certainly provided one of the chief incentives for the expansion of the Hittites' subject territories. As one historian of the Hittites has commented: 'Military expansion became an ideology in its own right, a true sport of kings.' But it was more

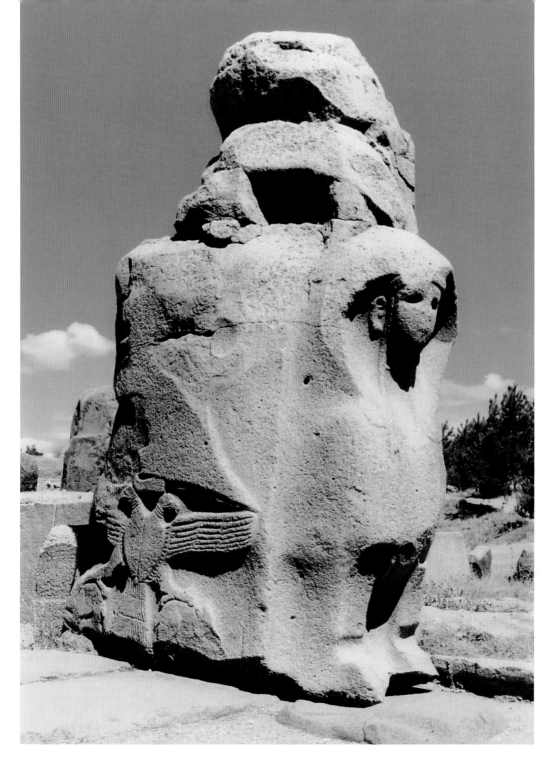

Sphinx Gate from Alaca
Höyük, Late Bronze Age.
Two such sphinxes flanked
the main entrance to the city.
Note also the representation
of the double-headed eagle, a
symbol of imperial power in
the Hittite world.

than just a sport. To maintain the respect and
support of his subjects, a king had to match his
predecessor's achievements in war, and if
possible to surpass them. Hattusili's military
enterprises far surpassed those of his
grandfather Labarna, and in his march across
the Euphrates he even challenged comparison
with the legendary Akkadian ruler Sargon. Yet
Hattusili was outdone by his grandson and
successor Mursili, who captured and sacked

Aleppo, a prize that had eluded his grandfather,
and then went on to destroy Babylon.

Seen in this light, the military campaigns of
the early Hittite kings have the appearance not
of empire-building enterprises, but rather of
personal adventures designed primarily for the
king's own aggrandizement. Indeed, there may
be some element of truth in this. The Syrian
campaigns of Hattusili and Mursili appear to
have been little more than large-scale raiding

The Hittite Army

The core of the Hittite fighting force was a full-time professional army, the majority of whose recruits came from volunteers within the Hittite homeland. Their numbers were supplemented by levies imposed by the king upon a number of his subject territories, and by transportees brought to the homeland from conquered lands and rebel states. Other able-bodied males within the homeland such as farmers could also be called up for military service when a major military campaign was to be undertaken. Mercenaries were sometimes employed, for example by the Hittite king Muwatalli in the battle of Qadesh. Infantry troops, who served as spearmen, made up the bulk of the army. But the elite fighting force, constituting about ten per cent of the total army, consisted of a chariot contingent. By the mid-13th century BC, the Hittite chariot crew was increased from two to three – a driver, a fighter armed with bow and arrow and spear, and a defender. The king was the commander-in-chief and frequently led the army into battle in person. But he sometimes delegated his authority to other high-ranking members of his family, generally one of his sons or brothers. Officers of lower status included lesser-ranking members of the king's family and other members of the nobility. Many of the latter were landowning nobles, who were given land-grants and a share of the spoils of battle (livestock, prisoners-of-war etc) in return for their service.

OPPOSITE: Relief scene from the Neo-Hittite city of Carchemish, on the Euphrates river, depicting charioteers charging into battle.

BELOW: Neo-Hittite reliefs of warriors. Both are probably gods. The left-hand figure is clearly identified as a god by his peaked cap. His long spear and short sword mark him out as an infantry man. He protects himself with a figure-of-eight shield. The right-hand figure appears to be wielding a slingshot.

66

Daily Life

Hittite art provides a few insights into their daily life. Reliefs and fragments of vases depict festival scenes showing a range of entertainers, from sword swallowers to musicians. Wedding ceremonies and elaborate funerary ceremonies are conducted for deceased members of the royal family. Slaves, often acquired through war, are shown performing a variety of functions.

expeditions which brought back substantial plunder to Hatti. No attempt was made to impose any form of Hittite authority over the conquered territories in Syria. After their destruction, the Hittite forces promptly withdrew. But strategic and economic considerations may have played some role in the campaigns. A number of the cities attacked by Hattusili lay on major routes linking Anatolia with Syria and Mesopotamia, and Hattusili may have been concerned to ensure continuing supplies to his land of tin, used in the manufacture of bronze, along the routes used by Assyrian merchant caravans to Anatolia during the Assyrian Colony period (20th–18th centuries BC). None of the surviving texts refer to such a motive, which is not surprising since those texts that do survive are devoted to extolling the king's military exploits. But plunder and personal glory may well have been the prime incentive for the Hittite kings' first ventures into Syrian territory. We should remember too that though the king was an absolute monarch, he needed the support of his military officers and other high-ranking officials with whom he shared the spoils of battle. Plundering expeditions conducted against wealthy cities provided a valuable source of income for the kingdom, and must have contributed much to the goodwill of the king's subjects towards him.

Constant military campaigning was also necessary to ensure the kingdom's survival. Hatti's core territory was landlocked, had no effective natural defences and was surrounded by enemy forces – most notably the Kaskan tribes in the Pontic region to the north, and the Hurrians in the southeast. The homeland's frontiers could be secured only by regular campaigns beyond them, led personally, whenever possible, by the king. The Hittite state needed a ruler at its helm whose paramount quality was that of a war leader. Even so, military victories provided no more than temporary respite from the constant threats posed by Hatti's enemies to the security of the homeland. There were also resource considerations. A far from unlimited supply of manpower meant that major campaigns conducted by the Hittites in distant regions seriously depleted the defence forces of the homeland, making it vulnerable to enemy attack. On a number of occasions, military victories abroad were offset by incursions into the homeland during the army's absence.

THE DIPLOMATIC ALTERNATIVE
Matters came to a head when, in the period following Mursili I's assassination, the kingdom lost many of its subject territories through rebellion, and the homeland fell prey to

OPPOSITE LEFT: Relief scene from Maraş (southeastern Anatolia) depicting a woman spinning wool and sitting opposite a scribe, from the 8th century BC.

OPPOSITE RIGHT: Neo-Hittite relief from a funeral stele found in Tel Halaf from the 8th–7th century BC, depicting a woman engaged in a domestic activity.

LEFT: Relief scene on a grave stele from the Neo-Hittite city Sam'al, depicting a deceased princess attended upon by a servant girl. The winged sun-disk above the figures indicates the deceased's royalty.

invaders. While Telipinu succeeded in winning back some of these territories, the strategically important state of Kizzuwadna in southern Anatolia remained independent. Rather than commit his troops to a costly and probably inconclusive conflict, Telipinu decided to come to terms with Kizzuwadna's ruler, a man called Isputahsu, by concluding a treaty with him. In effect, this marked a turning-point in the history of the Hittite kingdom. Although the treaty with Isputahsu seems to have been essentially in the nature of a compromise (it survives only in fragmentary form), it demonstrated that diplomacy could be at least as effective an instrument in maintaining the security of the Hittite kingdom and extending its influence as military force.

As we have noted, the greatest period in the expansion of Hittite power and influence came in the 14th century BC, during the period of the New Kingdom, in the reigns of Suppiluliuma I and his son Mursili II. Both kings carried out extensive conquests in Anatolia and northern Syria, and followed up their victories by reducing or restoring the conquered territories to subject status. But apart from Suppiluliuma's establishment of viceregal seats at Aleppo and Carchemish, the New Kingdom rulers never imposed direct rule upon their subject territories. Rather, they sought to maintain their authority over them through local vassal rulers and the treaties they drew up with them like that between Telipinu and Isputahsu. An important aspect of them was that they were personal compacts, drawn up between the Hittite king and his vassal. The vassal swore allegiance only to his overlord. He was thus bound to a person, not to the Hittite state, and was absolved of all his treaty obligations if the Hittite throne were seized by a usurper, unless he was called upon to help restore to the throne its legitimate occupant – i.e. his treaty-partner. As we have also noted, the king interfered in the internal affairs of a vassal state only in rare instances – for example, to help prop up a loyal vassal who had been removed from his throne by an anti-Hittite faction in the state, or on one occasion to threaten subjects in a certain vassal state with capital punishment for practising incest. Clearly, the Hittite policy of allowing almost complete autonomy to the subject states was pragmatically based. Hatti's kings simply did not have the resources to establish their own administrations in these states, or to ensure that they remained submissive to Hittite authority by installing permanent garrisons of Hittite troops in them.

Despite the largely 'hands-off' policy of Hittite kings towards the vassal states, anti-Hittite uprisings, especially in western Anatolia, were far from rare. And vassal rulers themselves frequently proved unreliable, or treacherous, sometimes consorting with foreign powers in their attempts to break their kingdom's ties with Hatti. On the positive side, the treaties gave a measure of stability to a number of regions where Hittite vassal rule was established. This provided Hittite kings with some relief, if only

for limited periods, from the need for constant campaigning in these regions, and the substantial commitment of resources which such campaigns entailed. In Syria, where Hatti shared a border with Egypt, the vassal states played an important role in maintaining a balance of power between the two Great Kingdoms. And control of the northern coastal states gave the Hittites direct access to the products brought by trade to the eastern Mediterranean ports.

A HITTITE 'EMPIRE'?

Whether or not the kingdom of Hatti warrants being described as an empire depends ultimately on how broadly this term is defined. Hittite kings claimed sovereignty over large expanses of territory throughout Anatolia and northern Syria. But in effect, there were only two regions where the Hittites actually ruled. One was the homeland itself in north-central Anatolia, the other consisted of those parts of northern Syria which were directly subject, from the reign of Suppiluliuma I, to the viceroys at Aleppo and Carchemish. Otherwise, the kingdom over which the Hittites claimed sovereignty was essentially a conglomerate of quasi-autonomous states, whose rulers signed personal contracts with the Hittite king and sometimes provided him with troops, tribute and military intelligence – unless they were rebelling or joining in alliances against him. The kingdom as such remained a fragile, tenuous structure, which fluctuated dramatically in size during the five centuries of its existence, and several times came close to extinction before its final collapse. But there is no doubt that Hatti played a major role in the history of the Late Bronze Age Near East, and at times profoundly influenced the course of events in this world. It was one of the four Great Kingdoms of the age, becoming for a time in the last half of the 14th century BC the most powerful of them all.

Neo-Hittite relief scene of the 8th century BC from Ivriz (southeastern Anatolia), depicting the local king, Warpalawas (right), offering prayers to the storm god, Tarhunda. There is evidence that in several of the Neo-Hittite kingdoms descendants of the earlier Hittite dynasty survived and continued to hold power.

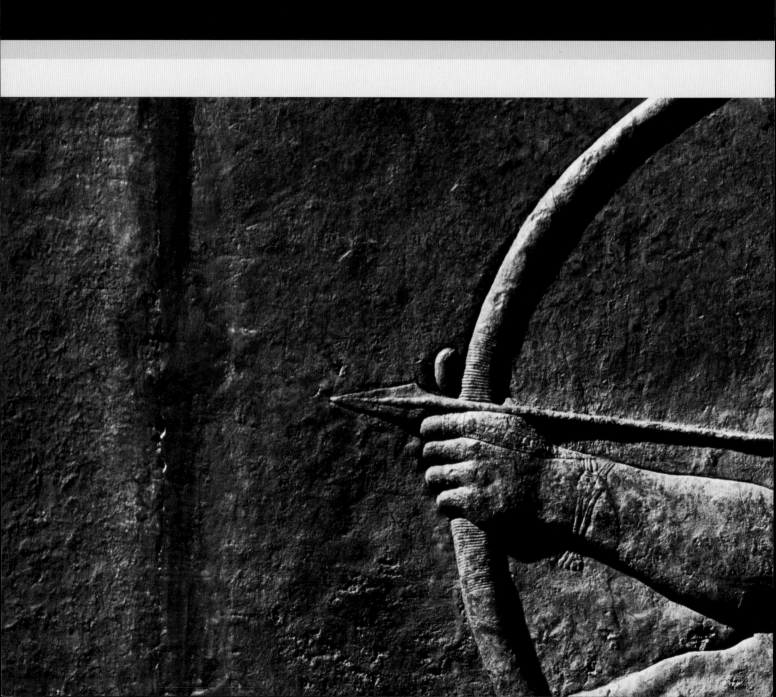

CHAPTER 3
THE EMPIRES OF
ASSYRIA AND BABYLONIA

900–539 BC

For most of the time since antiquity, the empires of the Assyrians and Babylonians have been synonymous with wanton cruelty and decadence. The reputations of their kings – the notorious Nebuchadnezzar, for example, derided in the Bible for his treatment of the Jews – were marked indelibly by the views of their victims and enemies, with little or no acknowledgment of the splendour of their written culture, the development of urban civilization, or the sophistication of their bureaucracies. Archaeological excavation and, above all, the decipherment of cuneiform in the 19th century have allowed us not only to hear the kings speak in their own words, but to appreciate the achievements of Assyrian and Babylonian cultures in their own terms.

King List

ASSYRIA

911–891 BC	Adad-nirari II
890–884 BC	Tukulti-Ninurta II
883–859 BC	Assurnasirpal II
858–824 BC	Shalmaneser III
823–811 BC	Shamshi-Adad V
810–783 BC	Adad-nirari III
782–773 BC	Shalmaneser IV
772–755 BC	Assur-dan III
754–745 BC	Assur-nirari V
744–727 BC	Tiglath-Pileser III
726–722 BC	Shalmaneser V
721–705 BC	Sargon II
704–681 BC	Sennacherib
680–669 BC	Esarhaddon
668–627 BC	Assurbanipal
627–623 BC	Assur-etel-ilani
622–612 BC	Sin-shar-ishkun

BABYLONIA

625–605 BC	Nabopolassar
604–562 BC	Nebuchadnezzar
561–560 BC	Amel-Marduk
559–556 BC	Nergal-Shar-Usur
556 BC	Labashi-Marduk
555–539 BC	Nabonidus

PREVIOUS PAGES: King Assurbanipal is shown here drawing a bow from a chariot during a lion hunt, depicted on the walls of his palace at Nineveh. The sculpture displays the intricate decorations of his headdress and garment and of his earrings, which resemble those found in the tombs of the Assyrian queens at Nimrud.

LEFT: This statue of King Assurnasirpal, excavated at his capital at Kalhu, is one of the few royal sculptures in the round preserved from Assyria. It was found in a temple on the city's citadel and shows the king in constant veneration of the god.

Assyrian empire in 859 BC
Annexations by Tiglath-Pileser III
Annexations by Sargon II
7th-century BC Assyrian raids
Babylonian annexations

0   100 km

0   100 miles

Sennacherib moves
capital to Nineveh
704–681 BC

Conquest of Babylon by
Persian king, Cyrus
539 BC

Shalmaneser III mounts
major campaigns
to extend empire
858–824 BC

Sargon II builds capital of
Dur-Sharrukin (Khorsabad)
713–706 BC

Elam ravaged, Babylonian
revolt crushed
668–627 BC

800 BC   700 BC   600 BC   500 BC

Tiglath-Pileser III reforms provincial
system and standing army
745–727 BC

Assyrian conquest
of Egypt
680–669 BC

Destruction of
Assyrian empire
614–605 BC

In 722 BC, the Assyrian king Shalmaneser V conquered the city of Samaria and terminated the royal house of Israel; in 587 BC the Babylonian king Nebuchadnezzar II did the same to the city of Jerusalem and the royal house of Judah. These events were not unusual nor of extraordinary interest to the victorious kings and their entourages. But they left a deep mark on the historical consciousness of the region and far beyond, because the victims described them in one of the great works of world literature, the Hebrew Bible. For centuries people read of these conquests and despised their perpetrators, though they knew little more about them than what was written in the biblical text. Other than that, only Greek authors of the 5th century BC and later provided a few garbled accounts and mostly fantastic tales

of Assyrian and Babylonian kings and queens. By the early 19th century AD the ancient tales of Assyrian and Babylonian violence and decadence perfectly fitted the then common perception of the Middle East as a dangerous and exotic place. Painters and poets delved into the stories to compose images of grandeur, indolence and cruelty that projected modern stereotypes onto the distant past.

Assyria and Babylonia were thus never forgotten, but it was the victims rather than the creators of the empires who shaped their memories. This situation changed radically in the mid-19th century AD, when archaeologists began to explore the ancient ruins of these cultures. The first great discoveries in ancient Mesopotamia, when the region was part of the Ottoman empire, uncovered the capitals of

First exhibited in Paris in 1828, this painting by Delacroix of the *Death of Sardanapalus* caused great commotion. The painter showed the last ruler of Assyria, whose name the Greeks rendered as Sardanapalus, in the guise of a stereotypical Middle Eastern potentate surrounded by harem women. He emphasized the king's moral depravity by showing him as totally indifferent to the massacre surrounding him.

74

Assyria (Assur, Kalhu and Nineveh) and Babylonia (Babylon). Monumental buildings came to light, often packed with works of art. Tens of thousands of ancient records, carved in stone or impressed on clay using a script called cuneiform, were excavated. Archaeologists filled newly built museums in London, Paris, Berlin and Istanbul with these objects and texts. Exploration has continued ever since, though political events in the Middle East, particularly in Iraq in the heartland of Mesopotamia, often make work difficult if not impossible. The material available to a historian of the Assyrian and Babylonian empires, however, is now abundant and varied. The decipherment of cuneiform in the mid-19th century allows us to read innumerable texts from the Assyrians and Babylonians themselves. Objects, buildings, cities and numerous other remains provide us with multiple sources to study their empires.

It is remarkable that, despite the abundance of sources that have become available in the last 150 years, these empires still have negative connotations that are often absent in the study of other ancient empires. It is obvious that they were of seminal importance to the history of the Middle East for some 400 years, from around 900 to 539 BC. How we judge them today should probably depend more on how we perceive empires in general – as systems oppressing many people over a wide area or as enabling great projects – than on the negative appraisal of people in the past who suffered from them. The Assyrian and Babylonian empires are examples of a long series of ancient empires, neither worse nor better. Their early date and the rich data available for them make them of special interest in the study of empires in history. While Assyria and Babylonia are mostly investigated independently and as two separate political structures, we shall discuss them here together, both because of the strong continuity in practices between the two and the fact that they ruled the same regions of the ancient world.

This aerial view of the site of Nimrud, ancient Kalhu, shows only a small part of the massive city. The citadel on the left was covered with monumental palaces and temples, on which archaeologists have focused their attention. In the background the Tigris river is visible.

OPPOSITE: These scenes from the so-called Black Obelisk of Shalmaneser III, excavated at Kalhu and dated to *c.* 828 BC, show the submission of defeated kings and the tribute Shalmaneser collected. The top panel displays King Jehu of Israel kissing the ground before Shalmaneser's feet. This is the only representation of an ancient Israelite king in existence today. The panel below shows the tribute of Egypt, which surprisingly includes two-humped camels, more commonly associated with Iran. The bottom panel contains a traditional Assyrian scene of a lion capturing a deer.

RIGHT: The cuneiform inscription that covers all the sides of the Black Obelisk relates the campaigns Shalmaneser mounted over 31 years and the loot he captured.

THE MILITARY DIMENSION

In the 10th century BC the entire Middle East was politically divided into small states. Many of the regions that had flourished in the 2nd millennium BC were now poor and disorganized, and political power had shifted to newcomers, principally to tribes from northern Syria with a nomadic background, the Arameans. The city-residents feared and loathed

these people, but it is clear that the Arameans had increased their influence everywhere and occupied much of the rural land as well as some cities, especially in the western part of the Middle East. It was in the west that they established small states around old urban centres, regularly in concert with other populations. In the east the old kingdoms of Assyria and Babylonia survived, but Babylonia in particular was unstable, with a quick succession of dynasties. In Assyria the same family occupied the throne for many generations, but the regional extent of their power was limited.

The Assyrians fundamentally changed this situation in the mid-9th century BC. Especially two men, Assurnasirpal II (883–859 BC) and Shalmaneser III (858–824 BC) rapidly expanded the kingdom's reach through incessant military campaigning, primarily in the west. Assurnasirpal systematically annexed all territories between the Assyrian heartland on the Upper Tigris in northern Iraq and the Euphrates river in western Syria. Shalmaneser crossed the Euphrates with his troops in order to confront the rich states further west. Opposition to their expansion was fierce. In 853 BC, Shalmaneser fought a battle against a large coalition of western states near a place called Qarqar and seems to have lost – though he never officially acknowledged this. Shalmaneser only recovered several years later, but by 841 he was able to raid numerous states of western and southern Syria and force them to pay tribute.

Assyria's success depended on stability in the centre and that faltered upon Shalmaneser III's death. Although his son Shamshi-Adad V (823– 811 BC) managed to take control – with the help of Babylon's king who imposed a humiliating treaty – provincial administrators gained much of their independence, and states across the Euphrates stopped paying tribute. Over the next 80 years Assyria's central power was limited. Theoretically the Assyrian king ruled all of northern Iraq and Syria from the area east of the Tigris to the Euphrates, but in reality local governors paid only lip service to him. At the same time powerful rival states emerged in the north and southeast: Urartu, which controlled

ABOVE: Prominent men in the provinces tried to portray themselves as independent kings when the Assyrian overlord was weak. This statue of Hadad-yith'i, from Guzana in northern Syria, probably dates to the mid-9th century BC. On it was carved the same inscription in the Aramaic and Akkadian languages. The first version calls the figure 'king of Guzana', the second 'governor'.

eastern Turkey and threatened Assyria's provinces in northern Syria, and Elam in southwestern Iran, which meddled in the affairs of Babylonia to its west.

In 744 BC, Tiglath-Pileser III (744–727 BC) initiated fundamental changes in the running of the Assyrian empire together with a long series of military campaigns. The reforms continued in subsequent reigns and reduced the powers of governors and state officials. The kings restricted their territories in size and forced them to share powers with others. Tiglath-Pileser's successors are the most renowned military men of Assyrian history: Shalmaneser V (726–722 BC), Sargon II (721–705 BC), Sennacherib (704–681 BC), Esarhaddon (680–669 BC) and Assurbanipal (668–627 BC). For about a century they campaigned almost annually in all parts of the Middle East. In the east and north they clashed with the states of Urartu and Elam, in the south they fought Babylonian opposition, in the west they gradually annexed more Syrian and Anatolian states, as well as the state of Israel. The furthest point Assyria reached was when King Assurbanipal sent troops to capture the Egyptian capital of Thebes in the year 664–663 BC.

Assyria's military strength may seem to have been unmatched, but this was the effect of the Assyrian propaganda, rather than reality. In fact, the struggles with major rivals were protracted and not always successful. The greatest challenge the empire faced was the control of its southern neighbour, Babylonia. Throughout the period when Assyria was gaining ascendancy over the Middle East under strong leaders, power in Babylonia was divided. Urban residents and tribal people from the countryside were competing for kingship, which had changed hands numerous times. During Assyria's second phase of expansion started under Tiglath-Pileser III, several of its kings captured Babylon's throne but when their attention was drawn elsewhere, local opposition managed to wrest it away. The solution of making another Assyrian or a faithful Babylonian king also failed. Either the local population removed them or they ended up defying Assyria. In frustration some Assyrian kings reacted with great violence: Sennacherib claims to have wiped Babylon off the face of the earth in 689 BC (an exaggeration, but he did cause much damage) after a tribal leader had seized the throne, and from 652 to 649 BC

RIGHT: The Assyrians often depicted their army's attacks on enemy cities and showed successive events as happening simultaneously. This view of an assault on a town in Egypt by Assurbanipal's troops displays the Assyrians still scaling the wall with ladders while they carry off bound prisoners and their families below. The river at the bottom of the relief is the Nile, shown with water creatures, such as fish and crabs.

Assurbanipal ransacked the entire country in a prolonged war against his own brother, who he himself had made king of Babylon.

These efforts to overcome Babylon were to no avail and in 626 BC, when Assurbanipal had just died, a leader of the Chaldean tribes, Nabopolassar, initiated a dynasty in Babylon that would last for almost 90 years, the Neo-Babylonian dynasty. Soon he was able to turn against Assyria, whose capital Nineveh he sacked in 612 BC. In order to replace Assyria as the regional superpower Nabopolassar's troops had to push westward for at least another seven years, mopping up Assyria's last resistance in 610 BC and confronting the Egyptians in a major battle in 605 BC at Carchemish, on the Euphrates river. He and his successors continued Assyria's policy of threats of military action followed by conquest as a last resort only in order to subdue territories at the fringes of the empire. Most notorious today is Nebuchadnezzar II's treatment of Jerusalem and the state of Judah, as the Hebrew Bible describes it in detail. Assyria had left Judah under local rule though

it had stripped the country of much of its territory. Nebuchadnezzar first attacked Judah in 597 BC, deporting part of its population. After a rebellion, he laid siege to Jerusalem for two years and finally destroyed the city in 587 BC, deporting yet more people. Even later the assassination of the Babylonian governor in 582 necessitated further military intervention. Nebuchadnezzar II annexed other previously independent Syrian states and his successors extended the empire into southern Anatolia and Arabia. These events are much less clear to us, as the Babylonians did not describe them in detail – unlike the Assyrians whose military actions dominate the official record. Still, there is no doubt that Babylonia was a worthy successor of Assyria.

From 605 to 539 BC the Babylonians were the masters of the Middle East from the Mediterranean Sea to the Zagros mountains. They could not control events in Iran, however, where the Persians from the southwest under King Cyrus II (559–530 BC) rapidly extended their powers northward to Anatolia. For some

This fanciful 19th-century reconstruction of the Assyrian capital, Kalhu, from the hands of James Ferguson, was published in 1853 by the British archaeologist Sir Austen Henry Layard. It is most likely inaccurate in its details but does represent the opulence of the city and its grandeur.

LEFT: These examples of the jewelry excavated in the queens' tombs beneath the palace of Kalhu show the amazing wealth of the women as well as the exquisite craftsmanship of the artists who made the pieces. The earrings (*TOP*), bracelets (*CENTRE*) and golden belt (*BELOW*) represent just some of the mass of objects placed on the bodies of the 8th-century BC queens.

OPPOSITE: In wells of the second citadel of Kalhu, archaeologists discovered ivories that originally decorated furniture looted by the Assyrians during their conquests. The pieces were crafted in various parts of the empire and beyond. This ivory was probably carved in Phoenicia on the Levantine coast and shows Egyptian influence in the depiction of the sphinx who wears a royal crown of Egypt.

Treasures from an Assyrian Capital

The palace residents and other elites surrounded themselves with the exquisite products of craftspeople both from the home countries of Mesopotamia and from the conquered territories. Most have vanished over time, but what remains gives us an idea of their splendour. In the late 1980s Iraqi archaeologists discovered several tombs beneath the largest palace on the Assyrian citadel of Kalhu (modern Nimrud). Although not all intact, they still contained an amazing quantity of grave goods from the late 8th century BC, given to several queens of the time. They are of gold (one tomb

contained 14 kg of gold), semi-precious stones such as lapis lazuli and carnelian, rock crystal and other valuable materials. Earlier archaeologists discovered in the same palace several wells in which ivory objects had been dumped. The workmanship of all the goods is superb. Jewellers carefully crafted objects using a wide array of techniques and sculptors carved ivories in exquisite ways. The styles reveal that the craftsmen came both from Assyria itself and from the western territories, and we can distinguish several workshops and artistic traditions.

seven years the Persian and Babylonian states shared a lengthy border from the Persian Gulf to the Mediterranean Sea. In 539 BC, Cyrus directed his troops against Babylon, whose resistance may have been weakened by internal resentment against the current king, Nabonidus. Soon Cyrus captured the city and almost the whole of its empire. The Persian empire was born, ending the 400-year-long dominance of Mesopotamian states in Middle Eastern history.

PACIFYING THE EMPIRES

Modern accounts of the Assyrian and Babylonian empires tend to focus on the military activity that led to the imposition of these countries' rule over vast areas. We describe conquests. But the greatest task empire-builders face throughout history is to make their successes last without having to maintain a massive military presence. In the study of the Assyrian and Babylonian empires we are confronted with great differences in the sources that these two cultures left behind. The Assyrians were explicit in their accounts of military actions and this detail enables us to determine how they pacified regions. They also left us correspondence from imperial bureaucrats that allows for the study of the administration of certain areas. The Babylonians, on the other hand, were much vaguer in their accounts of conquest and virtually no actual documents of the imperial bureaucracy exist. Yet, from sources such as the Hebrew Bible and some administrative records we can conclude that there was great continuity in practices between the two empires.

Both Assyria and Babylonia steadily expanded the limits of their empires. However, both seem to have done so reluctantly: their aim was not conquest but rather to gain access to the resources of regions on the periphery with the least direct interference in daily affairs. When encountering new territories they used their substantial military might to scare the inhabitants into voluntarily giving tribute, that is, annual payments of valuable goods. They kept local rulers on the throne as long as they obeyed and paid up. Yet, such arrangements tended to fail when vassals

took advantage of the absence of the imperial army and rebelled. After a second conquest the Assyrians and Babylonians selected a member of the local aristocracy who they thought would be more obedient to take on rule as a puppet king. Those men had often been educated in the imperial capital, and the fact that they were imposed on a country made them unpopular at home and more dependent on the empire for their survival. But they also regularly rebelled and thus triggered a final stage of submission, when the empires annexed the region and administered it directly through imperial officials rather than local men.

Both empires had sufficient flexibility to adjust their practices to local circumstances, but the sequence of vassal, puppet ruler and governor – each step triggered by rebellions – seems to have been at the basis of their policies everywhere. The Bible shows how this happened in the cases of Israel and Judah. Early in the reign of Tiglath-Pileser III, which started in 744 BC, the Israelite vassal King Menahem paid his tribute loyally. When an anti-Assyrian rebel, Pekah, seized the throne, Tiglath-Pileser intervened and made a puppet-ruler, Hoshea, king. Hoshea's later unwillingness to pay tribute to Shalmaneser V provoked another campaign, and in 722 BC the Assyrian annexed Israel as a province and destroyed its capital Samaria. Similarly in the case of Judah, the Babylonian Nebuchadnezzar II replaced the local vassal Jehoiachin in 597 BC with the puppet-king Zedekiah. Zedekiah's rebellion in 589 BC forced Nebuchadnezzar's return and in 587 BC he made Judah a province under a Babylonian governor.

The Assyrians and Babylonians employed fear to maintain obedience. Whenever the imperial armies were forced to act they did so with great violence. The Assyrians were careful to broadcast the misery their troops could cause in texts and images, with such success that these messages still shape the perception of their empire today. They narrated and depicted how they killed, flayed and beheaded people; burned and demolished cities, and washed away their ruins into the river; cut down orchards and ploughed fields with salt. While these depictions may have been hyperbolic, they were sufficiently realistic to terrify anyone who saw the Assyrians advance. It is likely that many submitted before a single arrow was shot.

One method of control and punishment that both the Assyrians and Babylonians used had a radical impact on the character of conquered regions and their inhabitants: namely mass deportations. The practice of moving groups of people from one end of the empire to another was common policy in both empires. This was done in different stages, first deporting selected people, mostly political leaders and skilled artisans. When regions remained defiant, large parts of the population ended up living abroad, including entire communities of men, women and children. The practice had several advantages for the empires. The fear of being uprooted probably pushed many to submit rather than fight. Deportation caused the people to end up in

foreign lands whose local populations resented them, so they had to rely on the empire for protection. At the same time the empire could use their labour in building projects or to develop new agricultural lands. Moreover, they could resettle other people in the regions the deportees left behind. Scholars estimate that the Assyrians moved around some 4.5 million people over three centuries, a staggering number for these early times. Figures for Babylonia are unavailable.

From around 900 to 539 BC, the Assyrians and Babylonians thus gradually converted the diverse regions of the Middle East into a more unified and homogeneous whole. They mixed populations and created provinces with similar administrative structures. Their policies had a great impact both on the core of the empires and on the peripheries that they annexed.

The Assyrians are famous for their vivid depictions of the punishments they imposed on defeated enemies. Here we see troops of King Sennacherib flaying two men from the city of Lachish in Israel, possibly Egyptians who assisted the Israelites.

A relief showing how the Assyrians deported entire families from Lachish. Women and children were allowed to sit on carts while men walked and carried their household goods.

THE IMPACT OF EMPIRE ON THE ASSYRIAN AND BABYLONIAN HEARTLANDS

The primary aim of the empires' expansion seems to have been to gain access to resources. Although Assyria and Babylonia had a rich agricultural basis, the conquered territories provided goods and materials that were rare or unavailable in the homelands, which naturally varied from region to region. In southern Anatolia, for example, there was metal ore, in the Lebanon mountains there was wood, and in the Zagros mountains there were horses. The conquerors found treasures that people had accumulated everywhere, which caused particular interest. Assyrian accounts detail the materials and craft products they looted from the palaces of defeated kings: silver and gold, semi-precious stones, woven textiles, furniture,

statues, vessels, weapons and much more. Some defeated countries were extremely wealthy such as Egypt. When Assurbanipal looted its capital Thebes, he boasted:

> 'My hands captured that city in its entirety with the support of the gods Assur and Ishtar. Silver, gold, precious stones, as much as there was in the holdings of his palace, brightly coloured and linen clothing, large horses, male and female residents, and two tall pillars made from pure silver, whose weight was 2,500 talents [75,000 kg] and which stood at the gate of the temple, I removed from their position and took to Assyria.'

All kings listed what they looted. It is clear that the conquests provided an influx of wealth, while the subsequent systems of annual tribute and taxation generated a constant stream of assets. At the same time the deportations supplied the empires with labour forces far beyond their core populations.

It is no surprise then that the Assyrians and Babylonians – at least the ruling classes – could shape their environment to reflect their empires' grandeur. Massive building projects took place whenever the empires flourished. Kings erected grand palaces with numerous rooms and large courtyards. They roofed them with cedar beams brought in from the distant mountains of Syria, decorated them with stone wall-reliefs and with panels of wood and ivory, furnishing them with elaborate fittings. They built and restored temples to their gods. They laid out gardens planted with exotic trees. They expanded and embellished cities. All these projects were possible only because of the empires' resources. The ruins of Mesopotamian cities and palaces today may not be very impressive, as their mud brick architecture is much decayed, their roofs and gates have disappeared, and their decorations were taken away. But in ancient times they would have been magnificent and clear signs of their builders' power and wealth.

Cities were not the only places that received attention. Both Assyrians and Babylonians developed the countryside and benefited agriculture through irrigation projects. The Assyrians laid out a system of canals to bring water from the mountains to cities such as Nineveh. Irrigation was much more important in Babylonia where rainfall was so scarce that no one could grow crops without watering them artificially. The Neo-Babylonian kings expanded and systematized the canal system to crisscross the entire southern region of Mesopotamia. The work initiated a long period of agricultural prosperity there that lasted many centuries after the dynasty's end. We have no documentation on who dug the canals and built other infrastructure, but it seems likely that imported labour played a great role in these massive projects.

The deportations had other effects on the core of the empires as well. The influx of people from regions all over the Middle East made the populations of Assyria and Babylonia more diverse. People from the west in particular seem to have been numerous and influential. Arameans had already started to migrate into Assyria and Babylonia in the early centuries of the 1st millennium BC, but the deportations from Syria increased their numbers by far. The Aramaic language became the commonly spoken tongue in Assyria and Babylonia. Since

LEFT AND OVERLEAF: The Ishtar gate of 6th-century BC Babylon was magnificently decorated with blue glazed bricks and coloured images of dragons and bulls thought to protect the city's entrance. The German excavators of the gate took it in its entirety to Berlin where it is now displayed in the Vorderasiatisches Museum as an example of the great buildings of ancient peoples of the Middle East. The next page gives a detailed image of one of the bulls, the symbol of the storm god, Adad.

they mostly wrote on perishable parchment rather than on clay tablets that preserve better (though some tablets inscribed with Aramaic exist), we know little of their actual writings. But representations of scribes in Assyria show men standing side-by-side writing Akkadian on clay tablets and probably Aramaic on parchment scrolls. The written Akkadian language of the mid-1st millennium BC shows influences from Aramaic, which may have been the language of daily use even in the court.

Other deported people likewise had an impact, albeit more limited. Documents from the centre of Babylonia in the 6th century BC show the presence of a large number of people with Hebrew names (Judean deportees), and the existence of villages of Anatolians, Arabs and Phoenicians. The enormous geographical reach of the empires and their dynamic economies probably also encouraged people to come to their cores voluntarily. Phoenician merchants from the

Mediterranean coast settled in Assyrian cities to conduct trade, and Egyptians came to Babylon. All these people brought their own languages and customs; they probably looked and dressed differently from the local populations, cooked distinctive foods, and behaved distinctively. Assyrian and Babylonian societies became more diverse.

Despite the great variety of people with different religions, intellectual traditions and habits, it cannot be said that Assyria and Babylonia were multicultural societies. Their high cultures were remarkably traditional and impervious to outside influences. Since the 2nd millennium BC Babylonian culture had been dominant in both countries. People read the same literature, they honoured their gods in similar ways (even if some deities were different), and they adhered to the same intellectual and scholarly traditions. Assyria's access to Babylonian writings increased when it controlled the south, and kings such as Assurbanipal sent out scholars to collect materials that were not yet available, but this was just an extension of the regular absorption of Babylonian culture. The influence was not

ABOVE: The alphabetic Aramaic script was usually written on parchment rather than clay tablets, but some exceptions, such as this one, exist.

RIGHT: This Assyrian relief shows the presence of two scribes working side-by-side. One impresses a stylus onto a tablet, writing cuneiform Akkadian; the other holds a pen to write alphabetic Aramaic on a parchment scroll. Both record the decapitated heads of soldiers handed in as part of their valour.

reciprocal: Babylonia accepted little Assyrian culture in return. Neither country paid much attention to the literatures and intellectual traditions of the regions they conquered, though both adopted the Aramaic language for some of their daily writings. The Assyrians also imitated artistic and architectural styles from conquered regions, but in cultural terms the empires made little difference to the Mesopotamians.

The empires were very large and complex structures, ruled in an autocratic way with the king as the ultimate source of authority for every decision. He needed to rely on a group of officials to govern, however, and the highest of those probably derived primarily from the empires' heartland. Despite the fact that we know many names and titles of Assyrian officials, the available documentation does not reveal clearly what each one did or even how many people were involved. But the numbers must have been large and grew with the empire. The Assyrian hierarchy had seven high officers at the top. The titles do not describe their functions accurately, however, as is the case in most palace organizations throughout history. They included the treasurer, palace herald, chief cupbearer, chief eunuch, chief judge, grand vizier and commander-in-chief. While titles seem to differentiate between civilian and military duties, in reality all were involved in both spheres of activity. These high officials must have spent much time in the capital where

they formed the king's cabinet, but they were also governors of strategic border provinces.

The Assyrian king personally chose his high officers. Although he probably selected men from the elites, he was not obliged to keep an office in the hands of one family. On the contrary, kings were careful not to make offices hereditary. Several of the highest officials were castrated men, who could not create dynasties in competition with the royal house. There is virtually no information on how people rose through the ranks. It seems likely that a king would have chosen men with previous experience to fill the highest posts, but the available data does not allow for the reconstruction of anyone's career path. Despite these shortcomings of the evidence, we should imagine that in the heartlands of both Assyria and Babylonia large groups of wealthy officials existed whose careers depended on the empires' success and who benefited from the conquests and the subsequent influx of resources. Their numbers must have risen in parallel with the expansion of the areas Assyria and Babylonia controlled. The growth of imperial elites affected their societies in many ways still invisible to us.

THE IMPACT OF EMPIRE ON THE CONQUERED TERRITORIES

Although Assyria and Babylonia were reluctant to take over the administration of the territories they conquered, increasingly more regions of

After his victory over the Elamite enemy Teuman the Assyrian king Assurbanipal relaxes in his palace garden with his wife sitting beside him. Attendants fan them and musicians entertain them, while the head of the slain king dangles from the tree above.

This colourful wall painting from Til Barsip shows in profile the heads of two Assyrian men. In the palaces of the capital cities the same images appeared but they were first carved on a stone relief which was then painted, while here the scene is painted onto the wall.

Dur-Shalmaneser, 'Fortress of Shalmaneser'. Excavations on the citadel revealed a huge 7th-century BC citadel with a throne room. The building was decorated with wall paintings that showed the same scenes as the stone reliefs in Assyrian palaces, which originally were also decorated with paint. In the provinces the imagery was the same, but the materials were less expensive, as a governor did not equal the king. Throughout the city existed houses of rich citizens, who adopted Assyrian customs. The house of one man named Hanni, for example, contained a group of cuneiform tablets in full Assyrian style. Hanni was also wealthy enough to own lavish furniture, which was decorated with the same type of ivories as those discovered in the palace at Kalhu. The decorations were not as varied as those in the capital, however. Til Barsip survived the transition from Assyrian to Babylonian empires intact, and its inhabitants maintained their earlier traditions inspired by Mesopotamia until they abandoned the city, possibly because Babylonia's neglect of the region made their lifestyle unsustainable.

In northern Syria east of the Euphrates river the Assyrians pursued a policy of replacing local traditions with Assyrian ones. For example, they used in their public inscriptions only the cuneiform script and Akkadian language; unlike others in ancient Near Eastern history (for example the Persians) they never displayed a multi-lingual inscription that would be easier to understand for local populations. Before the massive expansion of the empire starting with Tiglath-Pileser III in the mid-8th century BC, there existed a clear differentiation between regions that the Assyrians called 'the land of Assur' and those under 'the yoke of Assur'. The first term referred to areas whose economies and cultures had become fully integrated into the Assyrian, including in religious terms. The inhabitants of these areas gave offerings to the god Assur as if he were their god. The Assyrians interfered much less in the areas under 'the yoke of Assur', which remained under local rule, paid tribute and honoured their own gods.

When the Assyrians rapidly annexed territories after 745 BC, they gave up this clear

the Middle East became provinces of the empires. The presence of imperial bureaucrats led to changes in the provincial cultures and economies, partly enforced, partly because local populations willingly adopted the rulers' practices. We know much more about Assyria's impact than Babylonia's in this respect, as the latter empire left little evidence on the subject. The transition of power from one to the other does not seem to have caused drastic changes. Babylonia was less interested in the development of the provinces, however, and this neglect led to a reduction of the empire's impact, it seems, though much remains unclear to us.

When Assyria turned regions into provinces it installed an administration that mirrored the one in the capital. As representative of the king, the governor was surrounded with the same luxuries the court had in Assyria, but on a smaller scale. For example, after Shalmaneser III conquered the Syrian city Til Barsip on the Euphrates in 856 BC, he and his successors gradually turned it into an Assyrian town. Shalmaneser renamed the city distinction and may have tried to develop all the empire's assets as much as possible to their advantage. At Ekron in southern Palestine, for example, a region still under vassalage rather than annexed, they reorganized olive oil production, increasing the number of oil presses and standardizing their layout. The oil was no longer for local consumption only but for other parts of the empire as well. The Assyrians had realized that development of resources in the territories they already controlled brought in substantial benefits. The Babylonians, however, were different in that respect. During their conquests they ransacked regions such as Judah and Ekron, but they did not bother to redevelop them. The richer farmlands in the Babylonian heartland, which they actively expanded, may have made them less concerned with agricultural resources from the provinces.

In all their policies the Assyrians displayed great flexibility; political, cultural and military considerations influenced how they behaved. Even in neighbouring regions they varied their level of interference depending on local circumstances. Provinces adjoined vassal states, and the Assyrians left some areas alone because they were not interested in their resources, or because they wanted a buffer zone with enemies beyond. Sometimes a vassal state was closer to the core of the empire than a province because it was beneficial for the Assyrians to leave local structures in place. We cannot look at a map of the Assyrian empire and assume that the impact of the empire was uniform or extended in concentric circles from the core. It was a patchwork of regions that each had specific interactions with the core and consequently different mixtures of local and imperial elements.

The ideology of the Assyrian and Babylonian empires

Empires are systems of exploitation: a group of people imposes its will on others and forces them to submit. The creators of empires need to invest much effort into the enterprise, often manpower that only their own populations can provide. Throughout history there always was a need to convince audiences of the correctness

of the empire's existence and its behaviour. The audiences are varied both within the empire's core and in the regions it wants to control. Both contain elites – people who make decisions and impel others to act on them – and commoners, who often experience events more directly than the elites. They receive innumerable messages, some ephemeral, such as military parades, others more lasting as they are expressed in writing, images or the shaping of the environment. The study of ideological expressions of support for the Assyrian and Babylonian empires is multifaceted and must work with numerous lines of evidence. We can address only a few examples here to illustrate the riches of the Assyrian and Babylonian material.

In 714 BC, the Assyrian king, Sargon II, defeated in battle King Ursa of Urartu, Assyria's great rival to the north. Upon Sargon's return one or more courtiers composed a long account of the campaign, which was addressed to the people of the city of Assur. We do not know whether it was ever read out to them: written in high literary Akkadian it may have been incomprehensible to most people. It is clear, however, that some in Sargon's entourage devoted much effort to the task of constructing a document that was meant to show the king had been correct in his actions. One of the most remarkable aspects of the account is how it portrays the enemy kings as direct opposites. Ursa disobeys the gods, he is foolish and does not know his limitations; Sargon listens to the gods, he is wise and observes the limits the gods have set him. When the account narrates the battle between the two, it shows Sargon as a valiant warrior who massacres numerous enemies single-handedly. In contrast, Ursa is a coward, who despite his numerous troops runs away on the back of a mare and hides like a woman in the corner of the mountains. The end of the account describes how Ursa loses his mind: he tears off his clothes, pulls his hair, pounds his chest, throws himself on the ground and cries in constant pain. Ursa is not a true king but a madman, while his opposite Sargon is a wise ruler. Should we not agree then that Sargon was right in destroying Ursa?

Voices of Empire

Thanks to the discovery and subsequent decipherment in the 19th century of clay tablets impressed with cuneiform writing, we can now read innumerable texts from the time of the Assyrians and Babylonians themselves. These help to counterbalance the previously known biblical accounts which were written from the point of view of the conquered peoples. Imperial themes emerge of conquest and rebellion and the plunder of cities for their great wealth. The Assyrians made it a point to broadcast in text and image the misery their troops could cause, leading many to submit before a single arrow was shot. The Babylonians, like the Assyrians before them, deported vast numbers of conquered peoples from their homelands to other parts of the empire, most notoriously the Jews of Israel and Judah.

The Assyrians kept close track of all the goods they looted from conquered cities and their war reliefs regularly include the images of scribes who did so. The two men shown here represent the two types of scribes and writing systems in use in Assyria. The one closest to the viewer writes Akkadian in cuneiform on a clay tablet; the one to his right writes Aramaic in alphabetic script on a leather scroll.

King Nebuchadnezzar II (604–562 BC) attacks Jerusalem in this account from the Bible

'As the Lord had declared, Nebuchadnezzar removed all the treasures from the temple of the Lord and from the royal palace, and took away all the gold articles that Solomon, king of Israel, had made for the temple of the Lord. He carried into exile all Jerusalem: all the officers and fighting men, and all the craftsmen and artisans – a total of 10,000. Only the poorest people of the land were left.'

'With the support of the god Assur, my lord, I kept marching along difficult routes and over rugged mountains with the mass of my troops and there was no equal to me.' KING ASSURNASIRPAL

Letter to King Esarhaddon of Assyria (680–669 BC) by the people of Nippur, who support Assyria against the Babylonian rebels

'The king knows that all the lands hate us because of Assyria. We cannot step safely any of the lands. Wherever we go, we get killed with this accusation: "Why do you embrace the feet of Assyria?" Now we have barred my city gates; we do not go out to the open country. We have no water. Let us not die of thirst!'

King Nebuchadnezzar II describes how he fortified the city of Babylon

'On the outside of Babylon, on the other eastern bank [of the canal], I surrounded the city with a massive wall making a moat and raised its sides high with bitumen and baked bricks like a mountain. At the sides of Babylon I piled up great banks of earth and I surrounded the city with a large body of water. Great floods of destroying water like the great waves of the sea I made flow about it; with a marsh I surrounded it.'

The Assyrian king Assurbanipal (668–627 BC) boasts of looting the Egyptian capital, Thebes

'My hands captured that city in its entirety with the support of the gods Assur and Ishtar. Silver, gold, precious stones, as much as there was in the holdings of his palace, brightly coloured and linen clothing, large horses, male and female residents, and two tall pillars made from pure silver, whose weight was 2,500 talents [75,000 kg] and which stood at the gate of the temple, I removed from their position and took to Assyria.'

Tens of thousands of cuneiform scripts were excavated in Assyria's last capital at Nineveh. They illustrate numerous aspects of life: royal campaigns in annals, daily affairs in contracts, letters and administrative documents, scientific explorations in texts regarding astronomy and many other aspects of the world.

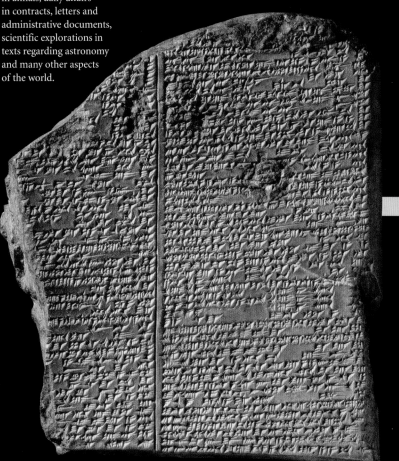

'I drove out of the cities 200,150 people, young and old, male and female, horses, mules, donkeys, camels, big and small cattle beyond counting and considered them booty.'

KING SENNACHERIB, referring to the kingdom of Judah

RIGHT: This English engraving from the early 19th century shows an imaginary Babylon dominated by the tower in the centre. Produced long before the city's excavation on the basis of classical descriptions, the artist unknowingly stressed one of the ideas the builders of Babylon themselves emphasized: the city was a model of order in an otherwise chaotic world.

OPPOSITE: This aerial view of the site of the ziggurat of Babylon shows the few remains left behind after Alexander of Macedon ordered the removal of the structure to make place for a new tower that was never realized. The new debris of the old ziggurat was dumped nearby and forms a hill called Homera today.

Slightly more than a century later kings Nabopolassar and Nebuchadnezzar used the wealth of their new empire to redesign their capital Babylon. They built new walls, gates, roads, and palaces. The plan of their city is striking because of its regularity. The inner city is a rectangle enclosed by two walls 7 m (23 ft) apart and respectively 3.7 m (12 ft) and 6.5 m (21 ft) wide. In the inscriptions the builders left behind they portray Babylon as a haven of order in a world of chaos. That order was far-reaching due to Babylon's contacts throughout the land. At every New Year's festival the gods of other cities visited the supreme god Marduk of Babylon and the king led them all into the city in a procession that displayed the war booty of the preceding year. An essential idea to the Assyrian and Babylonian empires was that they were forces of order and brought peace to their inhabitants. The empires were a benefit to the world, if not the entire universe.

RESISTANCE TO EMPIRE

Throughout history subjects of empires have defied them and have refused to obey the will of foreign rulers. Resistance can take many forms. It can be violent, including the assassination of imperial representatives; it can be civil disobedience; it can involve an unwillingness

to assimilate. It is hard to investigate these actions in the Assyrian and Babylonian records, since the sources give almost exclusively the empires' perspective and non-violent resistance in particular remains hidden. It is clear, however, that both empires had to deal with persistent opposition. The first task of many new rulers was to restore order in provinces that had taken advantage of the previous emperor's death to rebel and withhold taxes.

Consequently kings made efforts to improve relations with conquered people. Some Assyrians, for example, tried hard to placate their Babylonian subjects. Esarhaddon, whose father had devastated Babylon, funded the reconstruction of temples and cults and tried to present himself as a good Babylonian king. His policy was to culminate in the return of the statue of the Babylonian god Marduk to his temple in Babylon, but even the transport was difficult as Babylonians along the way rallied around the statue. We do not know exactly how they expressed their displeasure; they caused much trouble, however, and for a long time frustrated Esarhaddon's plans.

Violent opposition was ubiquitous. We read of the murder of governors and other imperial representatives, and the army had to return repeatedly to particular areas to quell

King Nabonidus

This stele of King Nabonidus, now in the British Museum, shows the king holding a ceremonial standard. Above him are the divine symbols of the moon-god Sin (closest to him), the planet Venus of Ishtar and the winged disc of the sun-god Shamash. The text on the stele celebrates the return of plenty after a drought.

The last ruler of ancient Mesopotamia who was independent from foreign control was a man called Nabonidus, one of the most unusual and controversial characters in Mesopotamian history. Nabonidus ascended the throne of Babylon in 555 BC after three descendants of Nebuchadnezzar II had ruled for a brief period each. He was not royalty and may have grown up in the north of the empire, near the heartland of Assyria. Soon he diverged from the usual religious practices of Babylonia, showing greater devotion to the moon-god Sin than to Marduk, the god of Babylon. He moved the capital to an oasis city in the Arabian Desert, Teima, which meant that the annual festival for Marduk, which required the king's presence, could no longer be celebrated. This and other actions infuriated traditionalists and writings appeared that foretold the wrath of Marduk against Nabonidus. The instrument of punishment would be the Persian king Cyrus, whom Marduk invited to capture Babylon. We know that Cyrus did indeed defeat Nabonidus in 539 BC and took over the Babylonian empire. A disenchanted part of the population may have encouraged him to do so, but this event ended Mesopotamia's independence.

uprisings. Certain regions were especially recalcitrant. For example, Babylonia never accepted Assyrian rule and even when Assurbanipal's brother was king of Babylon he led the country's fight against the Assyrian army. It is no surprise then that such resistance in the end led to Assyria's demise. An independent Babylonia turned against Assyria in the late 7th century BC, gaining the assistance of peoples from the Zagros mountains in the east, the Medes and Scythians (who may have been hired as mercenaries). The victims of imperial oppression took their revenge. Babylonia's end was of a different nature, although not necessarily because it was a less repressive empire. Its territory and riches tempted the Persians of Iran, who had never been under Babylonian rule. The outsiders captured a vast empire in one fell swoop.

THE PLACE OF THE ASSYRIAN AND BABYLONIAN EMPIRES IN WORLD HISTORY

When, in the mid-5th century BC, the Greek historian Herodotus wrote his account of the Persian wars, he contrasted his small country to the vast Persian empire, which could, he claimed, rely on two million soldiers. His investigation led him to search for Persian predecessors which he found in Assyria and Babylonia. But he knew little about them, especially Assyria. Already in the 5th century BC they were distant history. Today, when our knowledge of world history stretches much further down in time than Herodotus', we still see the Assyrian and Babylonian empires as the start of a long sequence of empires in the Middle East: Persian, Alexandrian, Seleucid, Roman, Parthian, Sasanid, Umayyad, Abbasid and Ottoman. All integrated part or the entirety of the regions Assyria and Babylonia controlled in their massive territories.

Yet, many scholars also use the term 'empire' to identify earlier political formations in the region. They speak, for example, of the 'first-world empire' in the mid-3rd millennium BC, or even of an informal trade empire in the late 4th millennium BC. Were Assyria and

Babylonia merely imitators of earlier empires? The answer is both yes and no: they took over practices that existed before but also introduced crucial innovations.

Here we may stress these novelties over the continuities. Many times before states had indeed imposed their wills on others, but these structures had been ephemeral and geographically limited. In contrast, Assyria and Babylonia unified vast areas for some 400 years and their actions fundamentally restructured life everywhere. The process had it highs and lows and only from 745 BC on was a fuller integration of the territories involved. The rulers experimented with a new system and had no earlier examples to follow. If the Egyptians (Chapter 1) and

(perhaps) Hittites (Chapter 2) of the late 2nd millennium BC had created empires previously, this was unknown to the 1st-millennium Assyrians and Babylonians. They showed inexperience in their efforts and learned the hard way that conquest was easier than pacification. Assyria's annual campaigning may be glorified in the official record (what official record does not glorify the empire's actions?), but it was exhausting and had diminishing returns. Empire builders had to learn how to follow up on their aggression, and neither Assyria nor Babylonia seem to have been good at it. Later empires in the region, such as the Persian, may have learned from them, but that is for another chapter.

The Tower of Babel story in the biblical book of Genesis fascinated people throughout history. This painting, which the Flemish Pieter Brueghel created around 1563, shows the tower reaching high in the sky surrounded by normal houses that look minuscule. Brueghel, who had no actual remains to work from, used the Colosseum in Rome as his model.

The history of the Achaemenid Persian empire (like that of the Babylonians) has usually been written from the vantage point of Persia's enemies or subjects – in particular the Greeks and the Jews. Writers like Herodotus and Xenophon, though they idolized the founder of the Persian empire, Cyrus, related vivid stories of the luxury and moral degeneration of the Persian court, and the violent actions of all-powerful Persian queens. Increasingly, however, the Achaemenid empire has come to be seen more dispassionately. As newly discovered administrative records reveal, Persian power depended not just on brute force but on its advanced system of roads, and on an immensely professional bureaucracy. The kings' own pronouncements also show that their pragmatism was matched at least by idealist rhetoric: in their religious tolerance, for example, or the claim that they were protecting their subjects from one another through a *Pax Persiana*.

Achaemenid King List

559–530 BC	Cyrus II (the Great)
530–522 BC	Cambyses II
522 BC	Bardiya (Smerdis)
521–486 BC	Darius I (the Great)
486–465 BC	Xerxes I
465–425 BC	Artaxerxes I
425–424 BC	Xerxes II
424 BC	Sogdianus
424–405 BC	Darius II
405–359 BC	Artaxerxes II
359–338 BC	Artaxerxes III
338–336 BC	Artaxerxes IV
336–330 BC	Darius III

PREVIOUS PAGES: Detail of the staircase leading up to the Apadana or throne-hall at Persepolis. Rows of soldiers, some in Persian 'court dress', and others in Median 'riding costumes', stand with spears in their hands. To the left, beneath a row of trees, a lion mauls the hind quarters of a bull, a powerful motif repeated frequently throughout Persepolis and in Achaemenid art in general.

LEFT: Panel of polychrome glazed bricks depicting a royal soldier from Susa. Dressed in an elaborately worked costume, perhaps a kind of royal livery, the soldier is equipped with a quiver and bow and holds a spear, the end of which rests upon his foot. This is one of a series of a procession of guards, perhaps the famous Immortals who made up the Great King's bodyguard.

Cambyses conquers Egypt
525 BC

Persians defeated by
Greeks at Marathon
490 BC

Final defeat for Darius
at battle of Gaugamela
331 BC

Conquest of Babylon by
Cyrus the Great
539 BC

Peace of Callias between
Persia and Athens
465/449 BC

Darius III escapes after
losing at Issus to
Alexander the Great
333 BC

500 BC   400 BC   300 BC

Cyrus dies in battle
530 BC

Xerxes defeats Greeks at
Thermopylae, but his fleet
is destroyed at Salamis
480 BC

Darius murdered; Persian
capital Persepolis sacked
by Alexander
330 BC

Construction of Persepolis
Palace begins
515 BC

First coinage; Persian
Royal Road built
500 BC

Artaxerxes I defeats rebel
army led by his brother
at Cunaxa
401 BC

In 2005 the British Museum produced a major exhibition on the history and culture of the first Persian empire, that ruled by the Achaemenid dynasty. Despite boasting such luminaries as Cyrus the Great, Darius the Great and Xerxes, the exhibition was entitled *Forgotten Empire* in an attempt to emphasize the notion that while the Achaemenid empire was the largest and most influential empire in the pre-Alexander period – a true world empire in fact – its impact on later history and scholarship has been (and continues to be) seriously misunderstood and undervalued. It is fair to say that if Persia enters into the historical

consciousness at all, then it is usually filtered through the classical or biblical imagination. By and large, the 'authentic voice' of ancient Persia has been either ignored or mistreated and we engage with the ancient Persians as either the champions of the Hebrew nation (the biblical slant), or the oppressors of the free world (the classical tradition). Moreover, today it is difficult to comprehend that the land we now call Iran once lay at the heart of a magnificent empire; its importance as an ancient world power and a cultural axis has been almost completely eclipsed by the Western media's obsession with the changes that have taken place within Iran since the Islamic revolution of 1978.

Thus, in the West, ancient Persia is best remembered for its war with Greece and its later invasion and ultimate defeat by Alexander of Macedon. For the Persians themselves, the Greco-Persian wars were little more than tiresome border skirmishes which took place over 2,000 miles from the heart of the empire in Iran. Yet so much of our understanding of Persian history is filtered through ancient Greek sources, especially the influential 'histories' of Herodotus, Xenophon, Arrian and Ctesias of Cnidus, that we find it difficult to separate the Greek fabrication of Persian history and culture from its reality. The Greek perspective on the history and nature of the Achaemenid empire pits Greek freedom and democracy against 'Oriental' (i.e. Persian) tyranny and despotism.

In modern popular Western culture the image propounded in the ancient Greek sources still dominates. Two recent Hollywood movies exemplify the trend in which the Persian empire is only viewed as a negative stereotype of 'Otherness'. Oliver Stone's movie *Alexander* (2004) displays all the familiar Orientalist notions about the inferiority and picturesqueness of Eastern societies. So much so, indeed, that in terms of its portrayal of East–West relationships, *Alexander* has to be seen as a stale cultural statement and a worn-out reflection of the continuing Western preoccupation with an imaginary exotic Orient. More interesting, however, is *300*, Zack Snyder's 2007 film version of the graphic novel by Frank Miller. Snyder's take on the

Thermopylae story and the slaughter of the 300 Spartans at the hands of the Persian army is a fantasy; it is created as the battle would have looked in the minds of the Greeks, as they mythologize the story of the 300's sacrifice. This is not history, and the 'Persians' of the film are a bizarre blend of sadomasochistic, effeminate, ninja-like cartoon villains (as equally bizarre are the Spartans' oiled and pumped porn-star bodies). However, *300* does nothing to promote the quest to locate and understand the real Persian empire.

Achaemenid art was once dismissed as repetitive and uninspired: thus George Curzon, the Viceroy of India, walking through the ruins of Persepolis in 1901 commented that, '1,200 human figures move in solemn reduplication upon the stones – what monotony and fatigue! It's all the same, and the same again, and yet again.' Now scholarship is beginning to reassess Persian art and to recognize not only the aesthetic timeless beauty of the artworks, but also the importance of art for understanding imperial ideology and Persian cultural norms.

Achaemenid art drew widely on Egyptian, Assyrian, Babylonian and Elamite motifs, and in turn the Persians exerted a strong influence on the arts of Greece. Achaemenid art is therefore an eclectic mix of styles and motifs drawn from different parts of the empire, but fused together to produce a harmonious look which is distinctly Persian. Egyptian and Assyrian motifs (like winged disks and winged *genii*, pediment shapes and designs, and even the canons for depicting the human figure) are frequently melded together so that Achaemenid art can be said to reflect, in physical form, both the diversity and unity of the empire as a whole.

Recent scholarship – based on a new understanding using ancient textual sources from all parts of the empire, together with analogies of Achaemenid art and archaeology – has recognized that classical authors displayed a heavy bias against Persian culture. We can now determine that in spite of revolts, succession crises and regicide, the vast empire nevertheless held together as a coherent unit for 230 years. It showed no signs of internal weakness or stagnation at the time when the Macedonians took over power from the last Achaemenid king Darius III. It is wrong to think of the first Persian empire as the 'Forgotten Empire', and it is more appropriate to re-label it the 'Misrepresented Empire'.

ABOVE: Xerxes, Great King and King of Kings – as conceived of in the Hollywood imagination. In Zack Snyder's movie *300*, Xerxes (played by the Brazilian actor Rodrigo Santoro) is depicted as an effete despot. With his shaved head and his naked torso adorned with jewelry, this Xerxes is a far cry from the official image of monarchy created by the Achaemenids themselves.

OPPOSITE: This raised relief (once painted) carved onto a door-jam at Persepolis shows an Achaemenid Great King processing through his palace in the company of two court officials. One shades the king's head with a delicate parasol, while the other carries a towel and a fly-swat. While these tasks may seem slavish, courtiers vied for the privilege of being the monarch's body servants, because close proximity to the king could result in personal gain and political advancement.

CHRONOLOGY OF EMPIRE

Made up of 23 lands (including Persia), the Achaemenid empire stretched from Libya to India and from southern Russia to the Indian Ocean. What was the process of acquiring an empire of this scale? It is fair to suggest that, in fact, there was never *one* Persian empire, but multiple empires, since throughout its 230-year history the empire was in a constant state of flux, expanding and contracting and expanding yet again. Provinces and peoples were added to the central government by force or coercion and were lost from Persian control through wars, rebellions and uprisings. Egypt, for example, was lost for almost 60 years before being re-conquered and forced back into the empire. After the reign of Xerxes, however, there was no territorial expansion, although there were still nationalist or localized revolts. A brief overview of the empire's history reveals how quickly the status quo could change.

ESTABLISHING EMPIRE

Cyrus II (559–530 BC), 'The Great', was ruler of the small southwestern Iranian kingdom of Persia, located in the modern Iranian province of Fars. He also styled himself 'King of Anshan', referring to an area in the foothills of the Zagros mountains and once ruled by the powerful and culturally sophisticated Elamites. It would seem that the earliest Persian monarchs regarded themselves as the natural inheritors of Elamite lands and perhaps even saw themselves as the custodians of Elamite culture.

Early in the reign of Cyrus, the Persians were one of several Iranian tribes who were vassals to the Medes. The powerful Median kingdom was expanding in the north of Iran to the point where its military might was strong enough to campaign against the wealthy region of Babylonia. Babylon itself was only saved from attack when in 550/549 BC Cyrus, supported by a coalition of south Iranian tribes, marched north to attack the Median king, Astyages. Following the sack of the Median capital, Ecbatana, Cyrus turned his attention towards northern Media, including the ancient kingdom of Urartu in the area of Lake Van. The chronology of this period is hazy, but it is possible that Cyrus also occupied Elam and claimed possession of its capital Susa. Cyrus also undertook a war in Bactria.

Following this a Persian campaign moved against the wealthy and powerful kingdom of Lydia in Asia Minor. Croesus of Lydia had brought the cities of Ionia under his rule and his wealthy capital, Sardis, benefited from extensive trade routes with Mesopotamia. The sack of Sardis meant that Cyrus was able to take other important cities along the Ionian coast, which were placed under the control of Persian satraps (provincial governors) and administrators.

By 540 BC Cyrus was ready to attack Babylon and moved his army into Mesopotamia, marching first on Opis and then on Sippar. He entered Babylon on 29 October 539 BC, having already taken its king, Nabonidus, prisoner. Apparently meeting no military resistance, Cyrus appointed his son, Cambyses, as the city's regent, although he maintained the status quo by allowing Babylonian officials to continue in their governmental and religious offices. Much of our knowledge of the fall of Babylon comes from the so-called Cyrus Cylinder – a clay foundation deposit written in Akkadian discovered near the sanctuary of Marduk in the city. It was presumably composed on Cyrus' orders, although the whole document is written from a Babylonian point of view in traditional Babylonian terms. As a piece of imperial propaganda, the Cylinder attempts to legitimize Cyrus' conquest of Babylon by representing the king as the

A barrel of clay inscribed with Babylonian cuneiform, the Cyrus Cylinder is an important piece of Persian propaganda. It declares that Cyrus the Great found favour with the Babylonian god Marduk, who championed the Persian king as a liberator of the oppressed Babylonians. The reality of Cyrus' conquest of Babylon may have been quite different. Today the Iranians often hail the Cyrus Cylinder as the first declaration of human rights, although in reality there is nothing in the text that suggests this concept.

champion of the god Marduk, who finds in Cyrus the city's saviour. It seems that the Babylonians benefited from Cyrus' capture of their city; certainly the Jews of Babylonia profited from his benevolence and were allowed to return to their homelands. Other peoples did not fare so well under Cyrus: the citizens of Opis were massacred *en masse*, and, following the fall of Lydia, the population was deported to Nippur in Babylonia, where a community of Lydians is later attested.

In the years following the conquest of Babylonia (538–530 BC) Cyrus was occupied gaining a truly international empire: Aria, Parthia, Sogdiana and Margiana fell to him on the eastern front, while near the Jaxartes river he founded a city which the Greeks called Cyropolis. In the west, Cilicia, Syria and Palestine came under Cyrus' rule and while he never held Egypt, he had clearly marked it out for conquest.

At Pasargadae in the modern Fars province of Iran, Cyrus constructed a tomb and a palace planted with a formal garden irrigated by myriad water-channels. The result was nothing short of a desert paradise – *pairidaêza* (Greek *paradeisos*) – which acted as an empire in miniature, as flora from all across Cyrus' conquered lands were brought together as a physical statement of Persia's ever-growing power.

EXPANDING EMPIRE

In 530 BC Cyrus died in a war against the Massagetae. He was succeeded by Cambyses (530–522 BC), who having been trained for the succession by his father ascended peacefully to the throne. A Babylonian text dated 31 August 530 BC names Cambyses as 'King of Babylon, King of Lands'. At his accession Cambyses appointed his younger brother, Bardiya, as a governor of Media.

Cambyses' greatest achievement was the conquest of Egypt in 525 BC, following the death of the last native pharaoh, Amasis. He was crowned according to ancient rites at Memphis with the pharaonic throne name Mesuti-Re. Following the conquest of Egypt, the

The tomb of Cyrus the Great at Pasargadae is a relatively plain structure: a small vaulted chamber built of a high stepped platform of huge stone rectangles. It resembles the kind of burial structures which Cyrus would have seen during his invasion of Anatolia. Standing a short distance from the palace complex and its extensive gardens, the tomb was certainly visited by Alexander of Macedon who revered Cyrus as a great military leader. Even today Cyrus' tomb is regarded as a hallowed site by many Iranians.

Voices of Empire

Before the 19th century, the popular image of the Persian empire was predominantly drawn from two important sources: the Bible and the works of classical authors. By and large, the Old Testament texts championed the Persians, because it was the Great Kings of Persia who freed the Jews from their Babylonian exile and allowed them to return to the Promised Land to build a new temple in Jerusalem. The classical authors, however, tended to depict Persia in a negative light. Great Kings are shown as lustful and mad tyrants, and the Persian empire was regarded as an oppressive challenge to the Greek love of Freedom. It was only from the 1850s, with the decipherment of the cuneiform language known as Old Persian, that the Achaemenid monarchs were able to speak for themselves. The Old Persian inscriptions, although somewhat repetitive, proclaim the heroic and militaristic qualities of the kings of Persia and place his rule within the shadow of Ahuramazda, the great god of the ancient Iranians. Other cuneiform texts in Babylonian, Elamite and Akkadian strengthen our knowledge of Persian history, and Egypt has also offered up information on Persian rule in hieroglyphic and demotic texts.

Cuneiform tablet with a text in Elamite. These baked clay tablets, surviving in their thousands (written in Elamite, Babylonian, Akkadian and Old Persian) are invaluable in reconstructing the administration of the Persian empire.

The Greek historian Herodotus explores the nature of the Persians' attitude towards their empire

'Persians most of all hold themselves in honour, then those that dwell next to themselves, then those next to them, and so on, so that there is progression in honour relating to distance. They hold least in honour those whose habitation is furthest from their own. This is because they rank themselves to be the best in mankind of everything and that others have a hold on virtue in proportion to their nearness; those who live furthest away are most base.'

'In the month of Arahsamna, the third day, Cyrus entered Babylon, green twigs were spread in front of him – the state of peace was imposed upon the city. Cyrus sent greetings to all Babylon.'

A Babylonian text known as the *Annals of King Nabonidus* recall the conquest of Babylon by Cyrus the Great in October 539 BC

In an Old Persian inscription from Persepolis Darius places himself and his people under the protection of the god Ahuramazda

'Proclaims Darius the king: this land of Persia, which Ahuramazda bestowed on me, which is good, whose horses are good, whose people are good, by the will of Ahuramazda and of me, Darius the king, it does not feel fear of any other. Proclaims Darius the king: may Ahuramazda bear me aid, together with all the gods, and may Ahuramazda protect this land from the enemy army, from famine, from the Lie … This boon I ask Ahuramazda, together with all the gods.'

In the Old Testament book of Isaiah, Cyrus of Persia is praised as the liberator of the Jews and the champion of Yahweh

'Thus says the Lord to His anointed, to Cyrus – whose right hand I have held – to subdue nations before him and loose the armour of kings, to open before him the double doors, so that the gates will not be shut: "I will go before you and make the crooked places straight; I will break in pieces the gates of bronze and cut the bars of iron. I will give you the treasures of darkness and hidden riches of secret places, so that you may know that I, the Lord, Who call you by your name, am the God of Israel."'

An Old Persian inscription from the tomb of Darius the Great at Naqsh-I Rustam in which he boasts of his military prowess

'I am a good bowman, both on foot and on horseback.'

'By the favour of Ahuramazda these are the countries which I got into my possession … Elam, Media, Babylonia, Arabia, Assyria, Egypt, Armenia, Cappadocia, Lydia, the Greeks who are of the mainland and those who are by the sea, and countries which are across the sea, Sagartia, Parthia, Drangiana, Aria, Bactria, Sogdia, Chorasmia, Sattagydia, Arachosia, Hinduš, Gandara, Scythians, Maka.'

At Persepolis, Darius records in an Old Persian text the extent of his empire

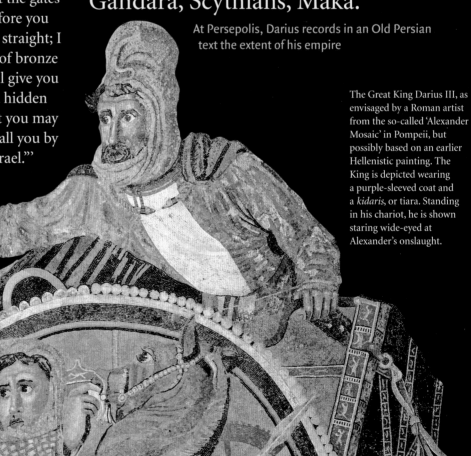

The Great King Darius III, as envisaged by a Roman artist from the so-called 'Alexander Mosaic' in Pompeii, but possibly based on an earlier Hellenistic painting. The King is depicted wearing a purple-sleeved coat and a *kidaris*, or tiara. Standing in his chariot, he is shown staring wide-eyed at Alexander's onslaught.

neighbouring countries of Libya and Cyrene offered submission to the Persian forces before Cambyses marched south, down the Nile, stationing a Jewish garrison on the island of Elephantine to protect Persian interests in the south. He then advanced and conquered at least a part of Nubia.

Greek sources tend to portray Cambyses as a mad despot, tyrannically oppressing his subjects and impiously debasing the religious traditions of his conquered nations. Much of this slander emanates from the accounts of Egyptian priests who were opposed to Cambyses' attempts to reduce their power and wealth. Archaeological evidence from Egypt suggests that Cambyses adopted a policy of religious tolerance – inscriptions from the Serapeum in Memphis (524 BC) confirm that he honoured the death of a sacred bull with due rites and rituals. Like Cyrus in Babylon, Cambyses co-opted the support of Egyptian nobles to maintain his sovereignty and was sensitive to Egypt's religious and cultural traditions.

REBELLIOUS EMPIRE

Cambyses' death occurred in Egypt in the summer of 522 BC. His brother, Bardiya, was assassinated after a few months' rule and was replaced on the throne following a violent and bloody palace coup, by Darius I, also 'the Great' (521–486 BC), the governor of Parthia, who solicited the support of six other Persian nobles. Immediately, rebellions broke out across the empire and turmoil quickly spread from province to province. Babylon, Media, Armenia, Scythia and even Parsa itself erupted in chaos as provinces tried to break free of Persian rule. Darius was ruthless in suppressing the revolts and bringing the empire to heel, an act which, amazingly, he accomplished in little more than a year. He captured and executed the rebel leaders and for the rest of his reign he was never threatened with an uprising again.

High above the Royal Road near Ecbatana, Darius had an account of the suppression of the rebellions carved deep into the rock face of Mount Bisitun. A huge raised relief dominates

In northeastern Iran, between Kirmanshah and Hamadan (ancient Ecbatana, the capital of Media), rises the Bisitun mountain, known in the Achaemenid period as Bagastana (place of the gods). Here on a rock about 60 m high there is a great monument to Darius I, the most famous Achaemenid king. It was no accident that Darius chose this site for his monument since the mountain evidently possessed religious-cultic significance in early history. In a trilingual inscription and an accompanying raised-relief, Darius describes how he quelled rebellions that had broken out in many parts of the empire at his accession.

the surface of the stone showing Darius standing at the head of a line of rebellious kings, each one fettered to the next by a rope. Darius is depicted on a larger scale than the other figures on the relief and he places his left foot upon the belly of the prostrate figure of the rebel Gaumata. In his left hand Darius clutches a bow, a symbol of his military authority, which is echoed by the presence of two armed guards standing to his rear. Darius' right hand is raised in adoration of the figure in the winged disk at the centre of the scene: this is probably Ahuramazda, the supreme deity of the Achaemenids; he offers Darius the kingship in the form of a ring.

CONSOLIDATING EMPIRE

In 518 BC, after confirming his hold on the empire, Darius I was able to expand its borders as far as the Punjab; in 513 BC he attempted to conquer the Scythians north of the Black Sea too. In Darius' reign the empire reached its zenith and extended from Libya to Bactria.

Darius was particularly concerned with implementing empire-wide building and engineering projects: in Egypt he was responsible for the creation of a canal between the Nile and the Red Sea, as well as for building temples to Egyptian gods at Hibis in the Fayum. In the Iranian heartland, Ecbatana and Pasargadae were expanded and embellished and he started a mammoth building programme at Persepolis. The Elamite city of Susa was afforded a new lease of life by Darius when he chose it as his administrative capital. An important inscription from Susa records how Darius enlisted workmen from all over the empire to build and decorate his palace in a truly international endeavour.

Late in his reign Darius came into contact with the Greeks, and while he may have had ambitions to incorporate Greece into the empire (and was certainly keen to punish Athens for its interference in Persian affairs), Herodotus' account of Greco-Persian tensions probably exaggerates the Persian response to

The Persians were a vital presence in the Greek imagination. Athenian vase paintings frequently represent Persian warriors or, in this case, Persian kings and courtiers. Possibly showing a scene from a Greek drama, the so-called 'Darius Vase' depicts the Great King, in his elaborate sleeved robe and high hat, sitting on a high throne. He is accompanied by a bodyguard. In front of him, on a platform inscribed with the word 'Persians' (*Persai*), is a messenger delivering news to the monarch.

The Palace of Persepolis

Darius I began the construction of the ceremonial palace of Persepolis around 515 BC, and it was added to by Xerxes and each of the successive monarchs thereafter. It was still in the process of being built when, in 330 BC, Alexander destroyed it in retaliation for Xerxes' sack of Athens. The buildings were built of locally quarried stone, although the craftsmen who worked at the site were drawn from every corner of the empire.

Persepolis consisted of a vast complex of military quarters, treasuries and storerooms, private living quarters, large reception rooms, audience halls, and hill-cut royal tombs. Yet Persepolis was not in continual use: the royal court moved between Susa, Babylon and Ecbatana annually, coming to rest at Persepolis for the Persian New Year in March. Darius planned Persepolis as a showcase of empire, for it was here that delegations from all over the empire would assemble each year to offer tribute to the Great King.

Ambassadors, nobles and courtiers would congregate in the Apadana, or throne-room, a 20-m (65-ft) high pillared hall in which the Great King held audience and received the obeisance of his court. Enormous courtyards were able to accommodate thousands of dignitaries and guards as they stood waiting to see the king, while impressive stairways and entrance gates, such as Xerxes' Gate of All Lands, guarded by colossal sculpted human-headed winged bulls, helped filter the crowds into the palace complex.

ABOVE: A beautiful small lapis-lazuli head, discovered at Persepolis, shows a Persian courtier. The identity is unknown and even the sex is debated. It is possibly a portrait of a youthful prince, or a representation of a eunuch or even of an Achaemenid queen or princess. The tiny sculpture is delicately and skilfully worked. Despite its size, this little head is a masterpiece of Achaemenid art.

RIGHT: The ceremonial palace at Persepolis sits on a man-made platform rising out of the Marv Dasht in southwestern Iran. This photograph shows clearly the layout of the palace complex, which included throne rooms, banqueting halls, treasuries and residential quarters. Cut into the mountainside above Persepolis are also several royal tombs.

the Greek resistance. However, before he could launch a Greek campaign Darius died and was buried in a tomb at Naqsh-I Rustam, near Persepolis. It was left to his son Xerxes to punish the Greeks.

TROUBLED EMPIRE

Xerxes (485–465 BC) took control of the empire, and, in all essentials, he continued his father's policies of expanding and strengthening the empire, although it must be noted that our knowledge of Xerxes' reign is almost totally confined to the western periphery of the empire, due to our complete dependence on Greek sources. Moreover, evidence for the events of the latter years of his reign is sparse and mainly conjectural. Because of his aggressive policy towards the Greek lands, classical sources depict Xerxes as a hubristic megalomaniac, but this is probably far from the truth.

Xerxes' first task was coping with a rebellion in Egypt, which had begun prior to Darius' death. He appointed his brother Achaemenes as satrap of Egypt, a policy frequently adopted by the Achaemenid kings whereby close family members were appointed to important satrapal positions, so much so that the running of the empire became a family concern.

In 481 BC Babylonia erupted in revolt. Again Xerxes drew on his close relatives for aid and the rebels were subdued by Megabyzus, Xerxes' cousin (who afterwards became one of the supreme commanders of the campaign against Greece). Xerxes responded to the revolt by dividing the huge satrapy of Babylonia into two: 'Babylonia', embracing all of modern Iraq and Syria, and 'Beyond the River', including Syria-Palestine and lands west of the Euphrates.

One aim, in which Xerxes ultimately failed, was to force the mainland Greeks to acknowledge Persian power. From the perspective of Persia's long-term Aegean policy, extending a measure of control to European Greece was logical and the importance of this Persian expansion is signalled by the fact that Xerxes himself led the expedition. Xerxes captured Athens in 480 BC, but his navy was then defeated by the Greeks at Salamis (see Chapter 5). The city was recaptured a year

later, although shortly afterwards the Persian general Mardonius was killed at the battle of Plataea and his army was heavily defeated. In August 479 BC the Greeks again routed the Persians at Mycale, causing the plan for the invasion of Greece to be abandoned. These battles were turning points in relations between the Greeks and Persians as it became clear that the Persian army was not invincible. During the following decades Persia lost much of its territory in Europe and the Greek cities of Asia Minor acquired increasing independence.

As Xerxes was marching his army into Greece in 480 BC, a second revolt in Babylonia broke out (the renewed unrest in Babylon would explain Xerxes' rapid departure from Greece). His rapid intervention in Babylonia was successful, since the province did not revolt again. However, according to Arrian, Xerxes punished the city by razing the temple of Marduk to the ground and removing the god's statue from the city. Is there any truth to this? Certainly the royal titles found in Babylonian texts of the period show a demotion in status of the city in the titulary of the king from 'Xerxes, King of Babylon, King of Lands' in regnal year 3 to just 'Xerxes, King of Lands' in regnal year 5. Yet there is no archaeological evidence to suggest that Xerxes destroyed Babylon's temples. Babylonia was probably not treated generously after two revolts, but exactly what form Xerxes' punishment took we do not know; its sanctuaries and cults suffered no noticeable decline and the New Year Festivals of Marduk went on uninterrupted.

In August 465 BC, Xerxes was murdered in a court coup. The events are obscure, but the plot seems to have been hatched by Xerxes' son, Artaxerxes, in cahoots with powerful eunuchs.

LATER EMPIRE

From the death of Xerxes on, and despite badly understood changes and developments in its infrastructure, the Persian empire can be classified as a fully mature and stable entity; far from being a time of stagnation, the late Achaemenid period saw a renewed spate of military activity and the re-conquest of rebellious territories.

When Artaxerxes I (465–425 BC) died he was followed to the throne by three of his sons in quick succession, his youngest reigning as Darius II (424–405 BC). With his wife, Parysatis, he eliminated all potential opposition so that the succession from Darius to his eldest son Artaxerxes II (405–359 BC) passed smoothly. Nevertheless Artaxerxes' younger brother, Cyrus the satrap of Lydia and Phrygia Minor, nursed ambitions for the crown and in this he was encouraged by the powerful queen mother, Parysatis. Royal women sometimes played a key role in the politics of the empire and although they could not rule in their own right, they had access to political agency through their intimate relationships with the Great Kings.

Cyrus gathered together an army of Persian nobles, troops from his satrapy, and a force of Greek mercenaries, including the Athenian soldier Xenophon, who has left us a valuable description of Cyrus' ill-fated revolt (*Anabasis*). The rebellious army met with Artaxerxes' troops at Cunaxa in Babylonia in 401 BC and Cyrus was killed. His bid for the throne had failed to gain more widespread support among the Persian nobility and Artaxerxes II's power remained unshaken.

At the same time Egypt attempted to break free of Persian control and successful campaigning led, between 401 and 399 BC, to the expulsion of the Persians. This was a serious blow to the Great King, and Achaemenid history for the next 56 years is dominated by the continuous efforts to regain control of this important province. The Persians turned their attention to ensuring that Syria-Palestine and Asia Minor remained under firm control and in 387/386 BC, Artaxerxes was able to impose a settlement on the Greeks (the 'King's Peace'), whereby they recognized that the cities of Asia Minor were under Persian control.

Artaxerxes II was succeeded by his son Artaxerxes III (359–338 BC). The major achievement of his reign was the re-conquest of Egypt in 343 BC, after hard and brutal campaigning. The re-conquest of Egypt had been preceded by the crushing of a revolt in Phoenicia, headed by the ruler of Sidon, Tennes; Artaxerxes' punishment of Sidon was swift: Tennes was executed, some of the city was destroyed and a part of its population was deported into Babylonia.

Artaxerxes' successor, Artaxerxes IV, reigned for only two years before a member of a collateral branch of the Achaemenid family seized the throne as Darius III (336–330 BC). Darius' reputation has suffered badly since he was fated to be the opponent of Alexander of Macedon, whose brilliant military victories spelled the end of the Achaemenid dynasty.

A Greek-style raised relief showing Greeks and Persians in battle. This type of scene was central to the Greek artistic output in the 5th century BC. The Athenians even envisaged their great mythic enemies, the Amazons, in Persian dress, so that in the Greek imagination Persians became effeminized as Amazon women.

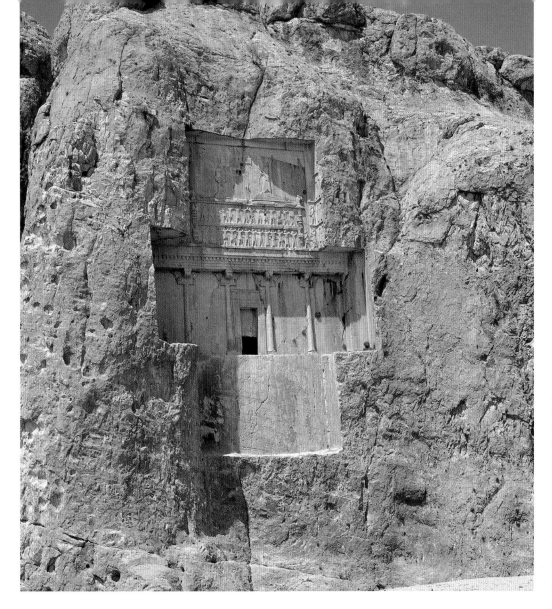

The tomb of Darius the Great at Naqsh-I Rustam, a few miles from Persepolis, gives us a good idea of how the façade of a Persian palace looked: a portico with bull-headed capitals and a large central doorway is depicted in high relief at the centre of the cruciform tomb. Above it is a representation of Darius standing on a high platform supported by subject peoples while he prays to Ahuramazda.

In reality, Darius was a brave soldier and an able administrator who posed a serious threat to Alexander's dreams of glory. He met Alexander in battle at Issus in 333 BC and again at Gaugamela in 331 BC but was defeated at both encounters. He fled to Ecbatana to try to raise fresh troops and thence to Bactria where he was killed by his satrap, Bessus, in 330 BC.

MAINTAINING EMPIRE: A *PAX PERSIACA?*

The longevity of such a vast empire is testimony to the Achaemenid policy of both tolerance towards its conquered peoples and its ruthlessness in maintaining power. The royal rhetoric recorded in the cuneiform inscriptions and disseminated widely across the empire, emphasized that all conquered nations were united in service to the Great King, whose laws they were required to obey and whose majesty they were obliged to uphold. The king was championed by Ahuramazda, the chief god of the Achaemenids, who granted the monarch the gift of kingship in order to put an end to chaos and bring about world order. The royal texts frequently used the motif that unrest and rebellion were linked to cosmic disorder and the growth of the Lie (*drauga*). The Great King was the champion of Truth (*arta*) and therefore crushed and quelled rebellious subjects so that order (also represented by the word *arta*) could triumph. Rebellion against Persian authority was therefore seen as a revolt against divine authority because the Great King served Ahuramazda's will on earth as the guarantor of justice and the maintainer of the social order.

Darius the Great, a truly brilliant bureaucrat, divided the empire's territories into administrative satrapies (provinces), under the

The Opulence of the Achaemenids

BELOW LEFT: Silver horn-shaped *rhyton* (drinking vessel) with a protome in the shape of a winged griffin with lion's paws. There is a drinking hole in the griffin's chest. The exquisite design of the *rhyton* attests to the quality of tableware enjoyed by the Persian elite throughout the empire.

BELOW RIGHT: A staircase relief from the palace of Darius the Great at Persepolis. Servants bring food and livestock into the palace – all of which is bound for the royal dinner table.

Achaemenid art, here displayed in masterpieces of gold and silver, also confirmed the royal ideology of the unity of the empire and promoted the image of the just monarch. A common motif, for example. shows the king elevated on a throne-like platform (see p. 113) which is lifted up by representative peoples from across the empire, each identified by ethnic dress and features. In his tomb inscription Darius I encouraged the passer-by to view the accompanying reliefs: 'If now you shall think "How many are the countries which King Darius held?" look at the sculptures [of those] who bear the throne, then shall you know, then shall it become known to you: the spear of a Persian man has gone forth far; then shall it become known to you: a Persian man has delivered battle far indeed from Persia.' The theme is also found in three-dimensional form in a sculpture of Darius from Susa. The interest in the ethnic make-up of the empire is also apparent in the kings' habit of listing their subject peoples (lists which made their way into the catalogue of the Persian empire in Herodotus' *Histories*) and, most spectacularly, in the sculpted reliefs on the staircases leading to the Apadana at Persepolis (below). Here representatives of the peoples of the empire are depicted in loving detail, and shown bringing tribute of precious metals, textiles, foodstuffs and livestock to the court of the Great King. The detailing of every delegate, every courtier and every soldier is overwhelming.

LEFT: A gold armlet (one of a pair) showing two leaping griffin lions. Cells used for inlays of glass or semi-precious stones are clear to see. The Persian empire was well known for its wealth and prosperity, and this form of elaborate jewelry confirms its reputation.

BELOW: Exquisite miniature model of a four-horse chariot, depicting a charioteer and a seated Persian nobleman. The front of the chariot is decorated with the head of the Egyptian god Bes, a protective deity whose popularity throughout the Persian empire can be confirmed by the number of amulets of the god's image found across the Achaemenid region.

'Saith Darius the king, these are the lands (*dahy va*) which came unto me; by the favour of Ahuramazda I was king of them: Persia, Elam, Babylonia, Assyria, Arabia, Egypt, [those] who are beside the sea, Sardis, Ionia, Media, Armenia, Cappadocia, Parthia, Drangiana, Aria, Chorasmia, Bactria, Sogdiana, Gandara, Scythia, Sattagydia, Arachosia, Maka: in all, twenty-three countries.'

control of satraps (governors), in order to maintain the levy of tribute required from each region. Darius' Bisitun Inscription (*c.* 520 BC) provides the oldest extant list of the constituents of the empire. It begins with two core lands, Persia and Elam. Then the order roughly follows the map of the empire in a clockwise fashion, first referring to the western provinces or satrapies, then those in the northern part, followed by the lands in the east of the empire. The ordering of the provinces of the empire here is interesting, since lands lying closest to the imperial centre (Elam, Babylonia) are privileged in the text over those at the periphery of empire (Ionia, Maka), suggesting an Achaemenid ideology of hierarchy: proximity to Persia signifies a higher level of civilization.

The impression we have of the administration of the Achaemenid empire is that the top posts were in the hands of a tiny group of men drawn exclusively from the highest echelons of the Persian aristocracy, especially from within the royal family. But satraps could come from more humble origins, and even non-Persian satraps are known, such as Metiochus, the son of the Athenian general Miltiades. The king was therefore at liberty to bestow the rank of 'Honorary Persian' on an individual not of pure Persian blood. The satrap enjoyed the privilege of being the Great King's representative. He was required to administer the collection of taxes and tribute and to raise armed forces when occasion required and, at a regional level, the satrap was also required to make all governmental decisions. For matters of international importance, however, he was obliged to consult the king and his chief ministers. As a representative of the king, the satrap kept court and maintained court ceremony based on that at the heart of the empire: he sat in audience, received petitions, observed religious rites and celebrated royal festivals.

Every satrapy covered an extensive area, ruled from a capital (which also acted as an administrative centre) where the satrap had a palace and a court. Thus, the satrapal capital of Media lay in Ecbatana, in Egypt it was Memphis, in Lydia it was Sardis, in Babylonia it was Babylon, in Phrygia it was Daskyleion, and in the satrapy known as Babylonia Beyond the River, it was Damascus. A palace discovered in Samarkand in Uzbekistan was probably the residence of the satrap of Bactria-Sogdiana. The palaces of the satraps, often acquired from local kings or nobles, were frequently set among villages and parks which helped support the feeding of the court and provided space for hunting expeditions. Many members of the royal family had private estates scattered throughout the empire which could be farmed by locals for the profit of the owners or leased out for fees. Satrapal palaces could also be utilized by the king and his court as they progressed across the empire on regular seasonal migrations: Babylon, Susa, Ecbatana and Persepolis in particular were routinely visited by the royal court.

The regional capitals were used to store the taxes that poured in from the satrapies; these taxes were paid in both coin and kind, the latter including foodstuffs used to maintain the vast satrapal court and its dependents. The Persepolis Fortification Texts attest to the fact that workers at the palace of the Great King were paid in food and wine rations, but not in coins or precious metals. However, taxation payments in precious goods and metals (especially silver) were widely used and one of the most important administrative jobs in each satrapy was the *ganazabara*, 'Treasurer'.

The treasuries were well guarded by soldiers and a record of goods going into and out of the storerooms was maintained in detail by an army of bureaucrats and scribes. The vast imperial treasury at Persepolis was a symbol of the Great King's power over his empire, and it is no coincidence that, in 330 BC, Alexander selected the treasury to be destroyed as a symbol of his conquest of the empire *en masse*.

The palaces were also centres for provincial administration; here royal orders were delivered to the satrap from the central authority. Royal decrees, identifiable by the king's seal, have been found as far afield as Nippur, Samaria and Artašat in Armenia, although the biggest horde of royal seals was discovered at Daskyleion in Anatolia. In his turn, the satrap issued decrees and statements which were disbursed throughout the province. Archives were kept of all royal and satrapal decrees so that they could form future reference. The Old Testament Book of Ezra, for instance, recalls how Darius I ordered that the royal archives of Babylon be searched for a copy of a decree issued by Cyrus the Great. In fact the document, an edict granting the Jews the right to rebuild the Jerusalem temple, was found not in Babylon at all, but in the archives of the palace at Ecbatana.

The satraps relied on a healthy interaction with local elites. In pursuing good inter-regional relationships, the institutions of marriage and concubinage should not be overlooked. Although we have very little information about the wives of satraps (let alone those of lesser-ranking Persian commanders and officials), there certainly were marriages between Persians and local women. Likewise, the marriage of the Paphlagonian prince, Otys, to the daughter of the Persian noble, Spithridates, recorded by Xenophon attests to the reverse practice of elite men taking Persian brides. Such alliances gave the local elite a foothold in the Persian honour system. In addition, both kings and satraps took women from among subject peoples into their harems as concubines. According to Herodotus, 'every man has a number of wives, a much greater number of concubines', and while this scenario of empire-wide polygyny cannot be taken at face value, it may well be representative of privileged members of Iranian society. Persian nobles, especially satraps, certainly imitated the royal polygynous custom: Pharnabazus, satrap of Phrygia, kept a court full of concubines at Sardis. The Great King's 360 concubines were, so to speak, physical manifestations of the Persian realm.

The Persian system depended very much on cooperation with local power-holders and they frequently used well-established regional administrative systems to work for them. Additionally, Persians often employed individuals who were familiar with localized government to work with them. The Egyptian nobleman Udjahorresnet is a case in point; a former naval commander under the last indigenous pharaohs of the Saite dynasty, he was stripped of his military rank under Cambyses but was accorded the privileged title of king's 'friend' along with a high rank in the temple of Neith at Sais. In other words, Udjahorresnet was denied any effective military power, but retained in royal service in a honorific position and could operate as a royal adviser.

The same system can be seen at work with the lesser kings and local dynasts. A good example is the use the satrap Pharnabazus made of the local rulers of Dardanus. When Zenis, the long-serving pro-Persian client-king of Dardanus, died, Pharnabazus had planned to bestow the satrapy to someone else. But Zenis' wife, Mania, petitioned Pharnabazus to bestow the province on her. The satrap took the unusual step of appointing a woman to the post to keep it within Zenis' family. Pharnabazus was delighted to find that Mania paid the tribute into the satrapal treasury just as regularly as her husband had done. These events illustrate the advantage of employing local elites to defend Persian interests. Conversely, dependence of the local dynasts on the satrap, and his power to strip the family of rank, kept them in check.

The smooth-running of the empire was facilitated by an excellent infrastructure. First-rate roads connected the main satrapal centres of the empire with the imperial core. The most important of these highways was the Royal Road which connected Sardis to Persepolis, via

OVERLEAF: Beautifully coloured glazed bricks were a feature of Persian palace architecture, although the tradition of making such bricks was Babylonian. Here from the palace at Susa a composite beast is represented with the head, body and forelegs of a kind of lion and the wings and hind legs of a bird. Rams' horns adorn its ferocious head. At Persepolis the Great Kings are shown mortally wounding such creatures in scenes of direct combat.

A silver tetradrachm of Artaxerxes III, 359–338 BC, minted in Egypt, following its reconquest and bearing the legend: 'Artaxerxes Pharaoh; life; health; prosperity.' On the obverse is the head of the Greek goddess Athena, while the reverse shows her sacred owl. This coin was probably issued on the order of the satrap of Egypt and was clearly intended to be used by Greeks as well as Persians and Egyptians.

Susa and Babylon; an eastern branch led first to Ecbatana and thence onwards to Bactra and on to Pashwar, while another road connected Persepolis to Egypt, via Damascus and Jerusalem. The roads were measured in 6-km (3.7-mile) intervals (*parasangs*) and road-stations were set up around every 28 km (17.4 miles) of the route to accommodate the quick change of fresh horses for any imperial messenger carrying official documents. Herodotus estimated that the distance from Susa to Sardis, 450 *parasangs*, could be covered in 90 days.

The Persians displayed no desire to impose their language or culture upon the conquered nations; the Great Kings utilized local languages for their decrees and employed Aramaic as a form of *lingua franca* throughout the imperial territories to help facilitate effective communication. In the realm of religion, too, the Persian kings were careful to appear as active upholders of local cults, if only to ensure control of the wealthy sanctuaries and the adherence of powerful priesthoods. Even in small administrative regions, like Jerusalem and Magnesia-on-the-Maeander, the Persians granted temple privileges and acknowledged the support their local gods had given them.

However, this seemingly *laissez-fair* attitude towards cultural autonomy needs to be balanced by the fact that the Persians could prove to be merciless overlords if crossed. Rebellious subjects and states were treated with ruthlessness: populations were uprooted and deported across the empire, and their holy shrines were burned and destroyed. Herodotus records the Persian destruction of the sanctuaries of Apollo at Didyma and of Athena in Athens. Artaxerxes III's reputation for harshness and cruelty is perhaps justified by his treatment of Sidon, while his violent re-conquest of Egypt is recorded on the stela of an Egyptian nobleman named Somtutefnakht: 'The Asiatic … slew a million at my sides', he recalls. As the heirs of the great Assyrian empire, the Persians inherited many kinds of savage punishment techniques documented in Assyrian and later neo-Babylonian sources: impaling, decapitation, killing of children,

burning, whipping, strangling, stoning, castration, blinding, cutting of a living body in two, cutting off breasts, nose, ears, lips, hands, arms, snipping out the tongue, branding, flaying, crucifixion and skinning alive. Thus in one passage of the Bisitun Inscription, Darius proudly proclaims: '[The rebel] Phraortes was seized and led to me. I cut off his nose, ears and tongue, and I put out one of his eyes.'

The empire was founded and maintained by military might. The army consisted of infantry, horse and camel cavalry, and elite charioteers. The Persians also routinely incorporated subject and mercenary Greeks in their army, each of whom received a monthly wage (a gold *Daric* per month in 401 BC). By the time of Alexander, these mercenaries had become a regular part of the army and their leaders had even been incorporated into the Iranian aristocracy. Other areas of the empire sent men to bolster the imperial army: Scythian charioteers and bowmen and Bactrian camel-riders are well attested.

The size of the imperial army was never as large as the Greeks suggested and historians now estimate that Xerxes' forces for the Greek campaign numbered around 70,000 infantry and 9,000 horsemen, while the army of Artaxerxes II at Cunaxa was probably around 40,000 in number. Darius III's troops at Gaugamela amounted to about 34,000 cavalry and some infantry. The army was led by a supreme commander, who was either the Great King himself or a close relative. Next in command was an officer in charge of a division of 1,000 men, subdivided into 10 battalions. The most famous of the army units was the crack fighting team known as the Ten Thousand (or 'Immortals'), a division of which served as the royal bodyguard.

A characteristic of the Achaemenid period is that commanders and dignitaries participated in actual fighting, and many of them died in action. Although imperial royal ideology propounded the peace and unity of the realm, Great Kings also emphasized their ability to rule by force. In order to be an effective ruler, the king had to be a brave soldier first.

THE PERSIAN EMPIRE TODAY

There can be no doubt that the first Persian empire was of enormous significance for the development of the idea of 'empire'. It made possible the first significant and continuous contact between East and West, and prepared the ground for Alexander the Great's vision of what an empire could be.

Within Iran itself, the debate on what the Achaemenid empire means in a modern framework is very much alive. Mohammed Reza Shah's obsession with the Achaemenid dynasty during the 1970s led to a backlash against the study of, and engagement with, the Persian past throughout the formative period of the Islamic Revolution. Yet today the monuments of ancient Iran are both studied and enjoyed by the Iranians, who appraise the Achaemenid empire as being at the apex of the history of Iranian civilization. Cyrus the Great is particularly revered as a visionary leader of great moral integrity and brilliance and the Cyrus Cylinder is frequently claimed as the first Bill of Human Rights. In Iran the first Persian empire is remembered with immense pride.

In the West, the study of the Achaemenid empire continues to expand and change, and, despite today's political tensions, the dialogue between Western and Iranian scholars is flourishing as never before. Textual studies of indigenous Persian sources continue to appear, and the archaeology of the empire is still producing unexpected finds which constantly force scholarship to rethink and re-mould their definitions of empire. Are the ancient sources on Persia really as Hellenocentric as they are often presented as being? Can we study the ancient Persian empire without forcing the subject to be viewed through the prism of Orientalism? Achaemenid studies stand at the threshold of new and interesting debates in which the concept of empire will play a key role.

Rows of Achaemenid soldiers fill the tourist bazaar at Shiraz in Fars Province, Iran. Tourism, though still in its infancy in Iran, centres around the ancient Persian sites of Persepolis and Pasargadae, and 'Achaemenid' souvenirs are big business.

By comparison with some other empires in this volume, the rule that the Athenians exercised over their fellow Greeks for three quarters of the 5th century BC was a short-lived and small-scale affair. Its origins lay in the naval alliance that defeated Xerxes' invasion of Greece: Athens' leadership of this alliance only transformed into unembarrassed 'rule' over time, with her grip tightening as allies attempted to secede. The city's power within the Greek world was confined for the most part to the islands of the Aegean and the cities of Asia Minor. The Athenian empire was more significant, however, than its scale suggests. Athens' power underpinned both the democracy and the extraordinary cultural achievements of 5th-century Athens. And in the main historian of Athens' rise to power, Thucydides, 'the father of international relations', we find one of the great theorists of empire.

Prominent Athenian Politicians

late 6th century BC: enacted reforms 508 BC	Cleisthenes
c. 524–459 BC	Themistocles
died c. 467 BC	Aristides
died late 450s BC	Cimon
early 5th century BC: responsible for democratic reforms 462 BC, murdered shortly after	Ephialtes
c. 495–429 BC	Pericles
died 422 BC	Cleon
451–404 BC	Alcibiades
died 388 BC	Thrasybulus
late 5th century BC to late 350s BC: played key role in foundation of second Athenian confederacy	Timotheus
c. 405–335 BC	Eubulus
c. 390–325 BC	Lycurgus
384–322 BC	Demosthenes

PREVIOUS PAGES: Detail of the West Frieze of the Parthenon. Young, heroic, beautiful, this rider encapsulates the ideal to which every Athenian male aspired. Athenian power may have rested on her fleet, but oddly it was the infantry and cavalry that Athens preferred to celebrate in her monuments as paradigms of the perfect citizen.

LEFT: Recovered from an ancient shipwreck off Riace in southern Italy in 1972, this statue is one of a pair of sculptures that were part of a cargo bound for Rome. Masterpieces of classical bronze sculpture, they possibly originally came from a monument set up to commemorate the Greek victory in the Persian wars.

Corcyra

MACEDONIA

THRACE

Thasos

Sea of Marmara

Aegospotami
Sestos
Sigeion
Tenedos

Lesbos
Mytilene
Arginusae Islands

Persian Empire

Aegean Sea

Scyros

Chios

Delphi
Chaeronea
BOEOTIA
Leuctra
Thebes
ATTICA
Megara
Eleusis
Marathon
Athens
Carystos
Salamis
Corinth

Peloponnese

Argos
Ceos

Samos

Delos

MESSENIA
Sparta
LACONIA
Pylos

Naxos

Melos

Rhodes

Athens and Attica

Allied states

0   100 km

0   100 miles

Persians defeat Athenians at Thermopylae, but are themselves routed in a naval battle at Salamis 480 BC

Formation of Delian League led by Athens 478 BC

Major building work on the Acropolis, including Parthenon 447–433 BC

Persia and Sparta confront Athens in the second Peloponnesian war 431–404 BC

Defeat of Sparta by Thebes at the battle of Leuctra 371 BC

Philip II of Macedon defeats Athens at Chaeronea, initiating Macedonian hegemony 338 BC

400 BC

300 BC

Greeks end Persian invasion with land victories at Plataea and Mycale 479 BC

Sparta revolts against Athenian domination in the first Peloponnesian war 461–446 BC

Capture of island of Melos 416 BC

Athenian expedition to Sicily 415–413 BC

Foundation of the Second Athenian League 378 BC

Assassination of Philip and accession of Alexander the Great 336 BC

Athenians besiege Samos after it attempts to secede from Delian League 440 BC

Greece emerged after the collapse of the Mycenaean civilization (*c.* 1100 BC) as a patchwork of individual city-states. Yet while these were important – they remained the 'atoms' of the political landscape – the trend from the 9th century BC onwards was for this autonomous isolationism to be gradually ceded to other institutions beyond the city-state. Greece gave itself over to a series of increasingly important and complex networks. Communities bound themselves in ties of mutual obligations through oaths. Cities sent out expeditions to establish independent communities in distant lands. These overseas settlements were often linked to their 'mother cities' through religious, cultural and political bonds. As the wealth of cities increased, elite members of society were not satisfied vying among themselves within the boundaries of their own states. They looked for new arenas where they could compete for honour and status, arenas that promised an international audience and even wider acclaim. Ambitious tyrants extended their influence through the creation of political alliances. States such as Sparta enslaved the neighbouring territory of Messenia and unified large sections of the Peloponnese under their leadership. Cities banded together to form religious unions to celebrate common cults or administer shared sanctuaries. This period of Greek history is characterized by an increasing trend towards centralization that unlocked the social, economic and cultural resources of the Greek world. It was a world ripe for empire.

That the agent for empire should be Athens was not, however, a certainty. Before the end of the 6th century BC, there were few signs that Athens would become the dominant power in the Aegean. Indeed, there were other candidates that were much more promising. Sparta dominated the Peloponnese. Corinth was wealthier and had more extensive trade connections; it was mother city to dozens of colonies throughout the Mediterranean and was an influential player in the Peloponnesian region. Corinth also had an ambitious elite who were not averse to the idea of extending their power. Yet these elements never translated into an empire. The story of the rise of Athens then is a story both about the inevitability of empire and the opportunities provided by chance.

THE BIRTH OF THE ATHENIAN EMPIRE

The immediate origins of the Athenian empire lay in the aftermath of the Greek defeat of the Persians after their invasions in 490 BC and 480/479 BC. This victory over Persia was certainly unexpected. Persian expansion in Asia Minor and the surrounding regions had gone largely unchecked for over a century (Chapter 4). Persian resources far exceeded those of Greece, and the size of the Persian army dwarfed that of the Greeks.

Within this story of opposition to Persia, Athens played a prominent role. It had responded to a call for assistance when the wealthy Greek cities on the coast of Asia Minor had risen in revolt against Persian rule in 499 BC. In 490 BC, when the Persians invaded mainland Greece under King Darius, they were stopped in their tracks just outside Athens on the coastal plains of Marathon. Athenian soldiers routed the Persian infantry, slaughtering soldiers in the boggy landscape, and driving the enemy into the sea. When Darius' successor, King Xerxes, returned with an even larger army in 480 BC, Athens was one of the leading members of the coalition of 30 or so states that opposed Persia. It even had the possibility of leading this coalition. However, to avoid disagreement and ensure the support of Sparta, it ceded overall command to the Spartans. In the final analysis, it was probably the largely Athenian naval victory at the battle of Salamis that contributed most to the eventual routing of the enemy.

Athens had every reason to oppose the Persians. For one thing, they threatened her newly founded democracy. The reforms of the Athenian statesman Cleisthenes in 509 BC had given Athens a democratic constitution and this democracy had been established in the wake of the expulsion of the previous tyrannical regime, the Peisistratids (c. 546–510 BC). One of the members of this dynasty, the former tyrant Hippias, had found refuge at the Persian court and his restoration was clearly seen by the

Persians as an ideal way to further their interests. He even accompanied the Persian forces to Marathon, ready to take over the running of the city following a Persian victory. In the first instance, Athens was fighting to avoid a regime change.

Yet the aim of saving the city and its newly formed democracy is only part of the story of Athenian resistance. This desire for self-preservation coincided with increasing ambition on the part of the state. The Peisistratids, like most tyrants, had been keen to make their mark on the wider Greek stage. Their extensive building works, their patronage of the arts, and their establishment of client tyrants on the island of Naxos and the city of Sigeion, had given Athens a taste of a world outside the borders of Attica. Indeed, there is much that is proto-imperial about the rule of these tyrants. The city was enjoying a period of increased prosperity prior to the Persian invasions. The tyrants had accelerated the unification of Attica, allowing Athens to fully exploit one of the largest hinterlands of any city-state in mainland Greece. The average city-state controlled between 50–100 sq. km (20–40 sq. miles) of land. The size of Attica is 2,650 sq. km (1025 sq. miles). This makes the state of Athens four times the size of its nearest neighbour, Megara, and twice the size of Athens' commercial rival, Corinth. Only Sparta, which controlled a region of 8,400 sq.km (3,250 sq. miles) exceeded Athens in size.

Athens was well positioned to provide alternative leadership to Sparta in the aftermath of the Persian war. It had not taken long for dissatisfaction with Spartan leadership to arise among the allied cities. In particular, they were dissatisfied with the Spartan reluctance to press their advantage over Persia and pursue an aggressive campaign of revenge. This, coupled with the perceived autocratic tendencies of the Spartan king, Pausanias, led the allies to approach Athens to lead them against Persia. Sparta recalled their king from the Hellespont where he was leading Greek operations against the Persians, and tried to send a replacement to take over the command, but they were too late. Events had moved on, and Athens was now the

OPPOSITE: Athens never forgot that democracy was formed out of bloodshed. At the central marketplace of Athens, in the early 5th century BC they erected a statue group (surviving in this Roman copy) to commemorate the actions of the tyrant slayers Harmodius and Aristogeiton who had killed the tyrant Hipparchus and so commenced the overthrow of the Peisistratid regime.

leader (Greek *hegemon*) of a new alliance designed to punish Persia, the Delian League.

It was the Delian League that would form the basis of the Athenian empire. The League offers a model of empire that stands in contrast to a number of traditional notions about empire. There were no governors of provinces. Athens allowed the majority of city-states under its rule in the League to remain autonomous in the conduct of their internal affairs. It instituted no universal system of laws. Nor did it ever extend its citizenship to anybody, except to a few honoured foreigners. Instead, the Athenian empire was one based on the recognition of the pre-eminence of Athens, and that certain privileges went with this status. These privileges included the right to demand and assess tribute to pay for the upkeep of the fleet, the right to arbitrate in disputes between members of the League, and the right to determine what lay in the League's best interest. Theoretically, members of the League also had a say in its administration. However, such niceties were not observed for long. It is telling that even today it is not possible to reconstruct the constitutional arrangements of the original League, so little historical impact did these arrangements have.

Once a city was admitted to the League, it was difficult to leave. Athens was ruthless in pursuing allies who abdicated their responsibilities. Under the pretext of maintaining the League, allied cities that revolted were crushed and new, more loyal regimes were instituted. At its height,

Athens considered itself to be leader of over 400 city-states, although only 190 seem to have been regularly paying tribute.

It is striking just how quickly Athens turned the actions of the Delian League to its own advantage. For example, immediately after taking leadership of the League and removing the Persian garrison from Thrace, the Athenian fleet attacked the Greek island of Scyros. The reason for this attack was supposedly to make the seas safer by destroying a nest of pirates. Such an action was defensible on a broad interpretation of the remit of the Delian League. Less defensible was the establishment of an Athenian colony on this strategic island, one that Athens had been eyeing for some time. The next Greek victim of the League was the state of Carystos on the island of Euboea. Its crime had been to assist the Persians (admittedly under considerable duress) in 490 BC. It had remained neutral during Xerxes' invasions. For such fence-sitting, Carystos paid a high price. The city was overrun, enrolled into the League and an annual cash subscription was levied. The unpleasantness of this incident is only magnified by the decision of a number of Athenian parents to name their children at this time, Carystonikos ('Victory over Carystos'). Exulting in the defeat of fellow Greeks takes off some of the shine of this supposed defender of Greek freedom.

It did not take long before a number of states decided to attempt to withdraw from the League. The first was Naxos in 470 BC. For such temerity, the city was besieged. When Naxos eventually capitulated, it was deprived of its fleet, re-enrolled in the League, and a cash contribution levied upon it. The capture of Naxos was regarded by critics of the empire as the first truly illegal act undertaken by Athens. Yet an even worse breach was to follow quickly upon it, namely the Athenian treatment of the island of Thasos. The cause of the dispute between Thasos and Athens was the Athenian intention to found a colony on the gold-rich coast off the island. This region had long been under the control of Thasos and was a considerable source of the island's wealth. Faced with this threat, Thasos seceded from the

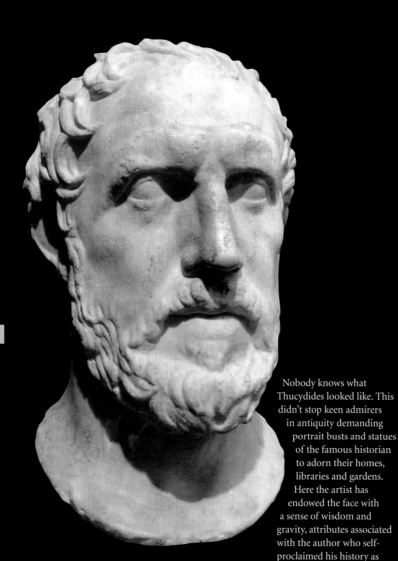

Nobody knows what Thucydides looked like. This didn't stop keen admirers in antiquity demanding portrait busts and statues of the famous historian to adorn their homes, libraries and gardens. Here the artist has endowed the face with a sense of wisdom and gravity, attributes associated with the author who self-proclaimed his history as a 'keepsake for eternity'.

Voices of Empire

The Greeks were fond of discussing the Athenian empire. Topics for debate ranged from the legitimacy of Athenian rule to the most efficient way to exploit the allies. The historian Thucydides records a number of speeches by prominent figures in his history of the Peloponnesian war. As a prominent Athenian general who was exiled by the Athenian people for his military failures in a campaign in northern Greece, Thucydides lived through the heights of the Athenian empire and witnessed its destruction by Sparta. The calculating pragmatism of so many of Thucydides' speakers has often shocked readers. Yet this strand of political opportunism can be found in other sources. Even in the 2nd century AD, the biographer Plutarch could recount stories of Athenians maddened by thoughts of conquest. Many benefited from the empire. According to the comic playwright Aristophanes, it was the politicians who gained most, while according to the 'Old Oligarch', an anonymous writer of a pamphlet highly critical of democracy, the empire was an elaborate scam to benefit the lazy and poor. Only Pericles seems to give us an insight to some of the justifications that Athens made for her empire.

The orator Cleon, as represented by Thucydides, berates the Athenian people for showing leniency to the people of Mytilene after they revolted in 428 BC
'I have had plenty of occasions to see that a democracy is not capable of governing others ... you treat the allies as you would your fellow-citizens. You forget that they are out to deceive you or you mistakenly pity them ... What you do not realize is that your empire is a tyranny over subjects who are unwilling to be ruled and who plot against you. They obey you not because of goodwill ... but because of your superior strength.'

'I am not blaming those who are resolved to rule, only those who show an even greater readiness to submit.'
Thucydides, *The Peloponnesian War*

'Our city is open to all, and we never practise deportation to prevent people observing our weaknesses or finding out secrets which might benefit an enemy. We rely on real courage and loyalty, not on secret weapons or stratagems ... We are the only city in Greece that performs acts of generosity without calculation. It is our belief in freedom that makes us act in this way. In short, our city is an education to Greece.'

During the course of his speech in praise of the soldiers killed at the start of the Peloponnesian war, Pericles praises Athens and defends her empire

Plutarch describes the people of Athens engrossed with plans of imperial expansion. As they busily plot the taking of Sicily, little do they realize that this ill-thought-out expedition will eventually cost them their empire

'Even before the meeting of the Assembly, Alcibiades had already corrupted the populace ... the young men in their gymnasiums and the old men in their workshops and resting-places would sit drawing maps of Sicily, charting the sea about it ... For they did not regard Sicily itself as the ultimate prize, but rather as just a stepping-stone. From Sicily, they proposed to take on the might of Carthage and get possession of both Libya and all of the sea west of the Pillars of Heracles.'

Here the 'Old Oligarch' exposes the Athenian reasons for imposing democratic political regimes on its allies

'As for the allies, the Athenians sail out and plot against their governments, especially those comprising local aristocrats whom they hate. For the Athenians realize that the ruler is always hated by the ruled and that if the rich and aristocratic men in the cities are strong, the rule of the people at Athens will only be brief. This is why they disenfranchise the aristocrats, take away their money, expel and kill them, and replace them with members from the lower class.'

In this comic scene from Aristophanes' *Acharnians*, ambassadors return from diplomatic duty and complain of the bitter hardships that they had to endure

'During the archonship of Euthymenes, you sent us to the Great King on a salary of two drachmae per day ... We suffered horribly ... Everywhere we were well received and forced to drink delicious wine out of golden or crystal goblets .... Sadly, the barbarians only regard big eaters and heavy drinkers as real men ... At the end of the fourth year we reached the King's Court, but he had left with his whole army ... after eight months he returned, then he entertained us and served us oxen roasted whole in an oven.'

It is through a diet of stories about gods and heroes that this Athenian youth learns to read. It is easy to forget that very few Athenians could read the great works of literature produced in classical Athens and so writers such as Thucydides tailored their histories to a select audience. His texts reflect their (and his own) elite prejudices.

League. The Athenians immediately sent a fleet to quell the rebellion. After three years of fighting they were eventually successful, and Thasos was once again enrolled into the League. In addition, Thasos was required to dismantle its walls, pay a cash indemnity to the League, and hand over control of the mineral coastline to Athens. This pattern of Athenian self-interest driving League activities was to continue for the next half century. It is no wonder that Athens eventually stopped referring to the League in inscriptions as 'Athens and her allies' and started calling it 'the cities which Athens rules'.

THE MACHINERY OF EMPIRE

The principal obligation required of members of the Delian League was to support the alliance through the maintenance of the fleet. This support could come through either the provision of money to Athens to buy ships and crew them or the provision of actual ships and crews to serve under Athenian control. The majority of states chose the former option,

handing over an amount of 'tribute' each year, and reducing the size of their navies accordingly.

That so many states effectively paid for their own enslavement and diminished their capacity for resistance reflects two factors. The first is the high cost and effort required to maintain a fleet. Even Athens, which enjoyed a number of economic advantages owing to its size, probably had little left over from the allied contributions after it had paid its fleet costs. Paying cash gave all the benefits of having a fleet (defence against Persia, removal of pirates) without the administrative difficulties.

The second factor is general acceptance of Athenian domination of the sea. It is extraordinary to see how quickly Athenian hegemony was accepted throughout the Aegean. Whatever the situation at the formation of the Delian League, it soon became apparent to the various states that nothing was going to happen in the Aegean without the consent of the Athenians. There was little point in maintaining a fleet because the sense of independence it

RIGHT: Festivals formed an important part of Athenian life and its allies were required to attend them and make contributions. The frieze of the Parthenon records one such festival, the festival for Athena known as the Panathenaia. Here four water-carriers are depicted taking part in the Panathenaic procession.

provided was illusory. Some states such as the large island states on Chios, Lesbos and Samos chose to buy into the illusion, enjoying the symbolism that supplying ships as opposed to money gave them. However, despite the symbolism, they enjoyed no greater autonomy than any of the money-paying states. When Samos and Lesbos rose in revolt, they were crushed with the same effectiveness.

The provision of tribute was not just about economic resources and the maintenance of military might. Tribute also served an ideological function. The hegemony of Athens was signalled from the very formation of the Delian League when it was granted the right to appoint its treasurers, a message reinforced when Athens moved the treasury from Delos to Athens. The symbolism of the act was not lost on anybody. Traditionally historians have regarded the act as the final sign of the complete destruction of the ideals of the Delian League. Athens tied a number of aspects relating to the tribute into its own civic calendar. They timed the reassessment of tribute to coincide with the Great Panathenaia, a festival held every four years that celebrated the birthday of Athena. Allied ambassadors were required to attend and bring offerings to the festival. Immediately afterwards they were told what their annual contribution towards the upkeep of the empire would be. Even more pointedly, tribute when it was collected was brought to Athens in time for the Great Dionysia, the annual dramatic festival in honour of Dionysus. Indeed, the display of tribute was one of the preliminaries to the dramatic festival. The money was piled up onto the stage for the contemplation and enjoyment of the satisfied Athenian audience.

In addition to its fleet, Athens employed a large number of officials to maintain order throughout its empire. According to one source, at its height in the mid-5th century BC Athens had over 700 officials devoted to the running of the empire. A considerable number of these were stationed in allied city-states. These officials served a variety of functions. They were involved in the transfer of tribute to Athens, liaising with local officials over the handling and collection of the money. They oversaw the carrying out of Athenian decrees. They reported to Athens on affairs within the local city, and acted as a contact point for Athenian embassies. In cases where a city had previously risen in revolt against Athens, there would also be a garrison of Athenian soldiers stationed there, responsible for keeping order and ensuring that the city remained loyal. Likewise numerous embassies and heralds were dispatched as the need arose to convey imperial policy to outlying city-states. Yet service as an official stationed in the allied cities does not seem to have been particularly popular among Athenian citizens. For this reason, those unlucky enough to have been allotted these postings were often tempted to try to excuse themselves or bribe another to take their place. Eventually Athens had to pass a law forbidding such practices.

The Athenians also enrolled a number of prominent locals into the service of their empire. These locals were awarded the title of 'proxenos'. These proxenoi were concerned with looking after the interests of Athenian visitors to a state. They provided hospitality, introductions to relevant individuals and institutions, and even in some cases financial support. In return, they were granted special privileges in Athens and legal protection against reprisals from their fellow citizens. Admittedly, this protection almost always came too late in times of revolt. Nevertheless, loyal proxenoi could rely on Athens to avenge their deaths.

CREATING CULTURE

There were few aspects of Athenian public life that were not affected in some way by the empire. It undertook a building programme that befitted its new status as an imperial capital. The empire made Athenians think differently about their history, and it impacted on the religious practices of the citizens and allies. The story of empire infused history and myth and this amalgam seeped onto the Athenian stage, into the visual arts, and ultimately into the minds of the citizens. For example, two of the most distinctive features in the classical period – its Athenocentrism and its focus on the barbarian – are both ideas developed in the service of the empire. Both these features acted to create a myth about Athens as the pre-eminent Greek state, one blessed by the gods whose rule was not only destined, but necessary.

It was not unusual for Greek city-states to promote heavily their own locale, so in that respect Athens' self-publicity was not peculiar. However, it is difficult to find a city that matches the Athenian effort in promoting the individuality and superiority of its institutions. The attempts are almost pathological, and suggest that Athens was desperately trying to cover up its own insecurities as *hegemon*. Athenian ideology tried to rewrite the historical accident that led to Athenian leadership of the Delian League into a law of nature, and the full panoply of the arts was devoted to this endeavour.

There are numerous instances of this Athenian sense of superiority at work. For

example, the special place that Athens enjoyed in the heart of the goddess Athena was a theme constantly reinforced in ritual, vase-painting, and most notably in the rebuilding work on the Acropolis. However, it was not just Athena who was depicted showing special favour to the Athenians. One of the claims that Athens liked to make was that Attica was the birthplace of agriculture. In the town of Eleusis, the goddess Demeter first taught the art of agriculture to prince Triptolemus, who then sped off in a winged chariot to teach the art to the rest of the world. This story, which makes Athens the cradle of civilization, was told in drama, art and ritual. Allies, for example, were required to send offerings of 'first fruits' of corn and barley to Eleusis in remembrance of this act of kindness. Although all these stories had existed long before the empire emerged, it was the empire that created a new and intense market for them, allowing them to be promulgated in ways and to an extent that had been previously unimaginable.

Similarly, tremendous focus was placed on the role of Athens as leader in the fight against the Persians. After all, this was the claim on which Athenian superiority rested. In Athenian hands, the Persian wars became a second Trojan war. Marathon became reworked as the most perfect of battles. Numerous monuments were erected around the city and throughout Greece

Athens was not only beloved by Athena, but all the gods. One popular myth in Athens was the story of the goddess Demeter commissioning the Athenian prince Triptolemus (here shown on a winged throne) to spread knowledge of agriculture throughout the Greek world. Through such stories, Athens portrayed itself as the founder of civilization and the centre of the world.

Athens gained its empire through its defeat of the Persians. It was a story that they never allowed any Greeks to forget. Athens produced numerous vases in which heroic nude Greeks vanquish their often outlandishly dressed (and in Athenian eyes effeminate) barbarian opponents.

to remind people of the Athenian role in the wars. It is no accident that one of the few dramatic tragedies that features an historical event takes as its subject the Athenian victory at Salamis. As a consequence of such ideas, the Persians came to be regarded as a breed apart, a group whose very nature was deficient. Classical art picked out every ethnic difference whether it was Thracian tattoos, the baldness of the circumcized Egyptians, or the soft effeminate dress of the Persians. Empire invented the barbarian, an ironic circumstance given the 'barbaric' flavour of so many of its own institutions (such as tribute).

All this activity attracted the attention of other Greeks. Artisans, poets and dramatists flowed into the Athenian harbour as well as grain

and timber. The increasingly wealthy Athenian elite developed a taste for novelty as a way of separating themselves from their fellow citizens. Talented foreigners were able to find many outlets for their skills in Athens, whether it was as teachers, musicians, poets, dramatists or even just semi-professional conversational partners.

Of course, one makes a mistake if one imagines that all this intellectual endeavour was just about supporting imperial ideology. Empire provided a spur to cultural development through the production of resistance as well as compliance. Art is different from propaganda, and one can easily see, especially in the art forms such as drama, a desire to question the excesses of Athenian imperial rule. Comedy was only too wise to the balance sheet of empire, and was

THE PARTHENON:
IMPERIAL TREASURY

One of the most enduring legacies of the empire was the large-scale building works commenced at the height of the empire's power. They ensured that the fame of Athens persisted long after the empire had fallen. In any account of this building programme, pride of place must be awarded to the Parthenon. Begun in 447 BC, the building took 15 years to complete. It measures 69.5 x 30.8 m (230 x 100 ft) and is composed of eight columns at each end and 17 on the sides. At its centre stood a 12-m (40-ft) high ivory statue of the goddess Athena, draped in over one tonne of gold.

More of a storage place for treasures than a temple, this building exemplifies the classical style. Its size, optical refinements and elaborate sculptural decoration were all aimed at proclaiming that Athens was a city whose greatness rivalled any of the important panhellenic centres such as Delphi or Olympia. Whether the allies whose subjection permitted the building of such edifices agreed is another matter. One suspects that their discussion of the Parthenon may have been less rapturous than that of the Athenians.

Indeed, even within Athens, such buildings were not without their critics. 'Athens is becoming beautified like a whore,' they complained. And in a sense they are right. Buildings like the Parthenon are irrational projects, the product of desire: the original lust-objects.

'If Athens were to be destroyed, the magnitude of its ruins would make one mistakenly think that its power was double what it actually is.'

Thucydides, *The Peloponnesian War*

For centuries the Parthenon remained largely intact, the most prominent building on the Athenian Acropolis. Converted first into a Christian church and later a mosque, its final use was as a Turkish gunpowder store. On 26 September 1687, a stray bomb ignited the store causing substantial damage to the building. Currently a major building programme is under way to help restore as much of the monument as the remains will allow.

At the heart of Athens lay its Agora. This space was a marketplace, meeting space and administrative centre. Here one could find traders and goods from all parts of the world. Its colonnaded pavilions were home to discussions of philosophy as well as the price of grain.

happy to point out its undesirable consequences and its grotesquery. Likewise tragedy, although conventionally setting its plays in the mythical past, often took violence and the abuse of power as its themes, concepts all too pertinent to the running of the empire. It is hard to imagine that many Athenians who witnessed the fall of Troy and the enslavement of the court of Priam in Euripides' *Trojan Women* weren't prompted to think of the massacre and enslavement of the island of Melos only a few months before, especially as a number of members of the audience would have had a reminder of this brutal act in the form of new Melian slaves in their households. Yet despite whatever questions these performances evoked, their effect is debatable. The comic Aristophanes who devoted numerous plays to the topic of peace never seems to have convinced his audience to abandon war.

OPPOSITION TO ATHENIAN RULE

One of the important functions of empires is the control and distribution of resources. As a consequence, every empire has both its beneficiaries and those who lose out. Many took advantage of the opportunities offered by the Athenian empire. The urban poor found themselves employment in the Athenian navy.

The wealth of Athens attracted merchants and craftspeople from all over the Greek world. Commodity exporters such as the wine-producers of Chios also did extremely well. In the marketplace of Athens it was possible to find Egyptian perfume sellers, Libyan grain merchants, Phoenician textile workers, and Thracian princes keen on enjoying some sightseeing. Wealthy Athenian citizens were not slow to see the potential under the empire for extending their landholding interests, and a number of citizens seem to have owned large foreign estates. Yet, all of these benefits came at a cost. Merchants were required to pay landing-taxes to help support Athenian religious cults. Foreigners who wished to live in Athens had to pay fees to the state. Athens could be rapacious in its demand for resources. We have already seen the consequences for Thasos that arose from Athenian desire to control its mines. Similarly, Athens endeavoured to secure for itself the best in timber and grain, even when those resources were much needed by its allies.

Allies did not always enjoy life under Athenian rule. Athenian officials stationed within cities could be a source of tension. Not bound by local laws, there was much potential for corruption and illegality. Athenian officials were infamous for their drunken debauchery and seduction of the wives of locals. Regimes that enjoyed the support of Athens used that support in the persecution of their opponents. If local elites showed disloyalty, Athens would often impose democratic regimes onto the states. Internal recriminations, bloodletting and exile were almost always the immediate consequences of these actions.

This occasional, but dramatic interference in their internal politics was one of the main grievances of the allies. Another was the confiscation of land and the imposition of colonies, that usually occurred after rebellion. The most famous case of such behaviour took place after the revolt of Mytilene in 428 BC. Mytilene was an important ally of the Athenians, and Athens took her betrayal to heart. The historian Thucydides presents us with an account of the passions roused following the revolt and subsequent capture of the island by Athenian forces. For him, the handling of the Mytilene affair exposed both the impetuousness of the Athenian people and their ruthless calculation in ruling their empire. In a meeting of the Athenian Assembly, the desire for revenge was strong and the Assembly voted to put to death all adult male citizens and to enslave all the women and children. Immediately a ship was dispatched taking these orders to the Athenian commander on Lesbos. However, the very next day, the Assembly had a change of heart, and it was decided that only the ringleaders of the revolt should be executed. Orders countermanding the previous ones were sent. Thucydides recounts how these two triremes raced across the Aegean, one bringing a death sentence, the

other a reprieve. The crew of the second trireme rowed without taking a break for meals or sleep and arrived at Mytilene just as the Athenian commander was about to carry out the massacre. The Mytileneans were spared, but Athenian 'leniency' was still harsh. The Mytilene fleet was commandeered into the Athenian navy, the city's walls were pulled down, over 1,000 men involved in the revolt were executed, and most of the island of Lesbos confiscated.

Yet, it was not just allies who were opposed to the empire. Some Athenians were not endeared to it either. As Athens developed its own foreign policy connections, it was venturing into an area that had previously been the sole preserve of elite aristocratic families. Many were happy to be co-opted, trading upon their family connections to secure positions on embassies or serve as generals to regions to which they had ancestral ties. However, a number resented this new democratic order.

This internal opposition to the empire took a number of forms. Most of it was just talk, yet sometimes talk translated into action. The most prominent act of urban terrorism in Athenian history seems to have been carried out by this opposition. One morning in 415 BC, Athens awoke to find that the much-beloved statues of the god Hermes had been mutilated. These distinctive statues took the form of a head of the god placed on a square pillar decorated with a set of male genitalia. They were dotted throughout the cityscape of Athens, clustering at crossroads and near people's houses. The mutilation was linked to the forthcoming expedition to Sicily, an attempt to establish Athenian dominion in the West. As Hermes was the god of travel, many saw the mutilation of

Almost every street corner or road junction in Athens had at least one of these markers which were dedicated to the god Hermes and called Herms. They were distinctively Athenian objects. The mutilation of these statues in 415 BC was seen by many as a protest against the Athenian expedition to Syracuse.

Since the 6th century BC onwards, Corinth had been one of the major rivals to Athens. An important commercial centre, it actively campaigned against the rise of Athenian influence in the Aegean. Archaeology has revealed much of the ancient city, including the impressive temple of Apollo, here shown against Corinth's highly defensive acropolis.

the statues of Hermes as a political protest against Athenian military expansion. Such was the climate of fear and distress caused by this act of sacrilege that the Athenians resorted to informers and torture to locate the culprits. A number of prominent Athenians were arrested, executed and their property confiscated.

Members of allied city-states who were opposed to Athenian rule were also known to resort to violence and Athenian citizens found themselves subject to occasional attack as they ventured abroad. In order to counteract these acts of brutality, a heavy fine was exacted on any city that allowed an Athenian to be murdered on its soil. Of course, such attacks are not surprising in cities where revolt had been crushed and new regimes installed. It is telling, however, that we find references to such attacks in even supposedly loyal communities such as those on the island of Chios. More significant

than random, sporadic acts of violence was widespread revolt. None of Athens' major allies were immune to the lure of revolt. Often they revolted more than once.

WAR WITH SPARTA

The war with Sparta and her allies, conventionally called the Peloponnesian war, represents the most significant historical event in the history of the Athenian empire. This war, lasting for over 27 years, divided the Greek world, and eventually would lead to the downfall of the Athenian empire.

To many, it seemed that Athens established its empire through stealing the hegemony of the Greeks from Sparta after the end of the Persian wars. Athens may have claimed that the leadership of the Greeks was not the exclusive domain of the Spartans and that it was given freely to Athens by her allies, but it is unlikely that these arguments ever held any sway outside the borders of Attica. Certainly, the Spartans were not pleased with Athenian imperial expansion. Their initial reluctance to oppose the Athenian usurpation of control owes more to their internal politics and an aversion to foreign campaigns than it does to a desire to see Athens in control of the Aegean. The Persian wars had gone on long enough, and the Spartans disliked the thought of continuing the fight against Persia. Spartan elites resented the tremendous power that Spartan kings wielded while on campaign, and so wished to recall the leaders home. Moreover, Spartans were wary of leaving their lands too long lest it encourage rebellion among their helot serfs. Sparta was content with the leadership of the Peloponnesian League, an alliance of states bound together by pacts of mutual defence. Where Sparta led, these states were obliged to follow. Yet, if Sparta expected gratitude for the ease with which Athens obtained the leadership of the rest of the Greeks, they were sadly mistaken. Throughout the first half of the 5th century BC, we see Athens continually aggravating Sparta and her allies, in particular the states of Corinth and Thebes.

Corinth was the other major power in the Peloponnese, and in many ways it felt the brunt of Athenian expansion far more than Sparta. Athens made alliances with rivals of Corinth. It threatened to upset the balance of power in the region by expanding its influence westwards. Between 461 and 446 BC, we see almost constant acts of hostility, both diplomatic and military, between Corinth and Athens.

Athens expanded northwards as well as west. It seems that Athens seriously considered the idea of establishing a land empire to match her naval one. For example in 457 BC, Athens captured a number of Boiotian towns and enrolled them as tribute-paying members into its empire. Although these towns were subsequently liberated, this action clearly indicated Athens' intentions in the area. It also ensured that it incurred the enmity of Thebes which regarded Boiotia as its domain.

As we can see, this period of 47 years after the formation of the Delian League is characterized by two features, namely the continued imperial expansion and 'bedding-down' of the Athenian empire, and a series of scrappy disputes between Athens and members of the Peloponnesian League and its allies. These disputes determined nothing, except to create a climate of hatred.

In such a situation, we may be forgiven for thinking that large-scale war between Athens and Sparta was inevitable. Certainly, the historian Thucydides, who chronicled the eventual conflict, thought so. 'The truest cause of the war was the growth of Athens' power and the fear this caused in Sparta.' Nevertheless, there is every reason to believe that when war did break out neither side imagined that it would extend much beyond five years, nor that it would extend to regions as far away as Sicily and Thrace.

The first phase of the war is generally called the 'Archidamian' war after the Spartan king, Archidamus, who led the Spartan army to invade Attica on three separate occasions (431, 430 and

One of the most important democratic leaders in Athens was the statesman Pericles. He oversaw much of the building programme for which Athens was famous. A skilled orator and talented general, he was the architect of Athenian defence plans in the early stage of the Peloponnesian war. Sadly, his death owing to an outbreak of plague meant that he was lost to Athens at the moment of its greatest need.

428 BC). This phase is typified by these annual invasions of Attica and the steadfast refusal of Athens to fight Sparta in open combat. This policy, attributed to the Athenian statesman, Pericles, was based on the idea that Athens could function effectively as an island behind its walls, relying on her port and command of the sea to provide her with the necessary supplies. Such a stalemate was unsustainable. Sparta was not used to such prolonged and indifferent warfare and, even with all its imperial wealth, Athens did not have the resources to maintain such a policy forever. Moreover, life on 'Athens island' was far from idyllic. The population of Attica was cramped into too small a space. The situation was not only uncomfortable, it was unhealthy.

An outbreak of plague swept through the city, with devastating effects. The population was decimated and the city lost many prominent individuals, most notably Pericles, the architect of the Athenian defence strategy.

Almost simultaneously, there was a change of policy by both sides. Sparta decided to strike at Athens' imperial resources directly, sending an expeditionary force to northern Greece to stir up trouble, and to impede the transport of grain to Athens so that hunger might force the city population out from its walls. Athens, for her part, decided to adopt a strategy of harrying the Peloponnesian forces through a series of piratical raids and the establishment of fortresses on the coastline. Both strategies met with a great deal of success. The Spartans in Thrace, led by the skilled tactician, Brasidas, liberated a number of cities from Athenian rule, and caused tremendous problems for Athenian control of the area. Meanwhile, in the Peloponnese, the Athenian commander Cleon managed, as much through luck as tactics, to capture a significant section of the Spartan army on the island of Sphacteria near Pylos. Curiously, in an attempt to break the previous stalemate, both sides had entangled themselves in another one of even greater complexity.

This lack of clear resolution meant that in 421 BC Sparta and Athens entered into a peace treaty to end the conflict between them. This so-called 'Peace of Nicias', named after the Athenian politician who had been instrumental in its negotiation, proved not to offer a long-term viable settlement of affairs in Greece. For a start, neither Corinth, Thebes nor Megara would agree to be bound by its terms. More importantly, it did nothing to introduce any structural mechanism to curb Athenian imperial ambitions.

Within a few years of the establishment of the treaty, we see Athenian expansion again causing problems with Sparta. In 419 BC, Athens entered into an alliance with Sparta's age-old enemy, Argos. In 416 BC, Athens attempted to bully the island of Melos, an island settled by the Dorians and technically neutral, into its empire. When Melos refused, Athens besieged the city and in conquering it inflicted a terrible price on the Melians for their refusal to acquiesce to Athenian demands (see box opposite). In 415 BC, Athens embarked on a

It was not just Athens who wished to commemorate victories in the Peloponnesian war. After the spectacular defeat of the Spartans at Pylos, the Messenian allies of Athens erected this statue of Nike, the goddess of victory, to celebrate the defeat of the Spartans. A reconstruction of this statue adorned the medals for the 2004 Olympic Games held in Athens.

Might versus Right – the Massacre on Melos

In the winter of 416/415 BC, an Athenian military force slaughtered all the adult males they could find on the island of Melos and sold the women and children into slavery. Thanks to Thucydides' dramatization of the Athenian and Melian negotiations prior to the massacre, this event has gone down in history as an example of the intense pragmatism that underpinned Athenian foreign relations.

In the course of these negotiations, the Athenian ambassador makes a number of chilling arguments. Melos had to capitulate, not because it posed a real threat to Athenian power, but because its independence just encouraged the enemies of Athens and made her look weak.

Empires govern through fear, they cannot afford to entertain ideals of justice or ethics. Interstate relations do not run on notions of honour and shame, but rather on profit and expediency. It is foolish to trust, as the Melians do, in the gods or blind hope.

The eventual massacre of the Melians seems to confirm the truth of these judgments. But was the Athenian ambassador really correct? The blood of the Melians has nourished many discussions among international relations theorists. It is a perennial question that governments of all types have faced – whether it is better to stay their hand or drive the knife in further.

Athens never allowed itself to pretend that war was anything other than bloody and cruel. Only months after the massacre on Melos, the Athenian playwright Euripides penned one of the great indictments against the brutality of war, the *Trojan Women*. The play tells the story of the murder and cruelty suffered by the women left after the defeat of Troy. Their horrible fate echoed that suffered by the women of Melos.

At its height, Athens had a citizen population of close to 200,000. Of these, 60,000 were adult male citizens. In addition, there were numerous slaves and resident foreigners. Not all lived in the city. Many Athenians chose to live in villages in the countryside. However, in times of strife, it was possible for the entire population of Attica to find shelter behind the city walls.

disastrous and overly ambitious expedition to seize control of Sicily. This expansion westwards was troubling to Sparta. If Athens had been successful in Sicily, Sparta would have found itself bracketed by Athenian controlled regions to the west and east and, with the wealth of the western Greeks at its disposal, Athens would have proved an almost unstoppable opponent. Sparta successfully aided the Sicilian opposition to Athens and the war continued.

The most significant factor in this second stage of the war is the courting of Persia by Athens and Sparta. Both sides realized that it was only the intervention of a major power like Persia that could settle the deadlock. Persia could provide Sparta with a fleet so that Athenian naval supremacy could finally be challenged. Persian resources could ensure that Athens need never worry about Spartan siege tactics or efforts to disrupt Athenian food supply. There had been attempts to court Persia from the very beginning of the war. However,

in this phase they took on a new intensity and urgency. Sadly for Athens, Persia decided to come down on the side of Sparta. At that point Athens' fate was sealed.

Persia provided funds to equip a fleet under the command of the Spartan naval commander, Lysander. The fact that Sparta, a traditionally land-based military power, was experimenting with the sea shows the extent to which the conflict promoted ingenuity and change. Indeed, one of the features of the Peloponnesian war is the way in which it provided opportunities for ambitious figures such as Brasidas and Lysander, people who might otherwise have been overlooked in the Spartan system.

Of course, the Athenians didn't know that they were living on borrowed time and consequently put up a spirited defence. Indeed, it was infuriating for the Persians how long it took for the Spartans finally to overwhelm them. At Arginusae, near Lesbos, the Athenian fleet defeated the Spartans, and another fleet had to be constructed with Persian money. Yet the Spartan opportunity eventually came at the battle of Aegospotami in 404 BC, when they managed to catch the Athenian fleet unawares while it was still beached. Only nine Athenian ships managed to escape the massacre. It was this defeat that effectively put an end to the Athenian empire. Athens was forced to enter a humiliating treaty negotiated by Lysander in which its walls were torn down and a brutal pro-Spartan military junta was installed to govern the city, the so-called 'Thirty'.

THE SECOND ATHENIAN CONFEDERACY

Power abhors a vacuum. Alternatively, imperialism is addictive. Whatever the explanation, the period following the defeat of Athens is not one of the peaceful co-existence of mutually autonomous states as Spartan rhetoric during the war promised. Instead, we see three powers, Sparta, Thebes and Athens, all jostling to dominate the Greek world. It was a time of shifting alliances, dramatic reversals of fortune, and complex diplomatic intrigue.

The imperialism of Sparta is surprising. Prior to the outbreak of the war, Spartan foreign policy had been distinguished by a reluctance to venture far from their traditional power base in the Peloponnese. Now the war had expanded their world view, and encouraged a new ambition.

This newly found ambition saw the Spartans turning on their former ally, the Persian king Artaxerxes. They backed a pretender to the throne, and when this failed they undertook to wage a war to free the Ionian cities now under Persian rule. This swaggering, imperialist Sparta was bad at making friends. In addition to incurring the enmity of Persia, Sparta now lost the support of her former allies, Corinth and Thebes.

The betrayal by Sparta persuaded Persia to start supporting Athens as a bulwark against Spartan aggression. They gave funds to the remnants of the Athenian fleet, and this fleet under the command of Conon, one of the survivors of the battle of Aegospotami, was successful in reducing the power of the Spartan navy.

In Athens, the oligarchic regime of the Thirty had only lasted for a couple of years. After losing the backing of its Spartan supporters, the regime had been removed and democracy restored. Athens seemed to be recovering from defeat. Indeed, it was recovering a little too quickly for Persia's comfort. The Athenian navy sailed the Aegean demanding funds and supplies from islanders and communities on the coast of Asia Minor. The Athenians encouraged rebellion in the Persian empire by inciting the Persian client king, Evagoras of Cyprus, to rebel.

This new-found enthusiasm of the Athenians needed to be checked. And so the former enemies, Persia and Sparta, joined forces to curb Athenian plans for expansion. In 387 BC, the Spartans captured the Hellespont and, faced with the possibility of starvation, the Athenians were forced to negotiate a settlement of their differences with Persia and Sparta, and in 386 BC a compromise was struck, the so-called 'King's Peace'. There was to be peace throughout the Greek world, but this would come at a price – there were to be no more Greek empires. Instead, all Greek states were to be autonomous.

In theory, this should have put an end to Athenian imperial ambitions. In practice, it seems only to have put them on hold temporarily and encouraged Athens to think of imaginative ways around this requirement. The Athenian solution initially was to construct a series of bilateral defensive treaty relations in which Athens and another state promised mutual support in the event of attack. Such actions were not excluded under the terms of the King's Peace. Out of these treaty relations blossomed the second Athenian Confederacy. Founded in 377 BC, this confederacy was designed to provide opposition to Spartan domination. The leader of this confederacy would be Athens, and the League was to be maintained through a series of 'contributions'.

The Athenian empire was back. Or was it? We possess the foundation document of this league, which makes for interesting reading. What is clear is that these allies knew the perils of entering into such an alliance with Athens. The document outlines what will constitute

ABOVE: It took a military and diplomatic genius such as Philip, father of Alexander the Great, to defeat Athens and strip it of its empire. Emerging from a troubled northern kingdom, Philip was able to expand his influence throughout mainland Greece. A brilliant strategist, Philip managed to bluff, confuse and eventually defeat in battle all his opponents. His plans for expansion were only stopped by his assassination in 335 BC. It was Alexander who fulfilled his plans for further conquest. This miniature head comes from a royal tomb at Vergina, thought to be that of Philip.

OPPOSITE: As the birthplace of democracy and the producer of some of western culture's finest art and literature, the appeal of classical Athens never diminished over the centuries. Following the fall of the Ottoman empire and the liberation of Greece in the 19th century, Athens once again became a place of pilgrimage and tourism. On the steps of the Propylaia, it was possible to imagine yourself in a city that was 'the education of Greece'.

unacceptable behaviour by Athens. Autonomy is guaranteed by the document. Tribute is explicitly banned. Athens is prohibited from establishing garrisons or governors. Athenian citizens are prohibited from foreign landholding. Any attempt to alter these conditions would result in the death of the proposer. Each member state of the confederacy was to have a vote in an assembly of allies, and this assembly had equal authority to the Athenian people.

In a symbolic gesture, a copy of the charter was erected in Athens beside the statue of Zeus Eleutherios (literally the 'Zeus of Freedom'). The charter of the Second Athenian Confederacy is an attractive package, and it is easy to understand why so many city-states were keen to sign up to it. The final tally of members is put as high as 70, and it can't have been much less than 60.

By and large, Athens kept the promises made in this charter document. There were a number of pragmatic reasons to do so. Athens was not nearly as strong as it had been in the previous century. Constant pressure from Sparta, and later Thebes, meant that it couldn't afford widespread dissension among the allies. Yet this didn't stop Athens using its position as the lead city to bully other city-states outside the league, or extracting advantages when it could. On liberating Samos from Persian rule, for example, Athens quickly imposed a series of colonies on the island so that the Samians were effectively displaced. The community on Sestos had all its adult males slaughtered and the rest of the population sold into slavery. Secession remained a problem. Ceos tried to secede and was brought forcibly into line. Military emergencies could cause Athens to bend its rule and establish garrisons at strategic points for the greater good. The extent to which Athens should be regarded as an imperial oppressor in this period will vary according to which city-state one might have asked. One suspects that the answer

from Sestos and Samos would have been very different from a state like Tenedos which remained a loyal member of the confederacy right until the end. What is perhaps significant is that the matter is debatable in a way that it is not for the 5th century.

Ultimately, the downfall of the Athenian confederacy came about thanks to the influence of other powers rather than any act on the part of Athens. In 371 BC, Thebes defeated Sparta at the battle of Leuctra, a setback from which Sparta never recovered. This newly emergent Thebes was not prepared to allow Athens to be the dominant power in Greece. It seems to have actively incited states to revolt against Athens. Persia, meanwhile, adopted a similar tactic for states close to the Persian sphere of influence. In 357 BC, these actions came to fruition and a number of important states, most notably Ceos and Rhodes, attempted to secede. This attempt initiated the so-called 'Social War'. This war demonstrates the weakness of the Athenian position. After a two-year campaign season, Athens no longer had the resources to continue and any ally who wished to secede was permitted to do so.

The last power to enter the stage is Macedonia, the state which finally put an end to the Athenian confederacy. The rise of Philip of Macedon is a supreme exercise in the art of diplomacy and double-dealing. He played Thebes and Athens off against each other, all the while extending his influence southwards and eastwards. By the time he effectively controlled Thessaly, Thrace and the Chersonese, it was too late for his enemies. Thebes and Athens allied themselves to oppose him, but they were routed by his superior military forces at the battle of the Chaeronea in 338 BC. This marks the end of Athenian imperialism. Athens and her allies were reorganized into Philip's new league, the League of Corinth. After the battle of Chaeronea, Philip is reported to have walked among the dead. Seeing the bodies of his opponents piled high, he wept for the loss of such brave men. No one we know apart from Athens wept for the loss of the Athenian empire; a new imperial age was beginning.

The dominance exercised by the various city-states of the Greek world only occasionally reached far from their borders. Greek writers, like Isocrates in the 4th century BC, itched for a champion to unite the Greeks in a war against the Persian empire. With the intervention in Greek affairs of the Macedonian king Philip II and his son Alexander, this aspiration was realized – beyond any reasonable expectation. Alexander's conquests transformed not only those lands he conquered – Egypt and the Near East as far as modern Afghanistan – but also the Greek and Macedonian worlds he left behind. At the time of his early death in 323 BC, however, he had only just begun to consolidate his rule over the former Persian empire: there were countless Macedonians hungry for power and wealth, but no convincing royal successors to his throne. It took around half a century for new dynasties to take firm root and for the shape of the 'successor kingdoms' to become set, giving rise to the Hellenistic world.

PREVIOUS PAGES: Detail from the so-called Alexander Sarcophagus. The sarcophagus from Sidon (Lebanon), now in the Istanbul Archaeological Museum, is the work of various Greek sculptors and dates to the late 4th century BC. The relief on the front side depicts the battle of Issus (333 BC) where Alexander defeated the army of the Persian king Darius III.

RIGHT: The Venus de Milo is allegedly the work of Alexander of Antioch (late 2nd century BC). The marble statue, discovered in 1820 on the island of Melos, is 2 m high and incomplete; the arms have never been found. It is now located in the Louvre, Paris.

King List

338–323 BC	Alexander

ANTIGONIDS OF MACEDON

306–301 BC	Antigonus I Monophthalmus
306–283 BC	Demetrius I Poliorcetes
283–239 BC	Antigonus II Gonatas
239–229 BC	Demetrius II
229–221 BC	Antigonus III Doson
221–179 BC	Philip V
179–168 BC	Perseus

SELEUCIDS

305–281 BC	Seleucus I Nicator
281–261 BC	Antiochus I Soter
261–246 BC	Antiochus II Theos
246–225 BC	Seleucus II Callinicus
225–223 BC	Seleucus III Soter
223–187 BC	Antiochus III the Great
187–175 BC	Seleucus IV Philopater
175–164 BC	Antiochus IV Epiphanes
163–162 BC	Antiochus V Eupator
162–150 BC	Demetrius I Soter
150–145 BC	Alexander Balas
145–142 BC	Antiochus VI Epiphanes
138–129 BC	Antiochus VII Sidetes
129–125 BC	Demetrius II NIcator
126 BC	Cleopatra Thea
125–121 BC	Cleopatra Thea and Antiochus VIII Grypus
125 BC	Seleucus V
121–96 BC	Antiochus VIII Grypus
115–95 BC	Antiochus IX Cyzicenus
96–95 BC	Seleucus VI Epiphanes Nicanor
95–88 BC	Demetrius III Philopator
95–83 BC	Antiochus X Eusebes
95 BC	Antiochus XI Philadelphus
94–84 BC	Philip I Philadelphus
87 BC	Antiochus XII Dionysus
83–69 BC	(Tigranes of Armenia)
69–64 BC	Antiochus XIII Asiaticus
65–64 BC	Philip II

ATTALIDS OF PERGAMUM

283–263 BC	Philetaerus
263–241 BC	Eumenes I
241–197 BC	Attalus I Soter
197–159 BC	Eumenes II Soter
159–138 BC	Attalus II
138–133 BC	Attalus III

PTOLEMIES

305–283 BC	Ptolemy I Soter
283–246 BC	Ptolemy II Philadelphus
246–222 BC	Ptolemy III Euergetes I
222–204 BC	Ptolemy IV Philopator
204–180 BC	Ptolemy V Epiphanes
180–145 BC	Ptolemy VI Philometor
145–144 BC	Ptolemy VII Neos Philopator
145–116 BC	Ptolemy VIII Euergetes II Physcon
139–101 BC	Cleopatra III
116–107 BC	Ptolemy IX Soter II
107–88 BC	Ptolemy X Alexander
101–88 BC	Cleopatra Berenice
88–81 BC	Ptolemy IX
80 BC	Ptolemy XI Alexander II
80–58 BC	Ptolemy XII Neos Dionysus
58–55 BC	Berenice IV
55–51 BC	Ptolemy XII
51–47 BC	Ptolemy XIII
51–30 BC	Cleopatra VII Philopator
47–44 BC	Ptolemy XIV
36–30 BC	Ptolemy XV

303 BC

→ Route of Alexander

Kingdom of Cassander

Kingdom of Lysimachus

Kingdom of Antigonus Monophthalmus

Kingdom of Seleucus

Kingdom of Ptolemy

0 ─── 400 km

0 ─── 400 miles

Foundation of Alexandria
332 BC

Alexander invades
Persian empire
334 BC

Alexander invades northern India
326 BC

Third Syrian war
246–241 BC

Battle of Actium
31 BC

Victory for
Philip of Macedon
at Chaeronea
338 BC

Death of Alexander
at Babylon
323 BC

Romans defeat Antiochus III
at Magnesia
189 BC

300 BC

200 BC

100 BC

0

Death of Philip
336 BC

Second Syrian war
260–253 BC

Roman sack of Corinth
146 BC

Persian king Darius
loses battle of Issus
333 BC

First Syrian war between
Ptolemies and Seleucids
274–271 BC

Romans defeat Philip V
of Macedon at
Cynoscephalae
197 BC

Huge victory for Alexander at
battle of Gaugamela
331 BC

Victory of Seleucus and
Lysimachus at Ipsos
301 BC

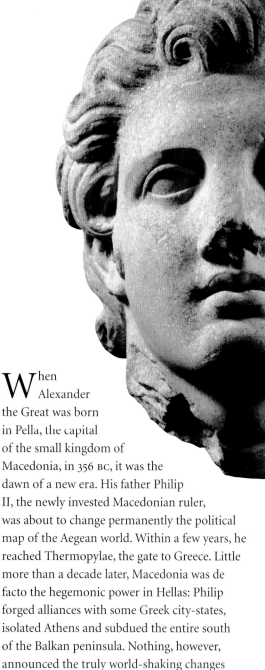

When Alexander the Great was born in Pella, the capital of the small kingdom of Macedonia, in 356 BC, it was the dawn of a new era. His father Philip II, the newly invested Macedonian ruler, was about to change permanently the political map of the Aegean world. Within a few years, he reached Thermopylae, the gate to Greece. Little more than a decade later, Macedonia was de facto the hegemonic power in Hellas: Philip forged alliances with some Greek city-states, isolated Athens and subdued the entire south of the Balkan peninsula. Nothing, however, announced the truly world-shaking changes that were imminent when Philip was murdered in 336 BC and Alexander came to power.

FROM PHILIP TO ALEXANDER

No single ruler changed the ancient world to the same extent as Alexander the Great. In the 13 short years of his reign, the tiny kingdom of Macedonia, at the periphery of the vast Persian empire of the Achaemenids, became the greatest power the world had seen so far. A new era had begun which we call 'Hellenism'; Greek language, culture and customs took off throughout the Near East and Central Asia.

When Alexander died in 323 BC, he had led his soldiers across the Hellespont and the Taurus mountains, through the deserts of Libya and the endless plains of Mesopotamia, across the Hindu Kush, into India and through the hostile Gedrosian desert in Iran. Thousands had died or been expelled from their homes, their cities plundered and their possessions confiscated. But after Alexander's death, his empire fell apart even faster than it had been built. One generation after the great conqueror, the Hellenistic world was divided into three major and a handful of minor kingdoms, all competing for the great prize: Alexander's legacy, universal power.

Alexander's conquests would have been impossible without the preparations laid down by his father Philip II (359–336 BC). It was he who had won for Macedonia leadership over Greece and the Balkans, amd he left to his son not only a stable and enlarged empire, but also a mission. In the battle of Chaeronea in 338 BC Philip had defeated the city-states that had allied under the leadership of Athens. There had been strong antipathies between the Greeks – living mainly in city-states – and the Macedonians, who lived under a king. The Greeks believed the Macedonians in general to be barbarians, though they made an exception for the Macedonian royal line and allowed them to participate at Greek festivals. After his victory over the Greeks at Chaeronea, rather than subduing the Greek city-states and integrating them into his kingdom, Philip chose to unite them under the umbrella of the Corinthian League, at the same time ensuring that the League elected him as its leader and general for life.

One of the first decisions taken by the League was a call to arms against the Persian empire. The official aim of this campaign was to be revenge: some 150 years earlier, as we saw in Chapter 5, the Persians had destroyed many sites in Greece, among them the Acropolis of Athens, and looted many important works of art from Greece. The campaign against the hereditary enemy fulfilled the Greek elite's desire for revenge and thus formed a basis for a cooperation between the Greek cities, conquered by Philip, and the Macedonian kingdom. This also explained the king's

second public declaration: it was his professed aim to 'free' the Greek cities in Asia Minor (the western coast of modern Turkey) from the Persian yoke – whatever 'freedom' might mean under Macedonian hegemony.

The Macedonian generals Parmenio and Attalus led a large army across the Hellespont, the narrow straits between Greece and Asia, in 336 BC. The timing of this venture was well chosen, as both the Persian king Artaxerxes III Ochus and his successor Artaxerxes IV had been murdered in 338 and 336 BC respectively. The dynasty of Iranian Achaemenids, which had ruled over an empire from the Hindu Kush to the southern border of Egypt, was thus ensnarled in internal strife (Chapter 4). From this, in 336 BC, Darius III emerged as the new Persian king, aged around 45 at the time of his accession – and his main goal, of necessity, was the consolidation of his empire.

Shortly after the campaign for 'freedom' had started, Philip fell victim to a murderous assault. He was succeeded by the 20-year-old Alexander, the third Macedonian king to bear the name. Philip had not had an especially close relationship with this son, after having married his second wife Kleopatra. The young man had

OPPOSITE: A marble portrait of Alexander, c. 320 BC. This fragment once formed part of a larger monument.

153

BELOW: Alexander (in hat and cloak) and his friend Hephaistion (or Krateros), hunting a lion: a pebble mosaic from Pella, Greece, c. 320 BC.

grown up under the influence of his mother Olympias, a princess from Epirus, and the Greek philosopher Aristotle, who had stimulated Alexander's great interest in Greek culture. With Aristotle, he had read the Homeric epics, and he was to keep a copy of the *Iliad* under his pillow for the rest of his life. An identification with the Homeric heroes became a major driving force for the young Macedonian prince, who idealized himself to be the Achilles of his own generation.

Tetradrachm of Philip II, King of Macedon, minted at Pella in 354 BC.

Alexander principally owed the relatively smooth transition from Philip to himself to his father's generals. Once made king, the young man had many of his internal rivals and enemies murdered, thus establishing his power in Macedonia. He dealt successfully with unrest on Macedonia's northern and western borders that had been provoked by Philip's assassination and the subsequent succession crisis: Illyrian and Thracian tribes prepared for an invasion of Macedonia, but were defeated in a campaign during which Alexander crossed the Danube in the north. From a Hellenic point of view, the river formed the border of the *oikoumene*, as the Greeks termed the inhabited, civilized world. This was the first of a number of times that Alexander reached and crossed a river that symbolically marked the end of the known world: similar turning points were to become the Oxus (Amu Darya) river in Central Asia and the Hyphasis (Beas) river in India. The act was, as we hear from ancient authors, motivated by Alexander's 'inner urge' – the same motive that underlay his campaigns against Persia.

When a rumour of Alexander's death in battle circulated, the important Greek city of Thebes left the Corinthian League and removed the Macedonian garrison. This prompted a sympathetic response from Athens, suggesting that the new order imposed on the Greek world by Philip was not one welcomed widely by the Greeks themselves. They wanted their freedom, rather than peace guaranteed by a foreign king. At the same time the Persian king was sending lavish gifts of money to politicians within Greece in an attempt to destabilize the Macedonian hegemony. When Alexander

reacted by razing the city of Thebes to the ground in 335 BC, no other Greek city went to help it. Instead, the members of the League congratulated Alexander on his victory and acquiesced in the destruction of the city. It was only to be rebuilt in 316 BC. Though the new king now reigned supreme and could start his war of aggression against Persia in the next year, the revolt reveals to what extent the rising empire depended on Alexander as a person.

CONQUERING THE PERSIAN EMPIRE

In the spring of 334 BC, a large army consisting of 30,000 men on foot, 5,000 on horseback and an elite of 12,000 experienced Macedonians crossed the Hellespont. As we have noted, it was officially a war of revenge for the Persian destruction of Greek temples and cities 150 years before. However, there were few contingents from the Greek city-states in Alexander's expeditionary force. This suggests that the motive of revenge on behalf of the Greeks was unlikely to have been Alexander's main priority when he set out on his expedition. Why he initiated his campaigns and how far he could have conceived of his subsequent success are ultimately matters for speculation.

It seems likely that Alexander at first thought only of 'liberating' the long-established Greek cities of Asia Minor. Even Alexander would have realized that such an army, however experienced, would not have been able to pursue larger geopolitical aims. The Persian king in the distant centre of his empire, on the other hand, regarded the small army of Macedonians and Greeks as a threat only to the outlying provinces (or 'satrapies') of his empire; it was not a problem that he would need to be involved in, and so he delegated the task of dealing with Alexander's threat to his satraps (governors) and the Greek admiral Memnon of Rhodes. Alexander, relying – as in all his military victories – on the speed and manoeuvrability of his army, defeated the satraps in the first large battle of Alexander's campaign at the river Granicus, and opened up the route towards the border of Syria. The Greek cities were thus, whether they wanted it or not, 'set free', as was the large

Persian horseman, a detail from a battle scene showing Greeks and Persians from the so-called Alexander Sarcophagus from Sidon, Lebanon, 330–320 BC. Today it is found in the Archaeological Museum in Istanbul.

non-Greek territory which now found itself under Macedonian rule. Only when Alexander crossed the Taurus mountains did the Persian king oppose him in person with a huge army at the Gulf of Issus – where he was duly defeated by Alexander. The celebrated Alexander Mosaic from Pompeii probably depicts the decisive moment, when the Persian king, attacked by Alexander, turns around to leave the battlefield. Darius fled with only a few soldiers across the Euphrates, while his camp, and with it his family, were taken over by the Macedonian conqueror. At Damascus the most important of Alexander's generals, Parmenio, managed to get hold of Darius' war chest, thus solving the Macedonians' previous financial problems.

Instead of pursuing and fully defeating the Persian king across the Euphrates, however, Alexander decided to march southwards, along the Mediterranean coastline towards Egypt. The city of Tyre, on an island off the coast of present-day Lebanon, welcomed Alexander's envoys but refused the Macedonian king's request to perform a sacrifice in the local temple of Melqart, the supreme god of the Phoenician city. Alexander put the island city under siege, which it resisted for seven months. Eventually the city was conquered when Alexander's engineers built a dam to the island. By now, the Persian king had realized the gravity of the threat that the Macedonian posed to his empire and his kingship, and asked for a peace on conditions which were very favourable for Alexander. The historian Arrian, writing at the height of the Roman empire but using near-contemporary sources, describes how Parmenio advised Alexander to accept the Persian king's terms, claiming that if he were Alexander he would be glad to stop the war under those conditions. But his advice was royally snubbed. Alexander retorted that he would also be glad to stop the war if he was Parmenio, but as he was Alexander, he would not. He claimed that all of Darius' money and empire belonged to him, and that in short, he aspired to become the king of Persia himself.

OVERLEAF: The Alexander Mosaic (c. 100 BC) was found in the House of the Faun in Pompeii. Whether the mosaic depicts the battle of Issus (333 BC) or the battle at Gaugamela (331 BC) is uncertain. At the centre, in a chariot, we see the Persian king Darius. Alexander is on the left, riding his horse Bucephalus, with a breastplate showing the head of Medusa.

Ruins of the village of Aghurmi that surrounds the temple of Amun-Ra in the Siwa oasis, Egypt. Here Alexander was proclaimed son of Zeus.

This ambition was to become a major factor in the subsequent alienation of the Macedonian elite. For the time being, however, Alexander was protected by the overwhelming success of his campaigns, and, now that the Phoenician-Cypriot fleet of the Persian king no longer posed a threat, he pushed on, largely unopposed, towards Egypt. There he visited Memphis, the ancient capital, where he conducted Greek-style games and made an offering to the Egyptian god Apis, a deity worshipped in the form of a living bull, and where we get a first glimpse of Alexander's constant endeavour to reconcile Greek and Near Eastern traditions. Leaving Memphis, he sailed down the Nile's westernmost branch and founded, on the delta's coast, a city named after himself: Alexandria. In the temple of Amun-Ra in Siwa, an oasis in the middle of the Libyan desert, he was proclaimed the son of Zeus.

The oracle of Amun-Ra at Siwa had been well established for several centuries. Greeks who had settled in nearby Cyrene in the 7th century BC had spread the oracle's fame, linking it to their own supreme god, Zeus. Here in Siwa, Amun-Ra announced with a nod his acceptance of the future pharaoh, Alexander. What exactly happened when Alexander entered the sanctuary is not known. Callisthenes, one of Alexander's earliest biographers who accompanied the king on his campaigns, provides a description of the events, extant in a fragment, which is rather cryptic: 'Hence the oracle of Ammon, which was formerly held in great esteem, is now nearly deserted …. Alexander was ambitious of the glory of visiting the oracle, because he knew that Perseus and Heracles had before performed the journey thither…. The priest permitted the king alone to pass into the temple in his usual dress, whereas the others changed theirs; … all heard the oracles on the outside of the temple, except Alexander, who was in the interior of the building; … the answers were not given as at Delphi …, in words, but chiefly by nods and signs, as in Homer: "the son of Kronos nodded with his sable brows," the prophet imitating Zeus. This, however, the man told the king in express terms: that he was the son of Zeus.'

The episode at Siwa determined much of Alexander's future reign; henceforth, his divine descent formed part of the monarch's officially divulged image. Being now Zeus Ammon's son he was separated from his fellow Macedonian aristocrats through a barrier, at first barely visible, but still decisive. No longer was he a military ruler elected by the army and bound by Macedonian tradition: his rule had become rooted in a Near Eastern theocratic tradition that went back several millennia. But his being the son of a god had probably more to it than the 'official' reading reveals: for a man raised with Greek myths the events of Siwa were designed to move him into one sphere with the Homeric heroes. Like Achilles, he had a divine pedigree himself now, and one which was even better: while the hero who had defeated the Trojan Hector had the relatively obscure sea god Nereus as grandfather, he, Alexander, could call Zeus himself his father. The evidence suggests that Alexander genuinely believed in his heroic mission.

In 331 BC the Macedonian king, leader of the Corinthian League and Egyptian pharaoh, revived the campaign against the Persian king, Darius. Having crossed the Euphrates and Tigris rivers, Alexander fought against Darius at Gaugamela and defeated him; his soldiers subsequently proclaimed him to be 'King of Asia'. He entered the two royal residences at Babylon and Susa, where he took over the unbelievable treasures of the Persian king. Early in 330 BC he finally reached Persepolis, one of the most important residences of the king and the empire's ceremonial capital. Then, shortly after a brief period during which he tried to find an accommodation with the local nobility, he set fire to the royal palace. Why did Alexander do something so apparently irrational? Some ancient authors suggest that

it was an accident, the result of a prostitute's late-night high jinx, others that it was an intentional political signal. The archaeological remains, however, reveal that the fire was clearly planned. One clue to the significance of the event is that immediately afterwards Alexander released the contingents in his army that had been drawn from the Corinthian League; this suggests that the destruction of Persepolis was presented as the fulfilment of the Greek's revenge for the Persian destruction of the Athenian Acropolis in 480 BC.

THE KING OF ASIA

Even though the campaign of 'revenge' had now been concluded, Darius was still alive and unwilling to yield to Alexander's power. Alexander pursued Darius through the east of his empire, in the mountainous regions of the Hindu Kush. But after Darius was murdered by one of his own men, the satrap of Bactria and Sogdia, Bessus, Alexander took the opportunity to adopt a new ideological mantle – that of the avenger of his former enemy. It was he who was the legitimate heir to Darius, a fact that was reflected in his homage to the murdered king.

Alexander was now the king of Macedonia, the Egyptian pharaoh and Persian king. He secured his conquests by founding cities in his name and by building military colonies for the Greco-Macedonian soldiers. As successor to the Persian kings he was also concerned to make his peace with the traditional elite of the Perian empire, and to integrate them into his imperial system. He adopted a ceremony whereby those who approached him had to fall to the ground like dogs, or *kynes*, which came to be known in Greek as proskynesis. This was a Persian court ceremony, and did not please his fellow Macedonian noblemen, who became increasingly uneasy about the direction his kingship was taking. It was also by an Iranian rite that he married Rhoxane, the daughter of a Sogdian chieftain from the mountains north of Afghanistan. The heir that was to be expected from this marriage could embrace both the West and the East in his rule.

Alexander the Great, portrayed as Pharaoh. A colossal statue of the Ptolemaic period from Karnak, Egypt.

The Persian kings' claim of absolute power, however, was incompatible with the traditional military monarchy. By following in the kings' footsteps, Alexander alienated himself from the people of his inner circle. He ignored them, and appointed increasingly more Persians to the highest offices, thus stirring envy among the Macedonians whose positions had previously been uncontested. It became obvious that the war – which had started as a revenge campaign against the Persians – was now being led by someone who was more and more influenced by Persian traditions and manners. The Macedonians who openly criticized Alexander, however, did not live for long; he either killed them himself or had them murdered. In 327 BC, seven young noblemen planned a plot against Alexander. One of them, Hermolaus, confessed when charged with treason and claimed before the Macedonians 'that he had conspired against the king's life, because it was no longer possible for a free man to bear his insolent tyranny'. The son of the Macedonian general, Parmenion, was duly executed as well. Alexander's new empire was Macedonian no more.

held a prominent place in Greek mythology. The son of Zeus-Ammon crossed the Indus river – as with his crossing of the Danube, crossing an apparently uncrossable border – and defeated King Porus in northwestern India in the last large-scale battle of the campaign, before he finally reached the river Hyphasis (Beas), today situated in the border regions of Pakistan and India.

Alexander still hoped to reach the eastern ocean, which at the time was believed to be the end of the world. But scouts reported that to the east of the river there were only endless fertile plains, and beyond them yet more mountains to cross. The soldiers' patience was wearing thin and mutiny was in the air: 'Conferences were held throughout the camp, in which those who were the most moderate bewailed their lot, while others resolutely declared that they would not follow Alexander any farther, even if he should lead the way'. In Arrian's narrative of the events, Alexander makes a final, desperate attempt to bring them back in line. After listing the lands they had conquered together, he goes on:

'If in addition to these, the river Indus flows through our territory, as do also the Hydaspes, the Acesines, and the Hydraotes, why do you shrink from adding the Hyphasis also, and the nations beyond this river, to your empire of Macedonia? Do you fear that your advance will be stopped in the future by any other barbarians?'

Aged 25, the king of what had been a petty kingdom at the periphery of the Persian empire had already changed the world. Yet the conquest of the Persian realm was not enough for him – he had, as the sources tell us, an 'inner urge' to pursue his conquests to the limits of the known world. He pushed his campaign eastwards, and no power, or so it seemed, was able to stop him. He believed that he was about to surpass Achilles and Hercules. In 327 BC, he crossed the Khyber Pass into India, following the god Dionysus' footsteps, whose expedition to India

His pleas were in vain; the soldiers insisted on returning to Babylon. Alexander gave in to the pressure and declared the Hyphasis (as a decade earlier he had declared the Danube), the border of the *oikoumene*. What lay beyond was no longer worth conquest. On their way back to Babylon, the bulk of the army had to cross the Gedrosian desert, a sunburnt, waterless hell in southern Iran, where more soldiers died than in any of his battles. On Alexander's arrival at Susa in 324 BC, a mass marriage was arranged in order to consolidate the fusion of the Greco-

Macedonian and the Persian elites: the king himself married two Persian princesses, and 80 of his most important courtiers found themselves forced to marry Persian women, as did 10,000 of Alexander's soldiers. The event contributed to further alienation of the traditional Greek and Macedonian circles. An edict ruling that the Greek cities had to re-accept those individuals who had been exiled from their communities led to yet more unrest; the edict was a clear breach of the traditional autonomy of the Greek city, and made it obvious that Alexander was only willing to respect the 'freedom of the Greeks' as long as it served his interests. Many Macedonians also opposed the king's apparent request to be venerated as a god.

When Alexander replaced the retired Macedonian veterans at Opis by Persians, his old soldiers mutinied. This was partly due to the fact that they would now have to fight alongside their former enemies, but mainly in objection to teaching the Macedonian art of fighting to the Persians. This implied a loss of their military supremacy, which had been one of the foundations of their privileged status that set them apart from other subjects in Alexander's empire. The king hoped to end the quarrel quietly, as Arrian reports: 'Alexander gave a public banquet, seated all the Macedonians round him, and next to them Persians and he himself and those around him drank from the same bowl and poured the same libations, with the Greek soothsayers and [Persian] Magi initiating the ceremony. Alexander prayed for various blessings and especially that the Macedonians and Persians should enjoy harmony as partners in the government.'

ALEXANDER'S EMPIRE

Alexander's empire, with its capital in Babylon, embraced three entirely different components: Macedonian-style kingship, Near Eastern-style empire, and the Greek league (in legal terms, at least) of independent cities. For his Macedonian soldiers, Alexander was legally nothing but a first among equals. For the subjects in the former Persian empire, however, he was a king

of nearly unlimited power, while for the Greeks he was a reluctantly elected leader. In the vast space of the former Persian empire, the king left the old territorial units unchanged, but gave the offices of the satraps to Macedonian officers, whereas subordinate officials were kept in place. After the victory over Darius at Gaugamela in October 331 BC he changed this policy and appointed members of the local elites to the highest offices, including that of governor.

It is obvious that Alexander envisaged an empire in which the ethnic origin and cultural affiliation of the ruling class mattered little, if at all. The theocratic approach to monarchy, which he had encountered at Siwa, and the autocratic style of government he adopted from the Persians, seemed to provide the appropriate tools for the integration of western and Near Eastern elements into the imperial layout. But the growing resentment among his own Macedonian soldiery, obvious at all levels, and Alexander's increasingly harsh reaction to it, make it doubtful whether the universal monarchy Alexander aimed for would have ever worked. Macedonian and Near Eastern concepts of leadership were by no means complementary, but mutually exclusive, and the readiness of the Greco-Macedonians to accept the quasi-divine escapism of their king had been dwindling long before the Macedonian phalanx mutinied at Opis. When Alexander died a premature death at Babylon, on 10 June 323 BC, the centrifugal forces got the upper hand. Asked on his deathbed who among his generals should succeed him, he reportedly answered: 'the strongest'. The empire was to fall apart.

Decadrachm of Alexander the Great, around 324 BC. This is the only image of Alexander to survive from his lifetime. Though Alexander's name is not mentioned on the coin, it is generally assumed that the coin forms part of a series issued by the king himself.

Voices of Empire

Sources for the history of Alexander the Great and his successors are relatively plentiful. In addition to reports by later ancient authors, there is a lot of primary evidence, including inscriptions, papyri and coins, as well as archaeological material. These sources present us with a direct view of the times and allow us to confirm, correct or supplement the later reports. Most of the texts are in Greek, which was the main language also in the Hellenistic Near East, replacing Aramaic as the language of administration. However, local languages did not die out – witness the Aramaic spoken by Jesus. In any case, to achieve social or economic success, every subject of a Hellenistic king would aim to know Greek. The texts not only present the conquerors' views, but enable us to take the perspective of the subject population in Aramaic, Egyptian or even Greek.

'What great and noble success could we have achieved, if we had sat at home in Macedonia and thought it enough to guard our homeland without effort?'

Alexander reproaches his mutinous troops at the Hyphasis river

Marble head of Alexander. The bust is a copy of the idealized image established by Alexander's favourite sculptor, Lysippus.

Alexander restores democracy in Chios, 332 BC
'From King Alexander to [the] citizens of Chios. All the exiles from Chios are to return; the form of government in Chios is to be demos. Law-drafters are to be chosen, who shall draft and revise the laws, in order that nothing may be contrary to the democracy or the return of the exiles; the results of the revision and drafting are to be referred to Alexander. The Chians are to provide 20 trireme-ships with crews at their own expense, and these are to sail for as long as the rest of the fleet of the Greeks sails with us.'

The Oracle of the Potter – an Egyptian anti-Greek prophecy
'The girdle-wearers [the Greeks] will destroy themselves as they are Typhonians. Then the Agathos Daimon will leave Alexandria and will come to Memphis. The city that will be founded as a city of strangers [Alexandria] will be empty. This will happen at the end of the evil, when in Egypt strangers will fall like leaves from the trees and the city of the girdle-wearers [Alexandria] will be emptied because of the evils they have done against Egypt.'

'In the reign of the young one – who received the throne from his father – lord of crowns, glorious, the one who established Egypt, and pious towards the gods … lord of the 30-years' feasts just as Hephaistos [Ptah] the great, king just as Helios [Ra], the great king of the upper and lower regions … living image of Zeus [Amun], Ptolemy Ever-Living, Beloved of Ptah.'

Part of the pharaonic titulature of Ptolemy V from the Rosetta Stone

The Old Testament Book of Daniel prophesies the rise and fall of Alexander's empire

'Then a mighty king will appear [Alexander the Great], who will rule with great power and do as he pleases. After he has appeared, his empire will be broken up and parcelled out towards the four winds of heaven [i.e. to the diadochi]. It will not go to his descendants, nor will it have the power he exercised, because his empire will be uprooted and given to others.'

Alexander's letter to the defeated Persian king Darius

'Your ancestors [i.e. Xerxes I and Darius I] invaded Macedonia and the rest of Greece and did us great harm … I have been appointed leader of the Greeks, and invaded Asia in the desire to take vengeance on Persia for your aggressions. … As I have conquered in battle first your generals and satraps, and now yourself and your own force … I hold myself responsible for all of your troops who did not die in the field but took refuge with me; they are with me of their own free will, and voluntarily serve in my army. You must then regard me as Lord of all Asia and come to me.'

The Rosetta Stone, a stela dating to 196 BC, found by members of Napoleon's expedition in 1799 near the Egyptian town of Rashid. The trilingual inscription translated by the British scholar Thomas Young and the French philologist Jean-François Champollion was crucial for the understanding of the ancient Egyptian writing systems.

Marble bust of Lysimachus (*c.* 355–281 BC), a Macedonian general who became King of Thrace after Alexander's death.

Octodrachm of Ptolemy I. Ptolemy, another general of Alexander, founded the Ptolemaic dynasty.

THE CONTEST FOR ALEXANDER'S LEGACY

Since Alexander's power had rested on his role as king of Macedonia, the assembly of the Macedonian soldiers regarded themselves as authorized to elect the next king. Two males were qualified through their descent:

Alexander's half-brother Philip Arrhidaeus, who was reportedly mentally ill, and the as-yet unborn child of Rhoxane, to be named Alexander (IV) after his father. Neither they nor Alexander's mother Olympias and Alexander's wife Rhoxane were to live for long. The generals took matters into their own hands: they divided the empire along the borders of the satrapies, but at the same time all paid lip service to the idea of a united empire, referring to themselves only as satraps. Lysimachus received Thrace, Antigonus a large part of Asia Minor, Eumenes of Caria got Paphlagonia and Cappadocia, and Ptolemy the prize of Egypt. Antipater was to be strategos, or general of Europe, which consisted mainly of Greece and Macedonia, while the unofficial ruler in charge of the overall empire was Alexander's former cavalry leader Perdiccas, who had also been responsible for distributing the satrapies. He assumed the administration of Asia for himself. The original provincial satraps, whom Alexander had held in high esteem, lost their importance, and the idea of universal monarchy was abandoned – as became apparent when most of the marriages formed at Susa were dissolved.

The satraps' intermediate position between monarchy and theoretical subordination under a central king led to problems in representation which are apparent from the 'Satrap Stela', a memorial set up by Egyptians priests. The leader of Egypt, Ptolemy, had given land to the Egyptian temple of the town Buto and this land-donation was recorded in the hieroglyphs on the memorial. On its upper section it depicts an Egyptian pharaoh sacrificing to the gods of Buto, a symbol of the land-donation to the temple. The cartouches of the king – that is, the rings into which the name of the pharaoh is usually spelled out – are empty, but we learn from the text that the king depicted is Pharaoh Alexander IV, and that Ptolemy himself is only his satrap. However, the whole text is then an encomium of the achievements of the satrap who fulfils a pharaoh's role: it is he who gives land to the priests of Buto, following the model of an Egyptian king called Chababash. By taking on the duties of a pharaoh, Ptolemy gave direction to the internal strategy of the dynasty of the 'Ptolemies' which followed him. For their Egyptian subjects, the Ptolemies represented themselves as pharaohs, for the Greeks and Macedonians, as Hellenistic kings. Modern scholars refer to this as the 'double face' of Ptolemaic rule.

Eventually, in the summer of 306 BC, Antigonus held an assembly of his army, which acclaimed him as king. As the insignia of his newly acquired kingship, he assumed the diadem. Not much later Seleucus, Lysimachus and Cassander, the ruler of Greece and Macedonia, followed: the 'year of the kings' (306/305 BC) gave the final blow to the fiction of a continuation of Alexander's empire. Two years later, Alexander IV was executed.

In only one generation, through a messy pattern of wars between the former generals of Alexander, the *diadochi*, or successors, gradually established and reinforced their control over their separate kingdoms. The largest part of Alexander's empire was taken by the former general Seleucus; his domain, which was to become the Seleucid empire, took up much of the former Persian empire, stretching from inland Asia Minor to the verge of India. Ptolemy had stood his ground in Egypt, and Antigonus' power base had shifted from Asia Minor to Macedonia. Alexander's empire was in ruins, but Macedonian dynasties remained in power in an area that stretched from the Ionian Sea to the Indus. Structurally, the emerging territorial kingdoms (Ptolemaic Egypt with parts of the Aegean; the Seleucid Near East; and Antigonid Macedonia) and the smaller units (Attalid Pergamum; the island of Rhodes; and a handful of petty kingdoms in Asia Minor) could hardly have been more diverse. In the west, the Greek city-states, the *poleis*, remained the dominant form of political organization. Their political scope began to increase again with the partition of Alexander's empire and the establishment of the relatively weak Antigonid dynasty in Macedonia.

The case of Rhodes demonstrates that even relatively small political entities could maintain their independence against far larger and more powerful territorial states. Rhodes had been a commercial hub in the eastern Mediterranean throughout the 4th century BC. Crucial for Rhodes' wealth was the grain route between Egypt and Athens, in which Rhodians acted as intermediate traders. In the year of the kings, 306/305 BC, Demetrius, the son of Antigonus, tried to put an end to Rhodian independence. The Macedonian, who had earned himself the surname Poliorketes (the 'besieger'), put in a great deal of effort and technological sophistication in the attempt to overcome Rhodes, but in vain; their victory yielded the Rhodians the respect of the entire Hellenistic world. Those who visited the island were welcomed by the Colossus of Rhodes, a huge statue, some 30 m (100 ft) tall, of the sun-god Helios, patron of Rhodes. The statue, erected by the sculptor Chares of Lindus, was finished in 280 BC: soon, it was counted among the Seven Wonders of the World. The statue stood for only 53 years, when it was largely destroyed by an enormous earthquake that hit the island and devastated its towns. However, the Colossus was a symbol for the Rhodians' quest for freedom, for their sea power and the wealth accumulated through trade: 'Not only above the sea they built him, but also atop the land, as a glorious light of unenslaved freedom. For theirs who grew from Heracles' lineage, is the sovereignty over sea and land.' Thus an epigram from the Anthologia Palatina, a collection of Greek poetry, praises the Colossus and its freedom-loving builders.

In the formerly Persian east, the word 'freedom' had a different tone. Here, the new rulers reinforced their entitlement to the land with the claim that the old Persian territory was 'spear won'. That meant in practice that

The Great Theatre in Pergamum in Asia Minor. Built by the Attalid kings of Pergamum in the 3rd century BC, it had a seating capacity of over 10,000. Pergamum was the capital of the eponymous state. The Attalids were close allies of the Romans from 190 BC onwards.

The temple of Horus at Edfu was founded by Ptolemy III in 236 BC, but not completed until 75 BC. This exceptionally well-preserved building is a striking example of architectural continuity in Ptolemaic Egypt.

indigenous landowners could be deprived of their property and replaced by Greek and Macedonian immigrants. Alexandria in Egypt became the model for a surge of new colonial cities founded by Alexander and his successors, mainly in Syria and Mesopotamia, but also in areas as distant as Central Asia. The influx of Greco-Macedonian settlers to Asia remained steady throughout the 3rd century BC. The concept of 'spear won' territory that turned parts of the Near East into urban landscapes dominated by Greek-style *poleis* had its intellectual forerunners in philosophers such as Aristotle and orators such as Isocrates, who had claimed that the inhabitants of the Persian empire were natural-born slaves and their land was a legitimate prize for Greek conquerors – an idea turned into practice by Alexander's victories.

On the other hand, the foreign-born dynasts had to come to an understanding with the local elites on whom they needed to rely. In Egypt, the indigenous temple priesthoods benefited from Macedonian rule by becoming economically more independent and were able

to commission large sanctuaries such as Edfu. But life under Macedonian rule also changed the cultural patterns of the Near Eastern societies. Some, like the Phoenician coastal cities in present-day Lebanon, had been in touch with the Hellenic world for centuries. But many inhabitants of inland Syria and Mesopotamia came into contact with Greek culture and Greek lifestyle only after Alexander's conquests. Many members of local elites began to emulate the invaders in some ways, while remaining distinct in others. A good example of the impact the political changes had on a local elite is the Jewish family of the Tobiads in present-day Jordan. Ever since the Jews had returned from the Babylonian exile in 538 BC, members of this family had served as regional administrators on behalf of the Persian king – a position they retained under the Ptolemies. Ancient papyri reveal the close relationship between Tobias and the king. When the Seleucids conquered Syria in the Fifth Syrian war, the Tobiads continued to play an important role. At Irak-el-Amir, Hyrcanus, Tobias' grandson, had a large palace built for himself, modelled on a Greek temple and imitating the now lost palaces of the Ptolemies in Alexandria and of the Seleucids in Antioch. The building illustrates how local elites gradually 'hellenized' themselves.

While the locals became more Greek, the Macedonian dynasties became increasingly local, thus culturally drifting further apart. What united them, however, was the importance kingship, dynasty and the ruler's personal charisma had for the coherence of the Hellenistic societies. Over and over again, Hellenistic kings had to prove their ability to convey to their subjects security, wealth and good luck. They had to be generous, fortunate and, above all, victorious in battle. The model was, not surprisingly, Alexander himself, who had possessed these qualities in abundance. Accordingly, Hellenistic monarchs boasted honorific names such as 'saviour' (*soter*), 'benefactor' (*euergetes*) or 'victor' (*nikator*) – even though, in most cases, the reality was more prosaic. Hellenistic kings had their subjects indulge in lavish jollifications. The processions put on stage by the Ptolemaic rulers in their capital, Alexandria, were famous. In the 270s BC, Ptolemy II honoured his deceased father with a procession that dwarfed anything the Greek world had seen so far. Carts with larger-than-life statues of Alexander and Ptolemy I were accompanied by a personification of *arête*, the rulers' virtue –

statues of deities and a statue with a golden wreath, symbolizing the city of Corinth. All this was followed by carts 'with richly dressed women, representing the cities which once had been subject to the Persians, in Ionia and elsewhere in Asia and on the islands. They all wore golden wreaths.' The spectators were duly impressed, but the treasury was afflicted with exorbitant expenses.

Another side effect of the Hellenistic rulers' pursuit of glory was their constant urge for war. Generations of Seleucid rulers felt the need to imitate Alexander by waging a major campaign (*anabasis*) to enforce their claim on the eastern satrapies. In spite of such efforts, these provinces continued to drift away from the centre. Still more devastating was the ongoing climate of tension between – and within – the Hellenistic powers; the Seleucids and the Ptolemies went to war over Syria as many as six times and the petty kingdoms of Asia Minor fought a constant war of attrition against the Seleucid empire. The Antigonid kings of Macedonia had a hard time holding the city-states of the Greek mainland at bay. Dynastic strife loomed as soon as a king seemed to betray his subjects' trust. In spite of the immense wealth, especially in the Ptolemaic and Seleucid kingdoms, these states were profoundly unstable, prone to overstretching their resources and to exhausting themselves in never-ending wars.

Ruins of a Hellenistic palace at Irak-el-Amir, Jordan. The structure, dating from around 200 BC, was built for a Tobiad notable, Hyrcanus of Jerusalem. The building is mentioned in the works of Flavius Josephus.

The 'Jockey' of Artemisium, representing a youth riding a horse. The bronze sculpture, dating from the 2nd century BC, was found in one piece in a shipwreck off Cape Artemisium on the island of Euboea. The sculpture was discovered underwater by two fishermen in 1926 and is now in the National Archaeological Museum in Athens.

Hellenistic Art

The end of the classical period and the replacement of the city-state, or *polis*, by large territorial states brought about major and contradictory changes in art. New themes emerged – the monarchs used art for self-representation on a hitherto unknown scale; they mobilized immense resources for building activity. The population had swollen and the social and cultural environment of Hellenistic cities were more diverse. The idealized style of classical art gave way to more individualized forms of expression: suffering, agony and failure all received their place in artistic representation.

The trend is exemplified by the Laocoön Group, a marble sculpture of two boys and their father, all entangled in a deadly fight against sea serpents. The father is the Trojan priest Laocoön. In the Trojan war, when the Greeks had offered peace to the Trojans and brought a giant horse as a gift, Laocoön had warned his fellow countrymen not to trust them. The Trojans ignored his warnings, however, and fell victim to the Greeks' deception. However, when Laocoön hurled his spear at the horse, Minerva sent the serpents to kill him and his sons.

The bronze statue of the 'Jockey' of Artemisium portrays a child riding a racehorse. The features of the youth are strikingly realistic and vivid: the full lips and curly hair evoke an African physiognomy; he may well have been a slave.

Laocoön and his sons being attacked by snakes. Nero added the sculpture to his collection in the Domus Aurea ('Golden House'), the colossal palace he built for himself in the heart of Rome. It was found there in 1506, almost intact: only Laocoön's right arm was missing. The sculptor Michelangelo amended it, pointing it upward in a gesture of defiance. The original arm was found in 1957; it is bent. A little less heroic than Michelangelo's vision of him, the 'real' Laocoön may be even more touching in his hopeless struggle against divine fate.

169

A CLASH OF CIVILIZATIONS?

Where people are moving, ideas also get in motion. As a matter of course, Greek concepts, ways of life and technologies spread with the Greco-Macedonian conquerors as they advanced through Asia and settled in new homes in Syria, Mesopotamia and Egypt. Our understanding of Hellenism in the east would be flawed, however, if we imagined cultures coming in contact with each other as a one-way process. Learning from each other and adopting ideas worked in both directions, as the example of Alexander at Siwa makes clear. What the Greeks did bring to the Near East, was their model of the self-governing, autonomous city, the *polis*, populated not by subjects, but by citizens. Greco-Macedonian settlers, among them many discharged soldiers, founded new, or took over existing, cities even in areas as remote as Bactria, in present-day Afghanistan. Though they were in the minority throughout, the Greco-Macedonians usually formed the dominant element of the population where they settled. On the other hand, the east had its own urban tradition, stretching back at least 3,000 years. Most of the indigenous cities in the former Persian empire continued to exist, virtually unchanged. But Greek personal names – adopted by local people – and some Greek political institutions even found their ways to cities like Babylon and Uruk, in the heart of Mesopotamia, where few, if any, Greeks ever settled.

Nowhere were the pitfalls of culture contact more tangible than in Jerusalem, once the city of Solomon's Temple and still the religious centre of Judaism when the Seleucids conquered Palestine from the Ptolemies in the Fifth Syrian war at the very beginning of the 2nd century BC. A substantial faction of the city's priestly elite, led by the high priest Jason, was profoundly 'hellenized' by the 170s BC and attempted to turn Jerusalem into a Greek *polis*. The Hebrew Bible's Book of Maccabees reports: 'And some of the people determined to do this, and went to the king [Antiochus IV]: and he gave them license to do after the ordinances of the heathens. And they built a place of exercise [a gymnasium] in Jerusalem, according to the laws of the nations.' Gymnasia, like theatres and stadiums, were emblematic for a city's 'Greekness'. In addition, they 'removed their marks of circumcision and repudiated the holy covenant'. Menelaos, who succeeded Jason through bribery, struck a deal with Antiochus and repeatedly allowed the Seleucid king – who was financially in dire straits – to loot the temple treasury. Menelaos was then ousted by his own predecessor, Jason, an action Antiochus could hardly tolerate. He duly issued a decree banning Jewish religious practice (167 BC), and thus provoked the Maccabean Revolt, named after the priestly family that sparked the uprising. The revolt virtually ended Seleucid rule in Judaea. What at first sight appears to be a cultural war between Greco-Macedonian rulers and Jewish subjects, at a closer look emerges as an inner-Jewish conflict in which Antiochus became involved. The 'hellenization' of the city of Jerusalem was a project that some of the Jewish elite could benefit from substantially. People like Jason and Menelaos hoped to steel their social hegemony by turning Jerusalem into a *polis*. Abandoning Jewish religious traditions was essential for their

A 3rd-century BC plaque featuring the Greco-Phrygian mother goddess Cybele, from Ai Khanoum in Afghanistan. Excavations here have revealed a Greek city, the most easterly one founded by Alexander and his successors.

scheme, and Antiochus was their natural ally. But the plan got out of hand and the Maccabees took over as a de facto sovereign dynasty of priests.

The greatest of all Greek cities in the Hellenistic east was Alexandria. Alexander the Great had founded his own city, on the westernmost branch of the Nile, during his campaign in Egypt. Its foundation led to a fundamental shift of the geopolitical 'axis' of Egypt towards the Mediterranean coast. The design of the city was probably the work of Deinocrates, who followed a rectangular (called 'Hippodamian', after the architect Hippodamus of Miletus) layout of the roads, not very different from modern Manhattan. A dam, called 'Heptastadium', connected the city to the island of Pharos, where Sostratus of Cnidus built a giant lighthouse, called simply 'Pharos'. It was later considered to be one of the Seven Wonders of the World. It was Ptolemy I, who – according to the 'Satrap Stela' mentioned previously – had moved the royal residence

from Memphis to Alexandria in 311 BC. Soon the new foundation became the most populous city of the ancient world, and the largest port of trade. Alexandria with its library that embraced the wisdom of the entire classical world, and the museion, an institution devoted to scholarship and the arts, became a cultural centre of prime importance, excelling in literature, philosophy and the sciences.

When Ptolemy I got hold of the satrapy of Egypt, he had Alexander's corpse transferred from Babylon to Saqqara, the necropolis of Memphis. His son, Ptolemy II, transported it to Alexandria, buried it in a tomb, called sema, and established the cult of Alexander-Ktistes. The cult of a *heros ktistes* ('founder hero') was a feature Alexandria shared with most Greek cities, especially the 'colonial' foundations on the Black Sea littoral and in the Mediterranean West. But Alexander was more than that: Ptolemy made him the founder god of his empire, with his own priest who featured second (after the king) in the ceremonial

Computer-generated view of Alexandria's Portus Magnus, based on real topographical data collected by the IEASM. The Pharos, one of the Seven Wonders of the World, watches the entrances to the city's port. Adjacent to the port are the – now immersed – royal quarter and the Hippodamic grid of the dwelling areas.

hierarchy of Ptolemaic Egypt. Coins issued under his rule portrayed Alexander with the attributes of Dionysus, Amun and Zeus. After Ptolemy Soter's death, Ptolemy II Philadelphus deified his father as Theos Soter ('God Saviour'), to whom the festivals called the Ptolemaia were dedicated. The dynastic cult allowed the Ptolemies to share in Alexander's charisma as the victorious king. Under Ptolemy II, the living royal couple was included in the ruler cult, a practice adopted also by later generations of kings.

Alexandria was thus closely linked to the dynasty, its cult and the royal institutions. But like any Greek *polis*, Alexandria had its own city law and autonomous institutions: officials, council, people's assembly. But Alexandria was not entirely Greek: Greeks and Macedonians were just one minority in the most multicultural city of the Hellenistic world, with other ethnic groups forming substantial minorities, too, notably the Jews. The vast majority of the kingdom's population, and probably even that of Alexandria, were native Egyptians. Egyptians, Jews and Greco-Macedonians formed three distinct civic

bodies within the city, each keen on maintaining their cultural traditions. Only Macedonians and Greeks enjoyed full citizenship.

The divide was not hermetic, though: Egyptians could rise in the ranks of Ptolemaic society by joining the army, or by learning Greek and taking on administrative responsibilities. There was intermarriage between the ethnic groups, and religious syncretism – the contamination of one faith with elements of another – was ubiquitous. Egyptians were quick to integrate the Macedonian dynasty into their own cultural and political framework. The earliest version of the so-called Alexander Romance, a compilation of popular fiction entwined around Alexander's life, has it that Alexander was the son of Nectanebo II, the last Egyptian pharaoh ousted by the Persians when they re-conquered Egypt in 342 BC. When Alexander conquered Egypt, it was the fulfilment of an oracle which once had announced that one day a rejuvenated Nectanebo would take possession of his ancestral throne. The story undoubtedly had its origins in a hellenized indigenous environment in Egypt, and was designed to reconcile the Ptolemaic dynasty with old local traditions. Egyptian inhabitants of Alexandria appropriated the founder hero of their city and the entire kingdom for themselves, thus laying the grounds for the locals to identify themselves with the Macedonian conquerors.

Recent fieldwork has brought to light much of Hellenistic Alexandria, which until a few years ago had been deemed to be lost forever. Large parts of the ancient city, especially the palace quarter next to the harbour, had sunk beneath sea level, probably due to a series of earthquakes. In 1996, a team of French underwater archaeologists embarked on a mission to map the royal quarter. A large building with a colonnaded esplanade, which stood on the island of Antirrhodos, was identified as the Ptolemies' Royal Palace. Statues and other artifacts found in the harbour reveal that the Macedonian rulers embellished their dwellings in an Egyptianizing style, which tied in with the ancient traditions of the kingdom

A Ptolemaic cameo, possibly of Ptolemy II Philadelphus and his wife. It is made of Arabian onyx, and dates from the 3rd century BC.

Alexander the Great
exploring the sea in a
diving bell lowered from
a boat. Miniature from a
manuscript of the Romance
of Alexander, France, 1445.

of the pharaohs. All this suggests that Ptolemy and his successors felt truly at home on the Nile, just as they were perceived by many of the local people as legitimate heirs of the pharaohs.

THE END OF HELLENISM

In 31 BC, in the naval battle at Actium, Octavian's admiral Marcus Agrippa won a decisive victory over his rival Mark Antony and Cleopatra, the queen of Egypt. Eleven months later, Mark Antony and Cleopatra were dead, Ptolemaic Egypt, the last of the Hellenistic empires, conquered by Octavian's legions. Was this the end of Hellenism? The answer is: yes and no. Yes, because Rome had proved stronger than any of the monarchies that had succeeded Alexander's empire. Their intrinsic political instability, conditioned by the charismatic character of monarchic rule and the fragile balance of power between them, had made them an easy prey for the expanding Roman Republic, in spite of the immense resources their rulers commanded. Political Hellenism was dead in 30 BC, the year when Egypt became

a Roman province, but it had been in agony since the middle of the 2nd century BC when Hellenistic monarchs became increasingly dependent on Rome.

Yet Hellenism as a cultural system, a lifestyle and a symbolic framework for art, architecture and town planning, as well as for literature, philosophy and religion, survived. *Graecia capta ferum victorem cepit* – 'conquered Greece defeated the savage victor'– thus versified Horace, the Roman poet writing under Augustus, the victor of Actium. Hellenism lived on in the uncounted cities that dotted the Roman empire, from the river Clyde to the Euphrates in Mesopotamia; it lived on in the self-representation of the Roman emperors, through buildings, inscriptions and coins; it also lived on in Christianity that, in Late Antiquity, absorbed many of the intellectual achievements of the classical world. Alexander's political legacy may have had inept heirs, but the cultural heritage of Hellenism shaped a world stretching from the Atlantic to the Indus far beyond Antiquity.

CHAPTER 7

The Parthian and Early Sasanian Empires

c. 247 BC–AD 300

Just as the classical Greek world was overshadowed by the looming threat of the Achaemenid Persian empire, so Rome's much greater power was also confronted with major eastern enemies. The Parthian dynasty eked out its position amid the ruins of the Seleucid empire (the main inheritors of Alexander's Near Eastern conquests). Like the Sasanians after them, the Parthians presented themselves as 'Kings of Kings' – in practice, they were often the leaders of a fairly loose configuration of peoples. Their dynasty was undermined by repeated internal conflict. But they earned themselves a formidable reputation for their military skills and (like the more aggressive Sasanians) for involving their Roman adversaries in a series of enormously costly eastern campaigns.

Parthian and Early Sasanian King List

PARTHIAN

238–211 BC	Arsaces I
211–191 BC	Arsaces II
191–176 BC	Priapatios
176–171 BC	Phraates I
171–138 BC	Mithridates I
138–127 BC	Phraates II
127–124 BC	Artabanus I
123–88 BC	Mithridates II
95–87 BC	Gotarzes I
90–77 BC	Orodes I
77–70 BC	Sinatruces
70–57 BC	Phraates III
57–54 BC	Mithridates III
57–38 BC	Orodes II
38–2 BC	Phraates IV
2 BC–AD 4	Phraatakes
8–12	Vonones I
10–38	Artabanus II
40–45	Vardanes I
40–51	Gotarzes II
51	Vonones II
51–78	Vologases I
55–58	Vardanes II
78–105	Pakoros II
80–90	Artabanus III
105–147	Vologases III
109–129	Osroes I
116	Parthamaspates
140	Mithridates IV
147–191	Vologases IV
190	Osroes II
191–208	Vologases V
208–228	Vologases VI
216–224	Artabanus IV

SASANIAN

224–241	Ardashir I
241–272	Shapur I
272–273	Hormizd I
273–276	Vahram I
276–293	Vahram II
293	Vahram III
293–303	Narseh

PREVIOUS PAGES: Relief from Bishapur, Iran, depicting the Sasanian king Shapur I on horseback, who grasps the captured Roman emperor Valerian with his right hand while another emperor, Philip the Arab, kneels before him, symbolizing his obligation to pay tribute.

LEFT: Statue of a nobleman from Hatra (Iraq), raising his right hand in an act of worship.

Extent of Parthian empire
Extent of Sasanid empire

Odaenathus of Palmyra defeats
Sasanians near Orontes
c. 259/60

Second campaign of Shapur who
invades Syria and captures Antioch
252–253

Gordian III killed in battle
against Sasanians
244

Septimius Severus captures
Parthian capital Ctesiphon
198

Traditional date of invasion
of Parthia by the Parni and
start of Arsacid era
c. 247 BC

First-ever crossing of Euphrates
by Roman troops when Licinius
Lucullus invades Parthian territory
69 BC

Roman general
Crassus defeated
at Carrhae-Harran
53 BC

200 BC   100 BC   0   AD 100   AD 200

Mark Antony's campaigns
against the Parthians end
in failure
36 BC

Trajan campaigns
against Parthia
AD 114–117

Parthian war
of Lucius
Verus
162–166

Shapur I
defeats and
captures
Valerian
(Shapur's third
campaign)
260

Great expansion of Parthian
empire under Mithridates I
171–138 BC

Artabanus IV, last Parthian king,
defeated; beginning of Sasanian rule
224

First campaign of
Shapur against the
Romans; fall of Hatra
c. 240–244

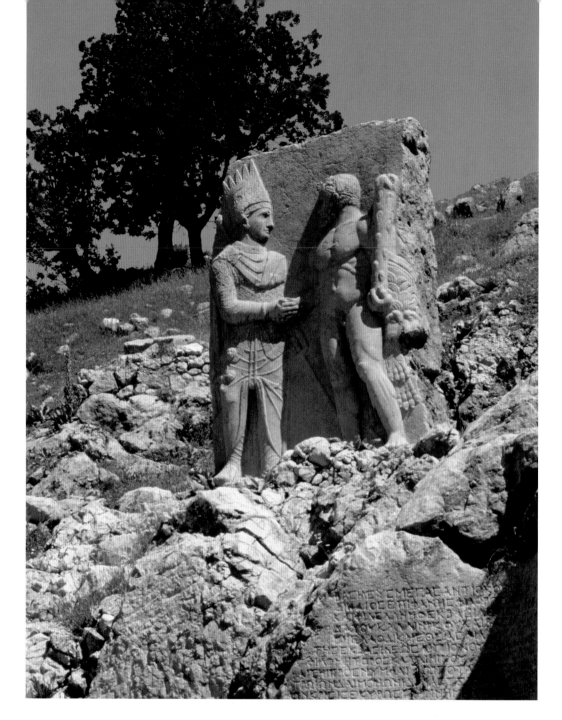

Forget about Gauls and Africans, Britons and Germans as Rome's most mighty enemy: from their first encounter in 92 BC – when a tête-à-tête between the Roman general Sulla and the Parthian envoy Orobazus took place – Parthia and its King of Kings swiftly came to be represented by Latin and Greek authors as the principal foe. Over the next 300 years, the two superpowers of the ancient world would regularly clash, especially over the mountainous region north of Syria known as Armenia, a famous breeding land for horses, and hence a potentially advantageous protectorate for both Parthians and Romans. Unfortunately, there are virtually no indigenous Parthian texts available to us, and we are therefore to a hazardous degree dependent upon classical sources, so that we have to study the Parthian empire above all through the eyes of its adversaries.

Ultimately replacing the residue of the once mighty Seleucids in Mesopotamia, the Parthians had their actual origins elsewhere. As the tribe of the Parni, part of a much larger nomadic confederation known as the Daha, they moved from the steppe area east of the Caspian Sea into the lands known as Parthava, in northeastern Iran, which had been known under that name as a satrapy of the Achaemenid empire (Chapter 4) since at least the later part of the 6th century BC. The original invasion of 'Parthia' by the Parni was traditionally set in 247 BC, under the chieftain Arsaces, after whom the Arsacid era and the Arsacid dynasty were later named, although this date is now heavily disputed. The campaigns by the 2nd-century BC kings, especially Mithridates I (171–138 BC), helped to install Arsacid rule over manifold territories which had their own cultural traditions and their own ruling families, and at its zenith the Parthian realm stretched from the Euphrates to the Indus. In less than a century and a half, the Arsacids had been truly transformed from nomads overrunning large parts of eastern Iran into world rulers, and in 113 BC Mithridates II took over the ancient Persian title 'King of Kings', proudly reflecting his domination over a patchwork of minor kings. However, the very presence of these vassal states, and the occasional efforts by their rulers to gain a larger degree of independence, made the Parthian empire vulnerable, especially in times of dynastic conflict, to which the house of the Arsacids seemed particularly prone.

A good example of the fluctuations in relations between the central Arsacid residence at Ctesiphon, situated on the Tigris in southern Mesopotamia, and the peripheral kingdoms elsewhere within the Parthian world is Hatra, a stronghold in the north-Mesopotamian Jazirah steppe. Hatra gained some notoriety for imposing losses on the Roman emperors Trajan and Septimius Severus, who both failed to take the city on different occasions. The material remains of Hatra's sophisticated culture only appear in our evidence in the late 1st century AD, when the city was ruled by a series of indigenous 'lords'. But in the second half of the 2nd century AD, this system of lordship was replaced by the installation of a royal house, and Hatra's rulers were henceforth known as 'King', or more specifically 'King of Arabia' and 'King over the Arabs', whatever that may have meant. This important change clearly implies that the Parthian overlords permitted the creation of a notionally new kingdom within the boundaries of their empire, or perhaps they were simply forced to accept it.

Our search for Parthian institutions and for typically 'Parthian' elements in their society is often frustrated by the lack of sufficient evidence. This is well illustrated by the example

OPPOSITE: 'Dexiosis' (handshake) relief from Arsameia on the Nymphaios (eastern Turkey), with Antiochus I of Commagene and the syncretistic god Artagnes-Heracles-Ares. Commagene was one of the kingdoms situated between Rome and Parthia in the centuries immediately before and after the beginning of our era.

ABOVE: Statue of the Hatrene king Sanatruq, *c.* AD 170, found in one of the many sanctuaries of Hatra. The hairstyle is particular to this locality.

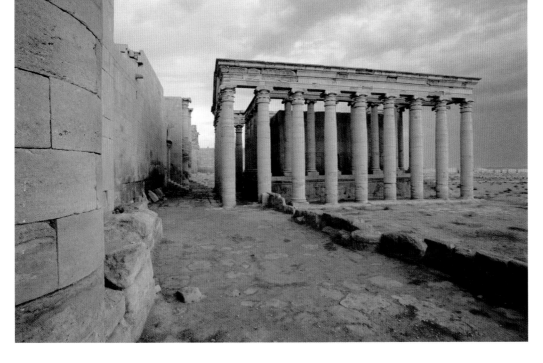

LEFT: The so-called 'Hellenistic temple' in the central temenos of Hatra, seen from the south.

Dura-Europos

Dura-Europos, originally founded as a Seleucid fortress on the Euphrates river, came to play a key role as a stronghold for the Parthians in their western frontier zone from the end of the 2nd century BC. The small town remained under Arsacid control until AD 165,

when it was captured by the Roman forces of Lucius Verus. Perhaps surprisingly, there is very little evidence for actual 'Parthian' culture in the centuries that Dura was under nominal control of the King of Kings. The main languages in use in the town were Greek and an Aramaic dialect, but there are hardly any traces of Parthian writing. The domestic and temple architecture of this period went back to ancient Near Eastern precedents instead. Durene reliefs and murals, often labelled with the modern misnomer 'Parthian art' on the basis of resemblances in style with sculptures from other places that once formed part of the Parthian world, were characterized by a frontality which cannot be linked with cultural developments in the Parthian heartland, but instead seems to coincide with the arrival of the Roman empire in the Near East. Even the Greek governmental structures of the town continued from its pre-Parthian past, and it is only the dating formula used in a number of Greek papyri and parchments, 'the year X as the King of Kings

of Dura-Europos, a small town on the Euphrates known among scholars as 'the Pompeii of the Syrian desert', thanks to its exquisite and important archaeological discoveries. Here there is very little that demonstrates Parthian occupation during the years under their control. The evidence for Parthian writing at Dura is scant, while its architecture harks back to early Near Eastern styles.

The documentary evidence from Dura clearly shows that the Parthians did not make major changes to previous administrative and societal structures. They did have their own language (Pahlavi), but Aramaic, the official language of the Achaemenid Persian chancellery, and Greek, the lingua franca of the Hellenistic world and later of the Roman East, remained more popular among the population of their empire. The impression gained is one of increasing decentralization and of opportunism on the part of the Parthian overlords. Their empire flourished through trade, and both Parthian and local merchants acted as

intermediaries between the Roman world and the Far East. From China and India they carried a rich assortment of colourful textiles and fragrant spices to the vassal kingdom of Characene on the Persian Gulf, from where they travelled up the Euphrates, and then made for the dangerous desert crossing to Palmyra in the middle of the Syrian steppe – still described by Pliny as an independent city in the 1st century AD, 'as it were isolated by Nature from the world, having a destiny of its own between the two mighty empires of Rome and Parthia, and at the first moment of a quarrel between them always attracting the attention of both sides'. In the 1st century AD, Isidore of Charax produced, typically in Greek, a list of fortresses and strongholds situated in the Parthian realm, including Dura-Europos. Although his *Parthian Stations* has sometimes been viewed as an itinerary following the Parthian trade route, it is in fact a description of the ancient royal road which was maintained in the first place for administrative and military purposes.

reckons', that hints at the fact that Dura actually formed part of the Parthian world. By the time the Arsacids gave way to the neo-Persian Sasanians the small town had long since been integrated in the Roman provincial system, and it was these same Sasanians that eventually heralded the end of its existence. The Roman troops now defending Dura-Europos thickened the walls and filled the adjacent street and its houses with sand and rubble with the effect that the buildings here – including the famous synagogue and Christian baptisterium – preserved their wall-paintings for posterity in a unique state (p. 217). The defence system notwithstanding, the Sasanians broke through the walls after a siege in 256 and the town was left to disappear under the desert sands until its accidental discovery by British soldiers in 1920.

OPPOSITE: The 'Palmyrene gate' in the western city wall of Dura-Europos (Syria).

181

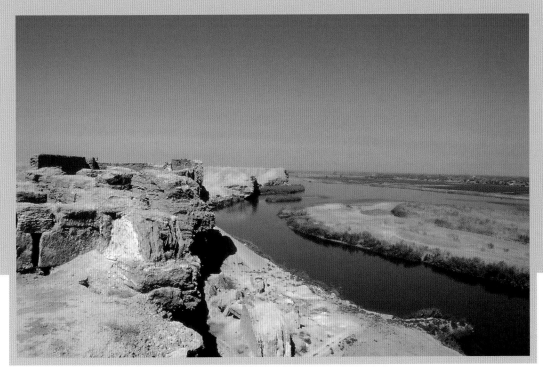

A spectacular view over the Euphrates towards the north, as seen from the citadel of Dura-Europos.

To what extent the Parthians understood their realm as an 'empire' in the way the Romans did theirs remains unclear. Whereas Rome ultimately wanted to occupy as much territory as was feasible, the Parthians seem to have viewed their domain more in terms of a collection of peoples answerable to the King of Kings, regardless of their level of independence. Some scholars have argued that Parthia was, in essence, similar to the Hellenistic kingdoms, while others prefer to follow the attitude of the Roman poet Horace, whose phrase 'Phraates has been restored to the throne of Cyrus' explicitly presents the Arsacids as rightful heirs to the Achaemenid Persians. In the end, perhaps the most lasting – and in any case the most visible – Parthian legacy was the peculiar dress code, which stood in sharp contrast to Rome's toga and tunic. The typically Parthian costume that became the mode over most of the Levant consisted of the famous baggy trousers that are often depicted on sculptures and frescoes, and local notables at cities such as Palmyra could appear on one and the same monument both in western and in eastern dress.

EARLY PARTHIAN CONFLICTS WITH ROME

The story of Rome vs Parthia gets under way in 92 BC, when the Roman general Sulla met with the Parthian envoy Orobazus in the presence of the Cappadocian nobleman Ariobarzanes, for whom the Roman commander acted as a patron. Three chairs were prepared, and Sulla is said to have given audience while seated in the middle, between the two other men. For this apparent act of complacency on the part of

Orobazus, who had openly acknowledged Roman superiority, he was put to death on his return by the King of Kings. When Sulla's former lieutenant Licinius Lucullus invaded some of the lands across the Euphrates in 69 BC, in the context of the Third Mithridatic war that Rome fought against the powerful monarch Mithridates VI of Pontus and his son-in-law Tigranes II of Armenia (who had himself annexed Parthian territories), this event – the first time ever Roman troops had crossed the river – was hailed by some as 'the greatest victory the sun had ever seen', as Plutarch records it later.

Only 16 years later, in 53 BC, did the unthinkable happen: no less than seven Roman legions were routed at the ancient city of Carrhae, also known as Harran and famous for its temple of the Moon, by Parthian opposition. The Roman commander Marcus Crassus – famous both for his secret alliance with Julius Caesar and Pompey the Great and for his corruptly acquired fortune – got caught in a trap and lost his life at the battle. Some 20,000 of his soldiers are said to have died with him, another 10,000 were deported by the Parthians, and the imperial army shamefully lost its eagles. Crassus' biographer, Plutarch, gives a vivid account of the horrendous end to the great man's life. He describes how the Parthian commander Sillaces arrived at the royal court with the decapitated head of Crassus, at the very moment that Euripides' *Bacchae*, which was being performed in the presence of the king, had reached the point where the head of Pentheus, king of Thebes, is supposed to be shown by his frenzied mother Agave. Plutarch poignantly states how Crassus' expedition therefore closed 'just like a tragedy': 'While the actor was receiving his applause, Sillaces stood at the door of the banqueting hall, and after a low obeisance cast the head of Crassus into the centre of the company.' The final act of Crassus' life thus also illustrates how the Parthian court proved to be populated by connoisseurs of Greek tragedy, which is a far cry

Marble portrait of the king Mithridates VI of Pontus, depicted with the lion-skin of Heracles, from the 1st century AD.

from the stereotypical image of the 'barbarian' generally encountered in classical sources.

The recovery of the lost standards of Crassus' army became a major issue for the Romans. Whereas in 36 BC the triumvir Mark Antony was unsuccessful in retrieving the eagles, Augustus could proclaim in the *Res Gestae*, his posthumously published list of achievements: 'I compelled the Parthians to restore to me the spoils and standards of three Roman armies and to ask as suppliants for the friendship of the Roman people.' This came about while Augustus was in the East from 22 to 19 BC. He settled the Armenian situation by installing as king a member of the indigenous royal house who had once been a resident at the Roman court and who could therefore be expected to be loyal. Augustus' stepson, the later emperor Tiberius, delivered the candidate to the empty throne in person, and in 20 BC a diplomatic agreement was reached with the Parthian king Phraates IV, who accepted the Armenian solution in exchange for Rome's promise not to interfere in Parthia itself. He also handed back the eagles lost by Crassus at Carrhae. Despite its diplomatic solution, the return of the standards was presented in Rome as a military victory, and the event became one of the cornerstones on which the ideology of the new principate was founded. The poet Horace wrote in the *Secular Hymn*, commissioned by Augustus specially for the 'Games of the Century', celebrating Rome's entering a new age in 17 BC: 'Now Parthia fears the fist of Rome, the fasces potent on land and sea!' State coinage referred to the recovered eagles by portraying kneeling Parthians, a triumphal arch was built on the Forum to celebrate the occasion (it is now lost, but we know it from imagery on coins), and on Augustus' return from the East in 19 BC the Senate consecrated an altar of Fortuna Redux, the good fortune bringing soldiers home, in his honour. Perhaps most famously, the return of the standards is shown on the cuirass which Augustus wears on a statue from Livia's villa at Prima Porta (see p. 198). A bearded Parthian hands over the eagle to a Roman soldier (or perhaps Tiberius) while the gods look on in approval: the sun-god in a *quadriga*, Caelus holding the firmament, the personifications of Dawn and Dew, the divine twins Apollo (Augustus' main deity) and Diana, and the earth goddess Tellus with a horn of abundance as symbol of prosperity.

When the rivalries began to resurface in Armenia some 20 years later, Augustus sent his grandson (and adopted son) Gaius Caesar to the East, where the young crown prince met with the Parthian king Phrataces, the bastard son of Phraates IV, on an island in the Euphrates. We have an eyewitness account by Velleius Paterculus, who wrote in his *History of Rome*: 'As for the meeting, first the Parthian dined with Gaius upon the Roman bank, and later Gaius supped with the king on the soil of the enemy.' The Euphrates had once again acted as the symbolic frontier between the two empires. Yet notwithstanding the mutual respect, as described by Velleius, the image projected at Rome was again different, and the cuirass worn by Gaius on a posthumously erected statue (he died in Lycia in AD 4) is decorated with the heads of the bearded 'barbarians'.

LATER PARTHIAN CONFLICTS WITH ROME

The fear of the Arsacids remained present in the Roman psyche, even though, in reality, after the 40s BC the military power of the Parthians was in fact hardly sufficient to allow offensive action into the now Roman-dominated lands of Syria and Anatolia. The great Roman historian Tacitus records how the Parthian king Artabanus II, 'despising [the emperor] Tiberius'

Arch and tower of the Ulu Cami, Anatolia's oldest mosque, at Carrhae-Harran (eastern Turkey), site of the famous temple of the Moon, where in 53 BC the Roman army lost its military standards to the Parthians and where general Crassus lost his life.

Voices of Empire

Nearly all our literary sources on the Parthians come from outside their empire, and the Arsacid realm can therefore be studied mainly through the eyes of its Roman neighbours. Imperial historians such as Tacitus and Cassius Dio kept the fear for the 'barbarian' power on Rome's Eastern frontier alive. The second half of Parthia's history is covered a great deal better than the earlier stages, and the precise date of the empire's foundation remains unclear. With the rise of the Sasanians in the first half of the 3rd century the tone changes somewhat, with Roman authors emphasizing the more aggressive attitude of the neo-Persian empire. From the reign of Shapur I comes a Sasanian account of the wars fought with Rome in the shape of a trilingual inscription, with words put in the mouth of the King of Kings himself. His achievements are furthermore illustrated with magnificent reliefs showing the humiliation of three Roman emperors.

'On an island in the Euphrates, with an equal retinue on each side, Gaius had a meeting with the king of the Parthians, a young man of distinguished presence. This spectacle of the Roman army arrayed on one side, the Parthian on the other, while these two eminent leaders not only of the empires they represented but also of mankind thus met in conference … it was my fortunate lot to see.'

Velleius Paterculus, writing during the reign of the Roman emperor Tiberius, describes a meeting he witnessed between a Roman crown prince and a Parthian king

Cassius Dio in his *Roman History*, writing at the beginning of the 3rd century, states how the Parthians had always been considered a match for Rome

'They are really formidable in warfare, but nevertheless they have a reputation greater than their achievements, because, in spite of their not having gained anything from the Romans, and having, besides, given up certain portions of their own domain, they have not yet been enslaved, but even to this day hold their own in the wars they wage against us.'

The Sasanian King of Kings Shapur refers to himself at the beginning of the trilingual inscription from Naqsh-I Rustam listing his achievements

'I, the Mazda-worshipping Lord Shapur, King of Kings of Iran and non-Iran, whose lineage is from the gods, son of the Mazda-worshipping divinity Ardashir, King of Kings of Iran, whose lineage is from the gods, grandson of King Papak, am ruler of Iranshahr, and I hold the following lands.'

The enigmatic *Thirteenth Sibylline Oracle* 'predicts' Odaenathus' victory over Shapur in poetic language

'... which time will reign over the mighty Romans two men, swift lords of war. One will have the number 70 [i.e. Valerian] and the other 3 [i.e. Gallienus]. And then a haughty bull, digging the earth with its hoofs and lifting the dust with its two horns, will do much harm to a dark-skinned reptile, dragging its coil by its horny scales. But he will perish with it … Then shall come one who was sent by the sun [i.e. Odaenathus], a mighty and fearful lion, breathing much flame. Then he with much shameless daring will destroy … the greatest beast – venomous, fearful and emitting a great deal of hisses [i.e. Shapur].'

The novelist Heliodorus of Emesa alludes to the reaction of Roman soldiers faced with their Eastern enemy

'Even from afar the pomp and show of Persia compelled the attention of every eye. From their gold and silver weapons lightning flashed and flickered over the plain, for the sun was not long risen and was shining full on the Persians' faces, so that their armour shone back with its own inherent brilliance, broadcasting an awesome coruscation into the furthest distance.'

This large rock-cut relief from Naqsh-I Rustam is a visual representation of the information given in the trilingual inscription at the site: Shapur I on horseback receives homage from the kneeling Roman emperor Philip the Arab, with the captured emperor Valerian standing behind him.

'A great battle took place beyond Carrhae and Edessa between us and Caesar Valerian and we took him prisoner with our own hands as well as the other commanders of the army, the praetorian prefect, senators and officials. All these we took prisoner and deported to Persis. We also burnt, devastated and pillaged Syria, Cilicia and Cappadocia.'

In the trilingual inscription at Naqsh-I Rustam, Shapur describes his third campaign against Rome, in which he captured the emperor Valerian old age as defenceless', threatened the Romans by 'bragging of the old boundaries of the Persians and Macedonians and that he would invade the lands once possessed by Cyrus and later by Alexander'. Cassius Dio describes how the Parthians had always been considered a match for Rome and discusses the Parthian equipment and aims and methods of warfare (see p. 184):

'The Parthians make no use of a shield, but their forces consist of mounted archers and pikesmen, mostly in full armour. Their infantry is small, made up of the weaker men; but even these are all archers. They practise from boyhood, and the climate and the land combine to aid both horsemanship and archery.'

The Romans not only learned from the surprise movements of the Parthian riders, but they also managed to take over many of their opponents' tricks by actually incorporating native troops as auxiliary units in the imperial army. Such units, filled with indigenous soldiers who continued to fight with their own weapons, were often employed far from their homeland. A 'cavalry unit of Parthians and Arabians' (*ala Parthorum et Arabum*) is known for example from the tombstone of an officer from the 1st century AD that was found in Mainz in Germany.

In the 2nd century AD Roman emperors still sought fame through war against the Parthians. Trajan created a series of new Roman provinces across the Euphrates (all of which were abandoned immediately after his death) and state coinage shows how the Parthian king receives his diadem directly from Trajan, with a legend saying *REX PARTHIS DATUS*, 'a king is given to the Parthians'. From AD 162 to 166, Marcus Aurelius' co-emperor Lucius Verus took nominal command of a military campaign in the East, although he is said to have left the actual fighting to his generals while he himself enjoyed a luxurious lifestyle in the cities of

Roman Syria instead. Wars between West and East seem to have resulted – like in more modern times – in an avalanche of historical publications attempting to satisfy a more general audience. In a wonderful piece called *How to Write History*, the famous satirist Lucian, himself of Samosata (formerly the royal capital of Commagene), criticized the way in which incapable writers hurriedly brought out books about Verus' Parthian war that were full of inaccuracies: 'Every single person is writing history; nay more, they are all Thucydideses, Herodotuses and Xenophons to us. Yet most of them think they don't even need advice for the job any more than they need a set of rules for walking or seeing or eating.' In any case Ctesiphon was conquered in AD 198 by Septimius Severus, who created (like Trajan, but this time lasting) the province of Mesopotamia and took the victorious title Parthicus Maximus.

THE RISE OF THE SASANIANS

The 2nd-century Roman campaigns weakened the Parthian power, which was further subject to infighting. But if the combination of war with Rome and dynastic conflicts was insufficient to bring the Parthian empire to its knees, ultimately it proved to be too vulnerable to rebellions and struggles for independence by vassal states. Some 475 years of Arsacid rule came to an end in AD 224, when a regional governor called Ardashir (or Artaxerxes, as classical sources name him) revolted against his Parthian overlords, defeated Artabanus IV, and in the process established the neo-Persian empire of the Sasanians. Named after Ardashir's ancestor Sasan, they would soon make Rome long for the days of the rivalry with their Parthian sparring partners. The Sasanians were far more aggressive and powerful than their predecessors on Rome's eastern borders, which is said to have caused the young emperor Severus Alexander to send letters to the Sasanian ruler to 'halt the invasion and check his expectations'. In the words of the 3rd-century historian Herodian, himself from the Near East: 'In these letters he told Artaxerxes that he must remain within his own borders and not initiate any action; let him not, deluded

The Parthian Shot

The Parthians gained a reputation as extremely skilful mounted archers. In his account of the battle of Carrhae in 53 BC, Plutarch describes how, while pretending to flee, they would suddenly turn around on their horses to shoot their arrows into their surprised pursuers: 'For the Parthians shot as they fled, being, indeed, more adept at this than anyone else except the Scythians; and it is certainly a very clever manoeuvre – to fight and to look after one's own safety at the same time, so that there is no dishonouring in running away' (*Life of Crassus* 24). It is clear that superb competence in the saddle was required to pull off the trick: with the horseman's hands holding on to his bow and arrow, he had only the pressure of his legs left to guide the animal. Graffiti from Dura-Europos and drawings from later periods depict the action clearly. This so-called 'Parthian shot' has become proverbial, distorted later into a 'parting shot', as the final insult hurled while departing. The 17th-century satirical poet Samuel Butler, in his *Hudibras*, has the protagonist writing to his lady 'You wound, like Parthians, while you fly, and kill with a retreating eye'.

A ceramic plaque of a mounted archer, now in London's British Museum, and a drawing of a horse archer exercising his 'Parthian shot'.

by vain hopes, stir up a great war, but rather let each of them be content with what already was his. By writing letters of this kind, Alexander thought that he would persuade the barbarian to remain quiet or frighten him to the same course.' The emperor's prose did not, however, have the desired effect.

Ardashir's son Shapur followed in his father's aggressive footsteps and benefited from the 3rd-century crisis in the Roman imperial system, where a series of so-called soldier-emperors reached the purple in rapid succession. In 244 the teenage emperor Gordian III died of his wounds following his army's defeat near Ctesiphon, and was succeeded by his praetorian prefect Philip, who was born in the Syrian Hauran region and has become known to posterity as 'Philip the Arab', and who was forced into a peace treaty with Shapur. In a second campaign, in 252, the armies of the King of Kings overran large parts of Syria, including the major city of Antioch, and in 260 the emperor Valerian was taken captive by the Sasanians. He eventually died in a Persian prison, having spent the remainder of his life

as a footstool to Shapur. For the Christian apologist Lactantius the King of Kings clearly acted as an instrument of God's punishment of the impious emperor, and he describes in detail the humiliation Valerian had to undergo in a pamphlet called *On the Death of the Persecutors*: 'He squandered the remainder of his days in the abject form of slavery: for whenever Shapur … chose to get into the carriage or to mount on horseback, he commanded the Roman to stoop and present his back; then, placing his foot on the shoulders of Valerian, he said, with a smile of reproach, "This is true, and not what the Romans depicted on their tablets and walls".'

We have the unique and invaluable reaction of Shapur himself in a trilingual inscription, written in Arsacid Pahlavi, in the Middle Persian of the Sasanians and in Greek. It is inscribed at Naqsh-I Rustam, north of Persepolis, where the Achaemenid kings had found their final resting-place, and is commonly labelled by scholars, in a witty reference to the famous *Res Gestae* of Augustus, as the 'Achievements of the Divine Shapur'. After introducing himself (p. 184), Shapur gives the neo-Persian perspective on the

OPPOSITE: Reliefs from the foot of the Arch of Septimius Severus in the Forum in Rome. The arch was built to celebrate the emperor's victorious campaigns in Mesopotamia (198/9). The reliefs depict Parthian prisoners.

189

THE PARTHIAN AND EARLY SASANIAN EMPIRES

Sasanian relief from Naqsh-I Rustam, showing how the supreme god of Zoroastrianism, Ahuramazda, hands a ring as a symbol of royalty to the King of Kings, Ardashir I. Under their horses' hooves lie defeated enemies.

consecutive wars: 'When at first we had become established in the empire, Gordian Caesar raised in all of the Roman empire a force from the Goth and German realms and marched on Babylonia against the empire of Iran and against us. On the border of Babylonia at Misikhe, a great frontal battle occurred. Gordian Caesar was killed and the Roman force was

Cameo showing the capture of the Roman emperor Valerian by the Sasanian ruler Shapur.

destroyed. And the Romans made Philip Caesar. Then Philip Caesar came to us for terms, and to ransom their lives, gave us five hundred thousand dinars, and became tributary to us.'

Shapur's second campaign is said to have been a reaction to further Roman falsehood: 'And Caesar lied again and did wrong to Armenia. Then we attacked the Roman empire and annihilated at Barbalissos a Roman force of 60,000 and Syria and the environs of Syria we burned, ruined and pillaged all.' His third campaign, in which Valerian was captured, is also described (p. 185).

As if this priceless document is not enough, we also have two exquisite visual representations of the events, which merge Shapur's three campaigns into one. A rock-cut relief (p. 185) at the same site of Naqsh-I Rustam shows the victorious King of Kings with two figures who have commonly been interpreted as Philip the Arab and Valerian, the one kneeling while the

other is grasped by Shapur. A similar relief, at Bishapur, shows the King of Kings, again on horseback, with no fewer than three Roman emperors: Gordian III is trampled under Shapur's horse, Philip the Arab is depicted as a suppliant, and Valerian stands captured.

The fact that both the relief and the inscription at Naqsh-I Rustam were cut in the rocks at the same place where the tombs of the Achaemenid kings were located is a good indicator of the length to which the Sasanians went to present themselves as the legitimate heirs to the 'old' Persians. Nevertheless, the claims by some Roman historians – namely that the Sasanians from the outset intended to take possession of all the lands once occupied by the Achaemenids – must be taken with a pinch of salt. The degree to which the Sasanians owed part of their legacy to that of the Arsacids is debatable, but their policy seems certainly to have been more aggressive and their attitude to religious freedom less tolerant.

The most famous religious victim was the prophet Mani, the founder of a gnostic world religion known as Manichaeism, which combined a dualistic system according to which the powers of Light had to fight the powers of Darkness with elements directly taken over from Buddhism, Zoroastrianism and Christianity. Born in the final years of Arsacid rule, Mani travelled to India once Ardashir had established himself as the first Sasanian King of Kings, possibly because Ardashir refused to provide proper patronage. On his return to the Sasanian empire, Mani found a protector in Shapur. A 10th-century Arab author describes their first meeting as follows: 'The Manichaeans said that when Mani came into his presence, there were on his shoulders two lights resembling lamps. And when Shapur saw him he was impressed and Mani grew in his estimation.' Shapur may well have viewed Mani's preaching – which incorporated elements from different cultural backgrounds – as a way to glue together, in a religious mould, his empire. His successor Hormizd, who only reigned for one year, also supported the prophet, but Vahram I, who became King of Kings in AD 273, showed a very different attitude towards Mani. Influenced by the Magians – the Zoroastrian priests whose lifestyle was directly opposed to much of what Mani taught (above all asceticism, including a condemnation of the great Persian pastime of hunting) – Vahram disliked him from the start. Mani was imprisoned and eventually executed.

The more aggressive Sasanian political and military approach is clear from Shapur's various incursions into Roman provincial territory. The fear that his soldiers could instill in their opponents is reflected by the novelist Heliodorus of Emesa (present-day Homs in Syria), who records, in the ninth book of his *Ethiopian Story*, the shock experienced by the Roman soldiers when they first laid eyes on the eastern enemy (p. 185). The historian Ammianus Marcellinus, who had experienced first hand the unsuccessful Persian campaign of the last pagan emperor, Julian 'the Apostate', was full of similar praise of the Sasanian army: 'Their military training and discipline, and their constant practice of manoeuvres and arms drill ... make them formidable even to large armies. They rely especially on their cavalry, in which all their nobility and men of mark serve. Their infantry are protected like gladiators and obey orders like slaves.'

PALMYRA AGAINST THE SASANIANS

Important developments within the Roman empire had taken place after the capture of Valerian. His son Gallienus had made the Palmyrene notable Odaenathus his official deputy in the East, with the new title of Corrector Totius Orientis, in order to create

Sasanian relief from Bishapur, showing the victories of Shapur over three Roman emperors. The horse of the King of Kings steps on Gordian III, who died in 244. Philip the Arab, Gordian's successor, kneels in front of Shapur, as a sign of his obligation to pay tribute to the Sasanians; and Valerian, who was captured alive in 260, stands on the left, with Shapur grasping his wrist. The later occasion was the first time a Roman emperor had ever been taken captive and resulted in a power vacuum in the East.

Sasanian Silver

ABOVE: Silver drinking vessel from Iran, depicting the head of a horse that possibly reflects a hunting scene.

BELOW LEFT: Sasanian plate with hunting scene from Iran, in silver with mercury gilding. The crown seems to identify the king as a 5th-century ruler, either Peroz or Kavad I.

BELOW RIGHT: A 6th or 7th-century carafe from Iran, depicting female dancers.

OPPOSITE: Silver plate showing a Sasanian King of Kings hunting lions. The crown identifies him as Vahram V, also known as Vahram Gur (420–438), who was famous for his hunting exploits.

The most famous works of Sasanian art, apart from the monumental rock-cut reliefs at Naqsh-I Rustam and Bishapur, are silver plates and vessels such as dishes, bowls and vases. Many of those beautiful artifacts were found in areas situated on the outskirts of the Sasanian empire, suggesting that they were sent as gifts from the King of Kings to vassal rulers (a theme also mentioned in some ancient texts). Scenes show the king in the act of hunting, possibly to reflect his invincibility and prowess. He is commonly depicted wearing a riding overall over his trousers and equipped with crown, fillet and globe. This motif, with the king fully armed and fighting with either sword or bow and arrow, became standard in the 4th century, which may be connected with Sasanian state control over the silver production from the reign of Shapur II (309–379). The hunting figure can in many cases be positively identified as a specific King of Kings, thanks to the elaborate crowns which were unique to individual rulers and which were known also from coin depictions.

194

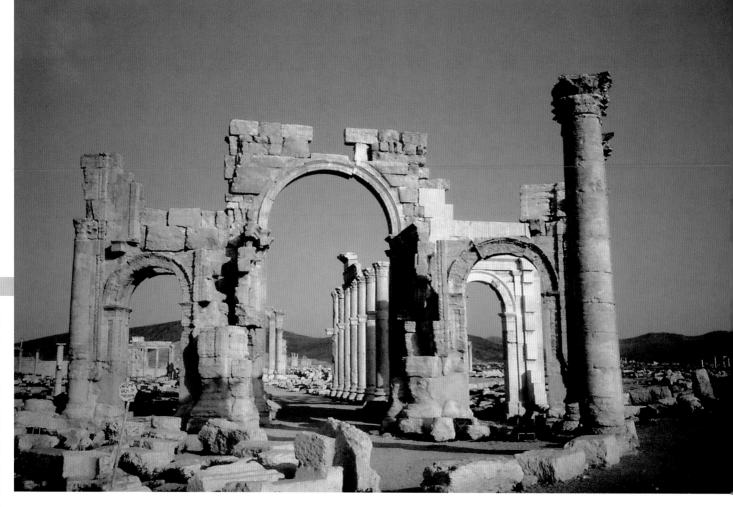

Palmyra, located in splendid isolation in the middle of the Syrian desert, developed into a monumental caravan city by the 2nd century. Originally situated between Rome and Parthia, it had long managed to play the two superpowers of the ancient world off against each other. From the early 1st century onwards, Palmyra was fully integrated into the Roman provincial system. The arch at the beginning of the central colonnade was built to celebrate the military successes of the local ruler Odaenathus and his son Herodian.

stability in the region. Palmyra (see also pp. 270–71) had been fully integrated into the Roman provincial system from the 1st century AD onwards. In 130 the emperor Hadrian visited the oasis in person, and in the early 3rd century Palmyra had acquired the prestigious status of a Roman colony. In the 250s Odaenathus came to the fore as the leading citizen, who also made it big time as a Roman senator and eventually consul. According to a late and not necessarily reliable source – the 6th-century imperial diplomat Petrus Patricius – Odaenathus was hoping to strike a deal with Shapur at the time of the second Sasanian campaign (when, as far as the trilingual inscription from Naqsh-I Rustam is concerned, Palmyra indeed seems to have escaped being pillaged). In any case, together with his son Herodian, Odaenathus won a famous victory over the Sasanians in 260.

As is shown by an inscription on an arch at Palmyra, the son (and we can therefore assume also the father) now took on the traditional royal title of the major power in the East: 'This statue was set up for Septimius Herodian, King of Kings, crowned near the Orontes with the diadem of royalty for his victory over the Persians.' In the late 4th century, Festus described Odaenathus, who had 'collected a band of Syrian country folk and put up a spirited resistance', as Rome's avenger, who even managed to capture Ctesiphon.

Odaenathus and his son remained loyal to the Roman emperor, but following their victory over Shapur, they considered themselves the rightful heirs to the royal diadem of the Sasanians. A mosaic that was recently discovered at Palmyra seems to echo the episode. The Greek mythological hero

Bellerophon, on his winged horse Pegasus, is shown (dressed in Parthian trousers) as killing the monstrous chimaera, while two eagles fly above him carrying a wreath, symbolizing victory. A second image, seemingly depicting an innocent hunting scene, has a horseman (dressed in the same way as 'Bellerophon') engaged in a fight with Persian tigers, again accompanied by an eagle with a wreath. Following the ingenious explanation of the archaeologist who discovered it, the mosaic – combining Greek mythology with local iconographic detail – is no less than an allegory for the victory of the Palmyrenes over the Persians, which earned Odaenathus and Herodian the title 'King of Kings'.

Following the untimely death of father and son under suspicious circumstances, Odaenathus' widow Zenobia ruled for their underage son Vaballathus and extended the Palmyrene kingdom over large parts of the Roman East. It was not to last for long, as the emperor Aurelian defeated Zenobia's troops and finally crushed Palmyra's power, bringing it back firmly in the bosom of the Roman empire. Rome's success rate on its eastern frontier would continue to ebb and flow, and the treaty with the Sasanians that followed the emperor Galerius' victory over them, in 298/9, resulted in Rome's greatest-ever extension of its territory across the Tigris. Nevertheless, the neo-Persian empire would finally come to an end only centuries later, following the Arab conquest of Mesopotamia and Persia.

Newly discovered mosaic at Palmyra of Bellerophon on his winged horse Pegasus, slaying the mythological monster chimaera (with a lion, snake and goat head). The image may well be an allegory for Odaenathus' victory over the Sasanians near the Orontes (260). The rider wears a non-classical outfit (the so-called 'Parthian trousers') and is being crowned with a laurel wreath by two eagles.

CHAPTER 8

The Roman Empire

27 BC–AD 476

For much of western history, the Roman empire has been the emblematic empire. Rome has spawned countless imagined successors: from the Carolingians or the Holy Roman empire to the Ottomans, the Russian Czars, or the founders of the United States. In part, this has been because of the scale and longevity of Rome's power: from small beginnings, carving out a position of dominance in central Italy, Rome mastered the whole Mediterranean world and more, from Hadrian's Wall to the Nile, from the Danube to the Libyan desert. Rome's potency is also a matter of its cultural influence, however. Unlike many other empires, Rome drew its subjects into its civilizing mission, assimilating the deities of the people it conquered, drawings its emperors from Spain and North Africa as well as Rome and Italy, and eventually granting Roman citizenship to all in its empire. At the same time, the machinery of Republican government under which its power had first spread became increasingly hollow, as power concentrated in the hands of a succession of autocratic rulers.

Roman Emperor List

Julio-Claudian Dynasty

31 BC–AD 14	Augustus
14–37	Tiberius
37–41	Caligula
41–54	Claudius
54–68	Nero

Civil War of 69

68–69	Galba
69	Otho
69	Vitellius

Flavian Dynasty

69–79	Vespasian
79–81	Titus
81–96	Domitian

Adoptive Emperors and the Antonine Dynasty

96–98	Nerva
98–117	Trajan
117–38	Hadrian
138–61	Antoninus Pius
161–180	Marcus Aurelius
(161–69	and Lucius Verus)
180–92	Commodus

Civil War of 193

193	Pertinax
193	Didius Julianus

Severan Dynasty

193–211	Septimius Severus
211	Geta
211–17	Caracalla
217–18	Macrinus
218–22	Elagabalus
222–35	Alexander Severus

Third-century Crisis

235–38	Maximinus Thrax
238	Gordian I
238	Gordian II
238	Pupienus and Balbinus
238–44	Gordian II
244–49	Philip the Arab
249–51	Decius
251–53	Trebonianus Gallus
253	Aemilius Aemilianus
253–60	Valerian
253–268	Gallienus
268–270	Claudius II
270	Quintillus
270–75	Aurelian
275–76	Tacitus
276	Florianus
276–82	Probus
282–83	Carus
283–84	Numerian
283–85	Carinus
260–69	Postumus
269	Laelianus
269	Marius
268–71	Victorinus
271–74	Tetricus

Later Roman Empire

284–305	Diocletian
(286–305	Maximian)
305–6	Constantius I
305–11	Galerius
306–7	Severus II
306–12	Maxentius
310–13	Maximinus Daia
307–37	Constantine
(308–24	Licinius)
337–40	Constantine II
337–50	Constans I
337–61	Constantius II
360–63	Julian
363–364	Jovian

House of Valentinian

364–78	Valens
/364–75	Valentinian
367–83	Gratian
375–92	Valentinian II
392–94	Eugenius

Theodosian Dynasty

379–95	Theodosius I
395–408	Arcadius
/395–423	Honorius
408–50	Theodosius II
/423–25	Johannes
/425–55	Valentinian III

The Final Emperors

455	Petronius Maximus
455–56	Avitus
456–61	Majorian
461–65	Severus III
467–72	Anthemius
472	Olybrius
473–74	Glycerius
474–75	Julius Nepos
475–76	Romulus Augustulus

PREVIOUS PAGES: In 13 BC, the Senate vowed to build a monumental altar to honour the peace Augustus brought over Rome and her empire. The Ara Pacis Augusta was completed in 9 BC. The altar's main frieze shows a religious procession, with Augustus and his family at the centre. Below, we see the four main priests (*flamines maiores*, left), followed by the *flaminius lictor* (with axe) and members of Augustus' family.

The marble statue of Rome's first emperor, Augustus, was discovered in the Villa of Livia, in Prima Porta, near Rome. The emperor is displayed in the pose of a victorious imperator. The centre of the composition on the breastplate shows the Parthian king returning a standard captured from Crassus in 53 BC.

MVNIF PL IX P M
AN XVIII

Extent of Roman empire in 1st century AD

0   400 km

0   400 miles

Hannibal defeats
Roman army
at Cannae
216 BC

Victory for Rome
in third and final
Punic war
149–146 BC

Title 'Augustus' conferred by
Senate on Octavian, who by
now is effectively first emperor
27 BC

Claudian
invasion
of Britain
43

Jewish War
66–71

Trajan's wars in Dacia
(modern Romania)
101–102/105–106

Diocletian divides empire
into east and west, each
with its own emperor
284

Defeat of Valens by Goths
at battle of Adrianople
378

Sack of Rome
by Goths
410

| 200 BC | 100 BC | 0 | AD 100 | AD 200 | AD 300 | AD 400 |

Caesar's conquest of Gaul
58–50 BC

Civil war: Caesar against Pompey
and the Senate
49–45 BC

Mark Antony and Octavian
defeat Caesar's assassins at
Philippi
42 BC

Great naval victory for
Octavian over Mark Antony
and Cleopatra at Actium
31 BC

Three legions destroyed
in Teutoburg Forest
AD 9

Civil war, Vespasian
becomes emperor
69

Citizenship extended
to whole free population
of the empire
212

Civil war, Septimius
Severus gains power
193–197

Vandals capture
Carthage
439

Vandals sack
Rome
455

Deposition of last
Roman emperor,
Romulus Augustulus
476

'Indeed, you best have proved that well-known saying, that the earth is the mother of all and the universal country of all. Now it is possible for both Greek and barbarian, with his possessions or without them, to travel easily wherever he wishes, quite as if he were going from one country of his to another … And what was said by Homer, "The earth was common to all", you have made a reality, by surveying the whole inhabited world, by bridging the rivers in various ways, by cutting carriage roads through the mountains, by filling desert places with post stations, and by civilizing everything with your way of life and good order … And now, indeed, there is no need to write a description of the world, nor to enumerate the laws of each people, but you have become universal geographers for all men by opening up all the gates of the inhabited world and by giving to all who wish it the power to be observers of everything and by assigning universal laws for all men and by stopping practices which formerly were pleasant to read about, but were intolerable if one should actually consider them and by making marriage legal between all peoples and by organizing the whole inhabited world like a single household.'

'Like a single household' – Aelius Aristides, an orator and intellectual in the 2nd century AD, could hardly have characterized the vast empire that stretched from the Firth of Forth to the Nile, from the Atlantic to the river Euphrates, more succinctly. In his speech 'On Rome' (*logos eis Rhomen*), probably delivered to an audience in the city of Rome during the reign of the emperor Hadrian (117–138), Aristides, a Greek from the northwest of Asia Minor, compares and contrasts Rome to preceding empires, beginning with the Persians. The juxtaposition with Persia is a favourable one for the Romans

Bust of Trajan in old age. Dacia, Arabia and Mesopotamia were conquered under the Spanish-born emperor (AD 98–117) and the Roman empire reached its greatest geographical extent.

as their empire is built on consensus rather than force, and turns subdued populations into shareholders of imperial rule. Unlike the Achaemenid Persian and Hellenistic empires, the Romans have much to offer their subjects. For Aristides, the Roman empire is synonymous with civilization.

This is certainly an idealistic perspective on Roman rule. After all it was the job of an orator to please his audience and to praise the empire of the city that hosts him. However, the image constructed by Aristides is not necessarily wrong. To be sure, Roman hegemony – like any empire in history – was established through force. But by the imperial period, Rome's elite was remarkably cosmopolitan, and the distinction between Romans and subjects had been diminished. People from the most distant parts of the empire had been admitted to the Senate. Trajan, the emperor under whom Aristides was born, was the first Roman ruler to be born outside Italy: his family, the Ulpii, came from the Roman colony of Italica in Spain. Still later, men whose mother tongues were Punic, Aramaic or Arabic could put on the imperial purple. These people were the living proof that the Romans had successfully 'romanized' their empire. But the repercussions of romanization were enormous: while the empire's non-Roman, non-Greek (hence 'barbarian') periphery became gradually more Roman, Rome itself became considerably more 'barbarian'.

In this sense, Rome indeed made the world 'common to all'. The empire created a universal framework of standards, values, role models, laws and means of communication that substantially reduced the distances between centre and periphery. The Romans gave local elites the chance to break the chains of parochial narrowness and rise to the higher echelons of imperial aristocracy. Having said that, Roman rule was quite different in its early days. The Roman Republic was as rapacious and keen on collecting revenues from its subject territories as any other expanding power. By the 2nd century BC, the recklessness of Roman tax farmers, private entrepreneurs who squeezed the provinces on behalf of the Roman state, was notorious throughout the Mediterranean.

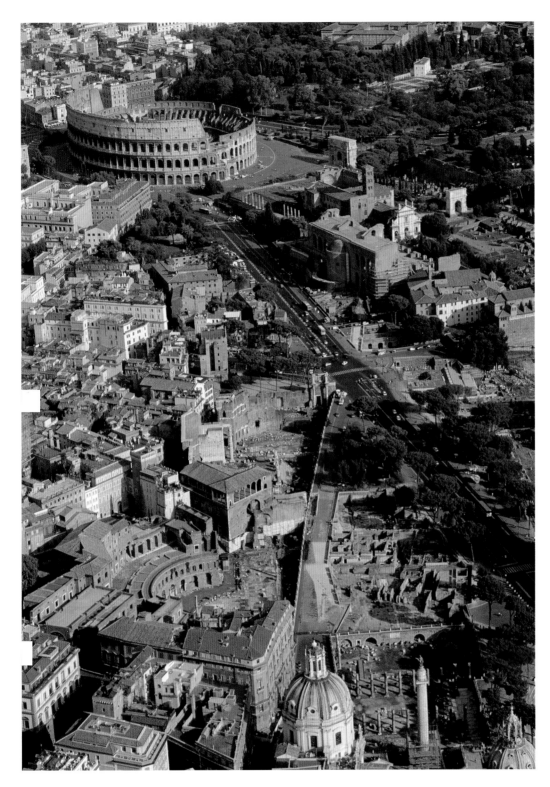

The imperial forums alongside the Via dei Fori Imperiali. Built in stages from the 1st century AD onwards, they were the work of emperors Augustus, Vespasian, Nerva and Trajan, and reflect the emperors' largesse. At the far side of the complex, now a UNESCO World Heritage Site, the Colosseum, or Flavian Amphitheatre, can be seen.

The transformation of this rapacious Republic into an empire that could be regarded at least as benevolent, if not praiseworthy, was largely the achievement of one man: Augustus, the first Roman emperor. His sole rule (31 BC–AD 14) marked a veritable watershed in Roman history and has duly been labelled the 'Augustan Threshold'.

THE 'AUGUSTAN THRESHOLD':
BEFORE AND AFTER

In his *Res Gestae*, the record of his accomplishments composed by the first Roman emperor towards the end of his life, Augustus describes the moment when the Roman Republic turned into a monarchy, and he himself was transformed from Gaius Iulius

Voices of Empire

The Romans left behind an immense wealth of literature – far more than any other ancient society. Much of it bears witness to imperial rule: historians like Tacitus, Suetonius, Cassius Dio and Ammianus Marcellinus provide us with biographies of rulers; poets like Virgil, Horace, Martial and Juvenal shed light on life in the imperial capital; philosophers including Seneca discuss ethical issues and moral standards; while orators like Aelius Aristides and Dio Chrysostom praise the empire in well-chosen words. The voice of the Roman aristocracy and the Romanized elites in the provincial towns is clear and distinct: Roman rule is tantamount to civilization as such, legitimate by definition and endless in space and time. The voices of other parts of society have mostly become silent. However, a few of them are still audible, most notably those of the Jews.

'Young Romulus
Will take the leadership, build walls of Mars,
And call by his own name his people Romans.
For these I set no limits, world or time,
But make the gift of empire without end.
Juno, indeed, whose bitterness now fills
With fear and torment sea and earh and sky,
Will men her ways, and favour them as I do
Lords of the world, the toga-bearing Romans.'

In Virgil's *Aeneid*, an epic in 12 books, the supreme god of the Roman pantheon, Jupiter, promises eternal rule to the hero Aeneas' descendants

The Virgil Mosaic from Hadrumentum (Sousse, in present-day Tunisia), dating to the 3rd century AD, shows the poet Virgil, seated in the centre and holding a script roll with the text of the *Aeneid*. He is flanked by the muses Clio (history) and Melpomene (tragedy).

Suetonius, who served in the imperial secretariat under Trajan and Hadrian, wrote a series of scurrilous biographies from Julius Caesar to Domitian. Here he gives a graphic description of the third emperor Caligula
'He was very tall and extremely pale, with an unshapely body … His eyes and temples were hollow, his forehead broad and grim, his hair thin and entirely gone on the top of his head, though his body was hairy. Because of this to look upon him from a higher place as he passed by, or for any reason whatever to mention a goat, was treated as a capital offence.'

The senator Tacitus wrote two influential historical works which cover most of the 1st century AD. In his *History*, he comments on the decline of the capital's political importance and the key role of the provincial legions in the making of a new emperor

'Welcome as the death of Nero had been in the first burst of joy, yet it had not only roused various emotions in Rome, among the Senators, the people, or the soldiery of the capital, it had also excited all the legions and their generals; for now had been divulged that secret of the empire, that emperors could be made elsewhere than at Rome.'

The historian Cassius Dio (born AD 160), who wrote a history of Rome, writes a sceptical note about the emperor Trajan's achievements

'[Trajan] used to say that he had advanced further than Alexander the Great, although he couldn't retain control even of the territory he had conquered.'

Rome's opponents among the Jews saw in the empire a robber in disguise

'"The boar out of the wood ravages it" (Psalms 80: 14). Why does Scripture compare Rome to a boar or pig? Just as the pig, when it lies down, stretches out its feet with their split hooves, as though to say, "Observe that I am kosher", so does wicked Rome, which violently thieves and robs, flaunt its legal system.'

The upper left corner of the *Monumentum Ancyranum*. The bilingual (Greek and Latin) inscription from Ancyra (Ankara) is the main surviving source for the text of Augustus' *Res Gestae*.

'I extended the frontiers of all provinces of the Roman people … I pacified the provinces of Gaul and Spain, and likewise Germany – the whole area bounded by the Ocean [Atlantic] from Gades [Cadiz] to the mouth of the river Elbe. I pacified the Alps from the region next to the Adriatic Sea to the Tuscan Sea, without waging war unjustly on any people.'

Augustus records his achievements in the *Res Gestae*, engraved on two bronze columns set up in Rome in AD 14, and now surviving copied on a Roman temple wall in Ankara, Turkey

Caesar (the name he inherited from his adoptive father Julius Caesar), *divi filius*, 'the son of a god', into *Augustus*, 'the venerable one', the sole ruler of the Roman world. This was when, in his sixth and seventh consulships (the year 27 BC), he transferred his extraordinary powers back to the Senate and the Roman people. In exchange, he received, among other honours, the title of Augustus from the Senate. 'After that time I took precedence of all in rank [*auctoritas*], but of power I possessed no more than those who were my colleagues in any magistracy.'

So he claimed. But who was this man who established the Roman monarchy? Born as Gaius Octavius (but today commonly known as Octavian), at the age of 18 he suddenly became a key figure in Roman politics: in his will, the great Julius Caesar, murdered by Cassius and Brutus on the Ides of March (15 March) 44 BC, had made Octavian his principal heir and adoptive son. Once Caesar was deified, Octavian became the son of a god and never used his name of birth again. Along with Caesar's name,

young Octavian inherited the dictator's fortune and the loyalty of his legions. Thirteen long years of unrest with changing alliances followed: in 31 BC, Octavian defeated his former ally Mark Antony in a naval battle at Actium, and was now the sole survivor of a century-long struggle for power which had split the nobility, Rome's governing elite, for almost five centuries.

But Rome was not yet ready for monarchy. Julius Caesar's obvious monarchic ambitions had cost him his life, and his adoptive son was determined not to make the same mistake. Despite internal upheaval that resulted in them splitting into factions, the members of the Roman senatorial aristocracy were united by a strong dislike of kingship. According to the foundation myth of the Republic, Brutus, a young Roman nobleman and supposed ancestor of Caesar's assassin of the same name, deposed the last Etruscan king – Tarquinius Superbus, whom the narratives unanimously depict as inept and cruel – in 509 BC. Brutus went down in history as a liberator, and kingship was discredited evermore: even in the 1st century BC,

The Gemma Augusta, a cameo gem, cut from Arabian onyx (early 1st century AD). The upper scene probably shows Augustus with Roma, seated in the centre, and, to his right, Oikoumene, the personification of the inhabited world. The lower tier shows the aftermath of a battle at one of Rome's northern frontiers.

a revived monarchy would lack any legitimacy. For this reason, the form of government that Augustus adopted was not a monarchy in the proper sense. The old Republican institutions were not abolished, and the Principate, as it was called, was more than a monarchy in disguise: Augustus did not assume the offices themselves, but he did assume their responsibilities. And the visible honours which were conferred on him – the laurels, the golden *clipeus virtutis* ('shield of bravery') and the *corona civica* ('civic crown') fixed to the entrance of his house – were all rooted in Republican tradition. Instead of overtly creating a monarchy, Augustus claimed to have 'restored' the Republic. Indeed, by labelling himself *princeps* ('first man'), Augustus 'took precedence of all in rank' without possessing any more institutional power than his colleagues in the magistracies.

The Roman Republic was a political structure no less puzzling than the Principate. The historiographer Polybius (*c.* 200–140 BC), a Greek politician who had been deported to Rome, admired its mixed constitution, with its checks and balances between monarchic, aristocratic and democratic elements. Government was divided between the people (voting in various assemblies), the two consuls (who held the supreme command in times of war and presided over the Senate) and the Senate (the council in which former magistrates convened). In theory, any Roman citizen could rise through the ranks of the *cursus honorum* – the hierarchy of public offices – and become a senator. In practice, access was largely restricted to a few powerful families. Social mobility into the senatorial class was less open than it appeared at first sight.

The nobility's unity was reinforced by a number of institutions that were not part of any written constitution, but were effective nevertheless. Senators were tied to each other by mutual bonds of solidarity (*amicitia*, 'friendship') or aversion (*inimicita*, 'enmity'), which were handed down from one generation to the next. They had at their disposal large groups of followers who owed loyalty to the senators and in turn received protection (*patrocinium*). Powerful patrons could easily

A wall painting of a Roman villa, found in the House of Marcus Lucretius Fronto in Pompeii, preserved by the ash of Vesuvius for almost 2,000 years.

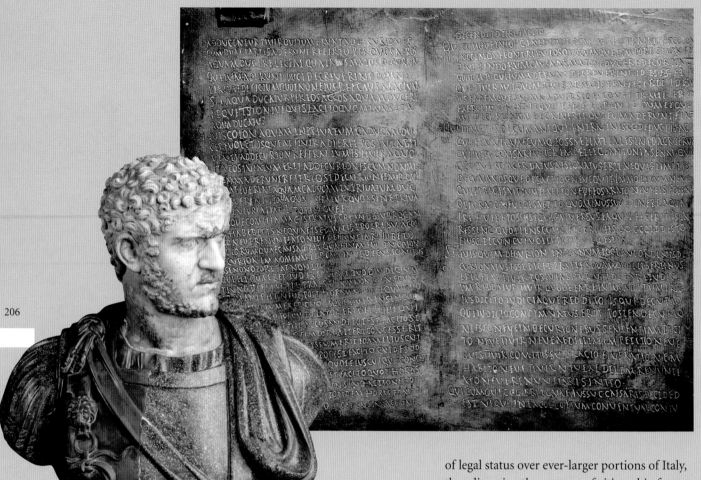

Citizenship

One of the key factors in Roman expansion was citizenship. While Greek city-states anxiously kept their civic bodies 'pure' and exclusive, Rome invented various categories of citizenship which could flexibly be bestowed on allies and subjects, without taking away their autonomy. The Roman territory was in fact a patchwork of municipalities with different statuses. Colonies (*colonia*) were settlements of Roman citizens and copies of Rome in miniature. *Municipia* were self-governing towns which retained their own citizenship. In some of them, the locals were full Roman citizens at the same time; in others, municipia of 'Latin' right, the inhabitants held a second-class citizenship which excluded the right to vote. Still other towns were purely indigenous in status. Gradually, Rome expanded the various forms of legal status over ever-larger portions of Italy, thus divorcing the concept of citizenship from its original ethnic or territorial implications. The co-existence of various forms of local self-government made Rome practically a confederation of autonomous cities to which a large number of functions of the state could be devolved.

In the long run, this flexibility paid off, having an overwhelmingly inclusive effect: subjugated populations turned into allies (*socii*), allies into Romans (*cives Romani*). The number of Roman citizens – and along with it the army which was composed of citizens and the allies' contingents – was in constant growth. Finally, the Lex Iulia granted Roman citizenship to all free males in Italy south of the river Po (88 BC). The law settled a long-smouldering conflict between Rome and its allies, who had demanded full citizenship and finally gone to war for it. In the imperial period, many people from the provinces became Romans by individual or collective enfranchisement. Still later, the emperor Caracalla extended Roman citizenship to virtually all free male inhabitants of the empire (212).

influence the crowds of their clients when it came to voting: candidates were supported both by their own clients and by those of their political allies. To increase the value of their patronage, aristocrats, whose economic basis was landed property, displayed overt pride in their ancestors, whose achievements would contribute to their own prestige. It was also every senator's mission to enhance his family's status through his own political and military achievements, and, by doing so, to accumulate *dignitas* ('dignity').

Even though the endemic strive for *dignitas* created a competitive social climate, the Roman nobility proved to be a surprisingly efficient political class. In little more than a century, between the First (264–241 BC) and the Third (149–146 BC) Punic wars, they turned the Republic into a truly imperial power and the Mediterranean into a *mare nostrum* ('our sea').

To understand this process, it is necessary to look back to Rome's early history, before the empire's growth began: in the 6th and 5th centuries BC, Rome was no more than a middle-sized city in central Italy which had cast off Etruscan dominance and maintained a close, albeit not always friendly, relationship to their kinsfolk in the towns in the hinterland of Latium. Just after they had eliminated their major regional rival, the Etruscan town of Veii (396 BC), the Romans lost a decisive battle against the Sennones, a migrating Gallic tribe, and Rome fell victim to the Gauls (387 BC). Only the Capitoline Hill withstood the siege, and the city itself was destroyed. The event was crucial for the Romans' political mentality – never again would an invader find Rome defenceless. Henceforth, the defeat and subjugation of potential enemies was the prime directive of Roman foreign policy.

By 300 BC, the Romans had tightened their grip on central Italy. They split the confederacy of Etruscan cities (357–353 BC), put down a revolt of the Latins (340–338 BC) and defended their sphere of influence against the Samnite League, a confederation of Sabellic tribes in southern Italy. In 280 BC, Rome suffocated the last pockets of Etruscan resistance. The

city's dominance was briefly threatened in the same year, when Pyrrhus of Epirus, a Greek warlord called by the people of the south Italian town of Tarentum to lead them in their war against Rome, entered Italy with a large army and defeated the Romans in a series of battles. In the long term, however, Pyrrhus was unable to benefit from his military successes and had to retreat from Italy. The south of the peninsula with its large Greek population thus remained defenceless and was gradually conquered by Rome, which controlled Italy from the river Po to the Ionian Sea by 265 BC.

Rome was not the only bellicose, expansionist power in the Mediterranean in those years. What distinguished the Romans from their rivals was the unique cohesion of their elites which, in situations of strain, immediately resolved any dispute and clustered around their leaders. Perhaps even more important to their success was the relative generosity with which Rome enfranchised its citizenship. The Roman state was growing continuously, and consequently so was its military potential. When it had to face the other great powers, beginning with Carthage (from 264 BC onwards), then Macedon (215 BC) and finally the Seleucid empire (192 BC), Rome had not only one of the largest, but also one of the most experienced armies of the Mediterranean world. Roman legionaries had engaged in battle almost every year between 326 and 267 BC.

What the Republic lacked, however, was naval power. After the conquest of the Greek cities in southern Italy, overseas expansion was the next logical step. The nearest target beyond the Italian mainland was Sicily, an economically and strategically rewarding prize. Here, Rome's interests inevitably clashed with those of Carthage, the period's maritime superpower. In order to overcome the Punic city and its empire, the Romans had to build a fleet from scratch and adjust to naval tactics. Amazingly, they succeeded: in 241 BC, the Carthaginians sought for peace and ceded Sicily to Rome. The island became Rome's first province: the Latin term *provincia* meant the administrative district of a Roman magistrate.

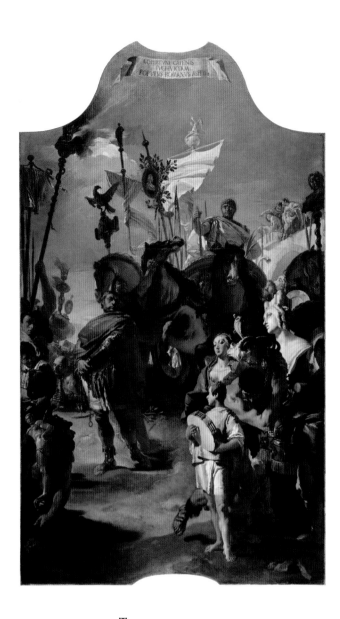

An oil painting that shows the Triumph of Marius, by Giambattista Tiepolo (1692–1770). Marius created the ultimate Roman fighting force by making drastic military reforms, including admitting citizens who did not own land into the army for the first time.

THE HARVEST OF WAR

The wars Rome waged overseas were prolific in terms of the establishment of new provinces: the islands of Corsica and Sardinia formed a province in 231 BC, northern Italy across the Po in 203 BC, Spain in 197 BC, Illyricum (former Yugoslavia and present-day Albania) in 167 BC, Macedonia and Africa (the territory of Carthage) in 146 BC, Asia Minor in 120 BC, and southern Gaul also in 120 BC. Defence and administration of the new provinces required an increasing number of soldiers and officials. By 133 BC, the Roman Republic had created an empire, but the impact that empire had on the Republic was ambivalent. Vast territories were annexed to the *ager publicus* (public land) and immediately occupied by members of the senatorial aristocracy, who accumulated enormous wealth by running large estates

specializing in the production of crops destined for the market. At the same time, many smallholders, not least due to the length of military service, became impoverished, lost their plots of land and had to move to Rome, where they increased the population of the urban poor.

The social strata of Roman society drifted apart at an enormous speed. Individual aristocrats could no longer resist the temptation to take advantage of the distressed many for the sake of their own ambitions. Tiberius Gracchus, by descent one of the most prominent members of the nobility, reinvented himself as an advocate of the stranded crowds, demanding land distribution and a fair deal for the landless poor, thus pioneering a new, populist style of politics (133 BC). At first, senatorial class solidarity proved stronger than the demagogues: Tiberius and his brother Gaius, who also did not shy away from unconstitutional action, were slain by furious senators. But in the long term, the aristocrats could not prevent individual members from making their names at the nobility's expense.

Towards the end of the 2nd century BC, the situation was aggravated by the military reforms launched by Gaius Marius, a *homo novus* from a small town in Latium. For the first time, Marius admitted the landless crowds to the army, thus transforming Rome's previous militia – the civic army recruited mainly from the landowning middle classes – into a professional army of soldiers who made their living with warfare. For the new type of soldier, the general was far more than a military commander. The legionaries' hopes for booty and the golden handshake they expected when – usually after 20 years of service – they were discharged from the army rested upon their leader: a new, exceedingly strong bond of solidarity was created. In the long term it proved to be stronger than the Republic.

Domestic affairs and the expansion of empire became closely interwoven. Correspondingly, military prowess was crucial for the rise of the late Republic's influential men: Marius, Sulla, Pompey, Caesar – they all first led huge armies against external enemies and then into civil war against their Roman rivals. Caesar's strategy to obtain the Senate's mandate to conquer Gaul was exemplary, and then he used the mandate as his personal basis of power. The Gallic war (58–50 BC) welded together general and army and fostered allegiance. Caesar could firmly rely on his soldiery when he marched them across the river Rubicon in northern Italy (49 BC). The Rubicon marked the boundary of Italy, where returning armies were meant to lay down their arms and disband before entering Rome. Caesar entered the city and chased his opponents, Pompey in particular, throughout the Mediterranean in a bloody civil war.

The rise of military men like Caesar proved to be fatal for the Republic, but beneficial for the provincial populations. When Cicero, the conservative senator and famous orator, in a case against the corrupt Roman governor of Sicily, Gaius Verres, took the part of Verres' Sicilian victims (70 BC), this was an exceptional example of political impartiality. Generals such as Pompey and Caesar not only annexed large portions of territory to the empire, they also worked as brokers for the locals. By extending the genuinely Roman institutions of *patrocinium* and *amicitia* to the provinces, they created, for the first time in Roman history, a lobby for the periphery in the empire's heart.

Both innovations of the revolutionary period, the new military with its generals and the relationship of *patrocinium* between conqueror and conquered, were universalized by Augustus when he came to power. Before he set off eastwards to defeat his rival Mark Antony, Augustus demanded an oath of

Reconstructions of Roman military men: from left, a legionary, a centurion and an archer.

The Colosseum

The arena of the Colosseum has the form of an ellipse, measuring 85 m by 54 m. Underneath the arena there was a subterranean maze of tunnels, cellars and cages (the *hypogeum*), from where a sophisticated system of pulleys and elevators transported men and animals to the arena.

The Amphitheatrum Flavium in Rome was, and still is, the largest amphitheatre of the entire Roman world. It received its nickname Colosseum or Coliseum from the colossal statue of the emperor Nero that stood here, on a site adjacent to the Roman Forum, until his death in AD 68. Built under Vespasian and opened in AD 80 under Titus to enhance the glory of the Flavian dynasty, the giant ellipse seated 50,000

people. No single building was better designed for the staging of communication between the emperor and the Roman people. The crowds were seated on the galleries' marble benches according to their social rank; a lavishly furnished box was reserved to the court and the emperor himself and guaranteed him visibility from all over the building. The spectators were protected from sun and rain by an awning supported by 140 masts. Eighty entrances gave access to the galleries. A sophisticated system of elevators and pulleys lifted gladiators and animals from the *hypogeum* into the arena. The arena could even be converted into an artificial lake where naval battles were staged. Spectacles did by no means cease with the Christianization of Rome: though the Colosseum was repeatedly damaged by earthquakes, they lasted well into the 6th century.

allegiance to be sworn by every single male inhabitant of the western provinces he controlled. This oath was later extended to the east, taken from the defeated Mark Antony, and formed the moral basis of the *auctoritas* Augustus refers to in his *Res Gestae*. He similarly inherited Caesar's veterans, to which he later added the surviving soldiery of the dictator's assassins, and still later Mark Antony's troops. His control of the army was Augustus' major asset when Rome's political structure was being reshuffled in the years following Actium. No senator could seriously compete with the man to whom all legionaries had personally sworn their oath of loyalty and whose image they bore on their legionary standards. Augustus also ensured loyalty by looking after the economic needs of his soldiers. He established no fewer than 28 military colonies in Italy alone, thus ensuring that the veterans received the arable land promised to them. (This practice was later abandoned and the soldiers received their discharge bonus in cash.) The Principate's heavy reliance on the army made it effectively a military dictatorship in disguise, illegitimate in the traditional and legal terms of the Republic. The new professional army was one of three decisive pressure-groups Augustus' successors had to reckon with.

PAX ROMANA: RULING A WORLD

In addition to the military, the senators (the representatives of the old Republic's ruling elite) and the *plebs urbana* (the crowds of the city of Rome) were decisive in the formation of the Principate. All three groups came to the emperor with their own particular concerns and expectations. The emperor on his part relied on the support and acceptance of each group. Failure to communicate with one or – worse – more of the three pressure groups inevitably resulted in serious consequences for the emperor: it meant in the final analysis his political – which in turn usually implied his physical – death.

The arena designed for communication with the Roman crowds was an arena in the most literal sense of the word: the amphitheatre. Gladiatorial games in Rome were far more

than a bloody form of entertainment for the urban masses. The arena was a formidable stage where the emperor could engage with the people, and they with him. Here was where his public image was created, and where unity between the emperor and the various strata of Roman society (who all had their allocated seats in the auditorium) was celebrated. The arena, where prisoners met their death and where gladiators and animals staged bloodthirsty shows, was a savage place in the heart of Rome, whereas the gallery, where the spectators were seated according to their social rank, encapsulated everything that was Roman. In the amphitheatre, the Romans met outcasts representing an outlandish and alien world – the nemesis of order, peace and stability for which their empire stood. The crowd carefully watched how the emperor dealt with the strange, savage world they encountered in the arena. The crucial moment came when a gladiator was defeated and the emperor had to make the decision as to whether he would live or die. An unpopular choice invariably cost the emperor credit among the people.

Communication with the senators also required sensitive handling. The nobility, while it had ruled the Republic over the centuries, had nurtured a powerful feeling of superiority and exclusiveness. Augustus himself, when creating the Principate, had not dared to style himself as the senators' master (*dominus*) – a term closely related to the institution of slavery – but chose to be called *princeps* instead. From the point of view of the senatorial aristocracy, the emperor was one of their own. Senators expected the emperor to communicate with them on an equal footing. When the emperor Domitian (AD 81–96) believed he could dispose of such conventions and redesign the Principate as a proper monarchy, he also changed the style of the dinners with the senators. In the banquet halls of his newly built palace on the Palatine, Domitian – who was the first emperor to insist on the title *dominus* – separated himself physically from his guests, thus making visible the enormous social distance between himself and the senators. He did not survive long; in AD 96 he fell victim to a plot in which

A mosaic from Nennig (Saarland, Germany) of the late 2nd or early 3rd century AD, showing a gladiatorial fight.

many courtiers and senators were involved. His successors hastened to undo Domitian's reforms.

Until 217, when the equestrian praetorian prefect Macrinus briefly became emperor, the Senate was the pool from which emperors were recruited. Since the dynastic principle was never firmly rooted in Rome, an emperor who lost acceptance could theoretically be challenged by any senator. Of particular importance in this game – and very dangerous for the ruling emperor – were those senators who commanded armies that were usually garrisoned along the distant frontiers. Once a ruling emperor had become unpopular with the soldiery, they would proclaim their own senatorial commander as rival-emperor. The pretender then usually marched on Rome and encountered his adversary on the battlefield. The first of a series of such usurpations happened when Nero's reign lay in ruins, in the Year of the Four Emperors (AD 69). Three generals from various areas of the empire tried to seize the imperial purple, but all failed. Only when Titus Flavius Vespasianus, Rome's successful supreme commander who put down

Relief from the Arch of Titus, built under Domitian (AD 81–96). The relief shows Titus' triumph after the capture of Jerusalem in the First Jewish Revolt (AD 66–70). Soldiers carry cult objects from the Temple of Jerusalem, most notably the menorah, the seven-branched candelabra.

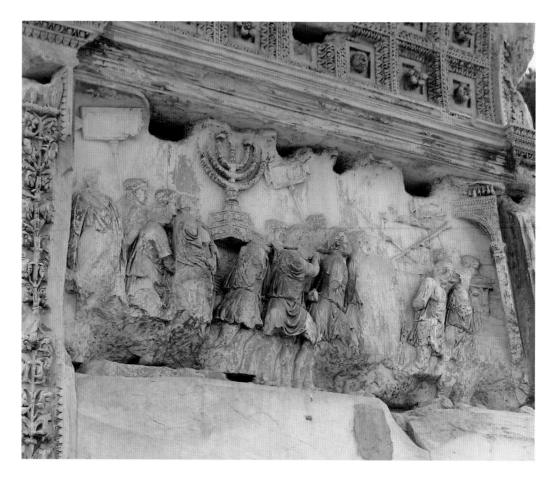

the Jewish revolt in Palestine, appeared on the scene, did political stability return to Rome. Whereas the Principate had worked smoothly in the relatively calm 1st and 2nd centuries AD, its flaws – an inherent tendency towards usurpation and civil war – became apparent as soon as more troublesome times began for the empire.

In the late 2nd and early 3rd centuries, during which the Principate relied even more heavily on the military than previously, it was the senators who suffered. In relation to the other pressure groups the senatorial aristocracy lost substantial ground, being ousted from most of the administrative top jobs and military commands they previously had held. These positions were instead taken by members of the equestrian order, who were socially inferior to the senators but were more capable with regard to military affairs. Rome was increasingly being challenged by external enemies, so the emperors reacted by making the army larger and more efficient, but the improvement of Rome's military power was only available at a high price: an increase in numbers and pay weighed

heavily on the budget. Furthermore, in a scenario with many theatres of war, the emperor as supreme commander could not be present at all the frontiers. This led to the appointment of professional officers to control large portions of the frontiers and armies in his stead. Those who were successful would then, in turn, direct their troops against the ruling emperor. All these factors contributed, directly or indirectly, to the weakening of the central government: the 50 years between the assassination of the emperor Severus Alexander (235) and Diocletian's accession (284) saw no less than 17 emperors coming and going, not including innumerable usurpers that were not recognized by the Senate.

MILITARY ANARCHY

These 'soldier emperors' fought a seemingly hopeless battle against migrating Germanic tribes, both along the Danube and the Rhine and also against the Sasanians in the East, who had replaced the far more defensive Parthians in 224. Neither the Sasanians nor the tribal groups had the potential to conquer Roman territory permanently, but they were able to overrun the frontier provinces, to raid and loot cities, and to disappear loaded with booty. It took Rome a generation to develop a strategy against the twofold threat that was in part a response to Roman expansion itself: the fall of the Parthian empire was largely a long-term consequence of repeated Roman aggression in the East, and the formation of new Germanic tribes that were much larger than the groups preceding them was at least to some extent a reaction to Roman campaigning, diplomacy and trade: the soaking of Roman commodities, concepts and know-how into Germany, combined with Germanic tribesmen joining the Roman auxiliary forces, changed social patterns across the Danube and the Rhine. What emerged from the change were compact, highly mobile groups that had personal allegiance to charismatic leaders and the belief in a commonly shared ancestry, and were far more dangerous to Rome than the petty chiefdoms that had dominated the scene in Caesar's day. By 260, Germanic tribes had repeatedly overrun Gaul and the Danube provinces, had crossed the Black Sea, devastated Greece and Asia Minor and some had even

ravaged Italy, before the emperor Aurelian (270–275) had finally driven them out.

No less dangerous for Rome were the events in the East, where the Sasanians first took the stronghold of Hatra in present-day Iraq (240), and then repeatedly invaded the provinces of Mesopotamia and Syria, where they skirmished with the Romans but avoided a major battle. The direct clash between Rome and the Sasanians became unavoidable when the emperor Valerian (253–260) entered the eastern theatre with a large army in order to corner the Persian king Shapur (241–272). The consequent battle of Carrhae brought a disastrous defeat for the Romans – for the first time in Roman history, an emperor was captured by the enemy. Valerian's army was annihilated and the Roman eastern provinces became a power vacuum.

When Aurelian gained power in 270, the outlook seemed dismal for the new emperor. The situation along the Roman frontiers appeared bleak, with Germans raiding the Balkans, Greece, Asia Minor and even Italy, and separatist dominions had been established in Gaul and the East. It was only a question of time

The triumph of the Persian king Shapur I (241–272) over his Roman enemies, as depicted in a rock relief at Naqsh-I Rustam near Persepolis in present-day Iran. Shapur on horseback grasps the captured emperor Valerian who stands behind the kneeling Philip the Arab.

before another usurper would take on Aurelian. Public finances were in a perilous state. And yet the impression of a universal crisis may be illusory. The 'barbarian' invasions affected only relatively restricted areas and rarely fortified cities. The expansionism of the Sasanian empire had come to a halt. And the economic conditions in the provinces were by no means uniformly bleak. On the contrary: whereas some of the western heartlands of the empire – namely Italy and Gaul – may have been in gentle decline, the provinces in North Africa, Syria, Asia Minor and the Balkans were clearly flourishing.

BECOMING ROMAN:
LOCAL AND IMPERIAL TRADITIONS

All over the empire, 'romanization' had – by and large – been a success story. Roman material culture – with its luxury commodities, imperial and domestic architecture, water supply and drainage systems, roads and other means of communication, Roman citizenship, the sophisticated lifestyle of the elites – was sufficiently attractive to local populations, in particular the petty aristocracies of tribes and cities, to be adopted and adapted with enthusiasm. The urge for romanization came, therefore, from the periphery rather than the imperial centre: the locals themselves competed for the most convincing display of their Roman identity. Rome hardly had to impose its civilization upon its subjects. But becoming Roman did not mean that Greeks, Gauls, Syrians or North Africans had to abandon their own traditions, customs and convictions – or indeed their religious faith, which was usually incorporated into Roman religion. Roman tolerance allowed indigenous populations to insert their ancestral traditions into the wider imperial framework.

Local reflections of this cohabitation can be found everywhere from Roman Britain to Roman Egypt, mostly in the material culture, as literary evidence for the imperial periphery is generally scant; Tacitus' works on contemporary Britain and Germany are rare and precious exceptions. Artifacts such as statues of Apollo found in Gaul, in which the image of the Greco-Roman god combined with that of local deities, the representations on family tombs in the Libyan desert and the stunning wall paintings from several buildings in the Near Eastern town of Dura-Europos have been misinterpreted as abortive attempts to emulate Roman models. Recent scholarship tends to regard them as complex expressions of 'hybrid' cultures in which elements of both, the little and the great,

Roman material culture was eagerly adopted in the provinces. The Pont du Gard, a Roman aqueduct in southern Gaul (50 m high and 275 m long), was probably built in the 1st century AD to supply the city of Nemausus (Nîmes) with water.

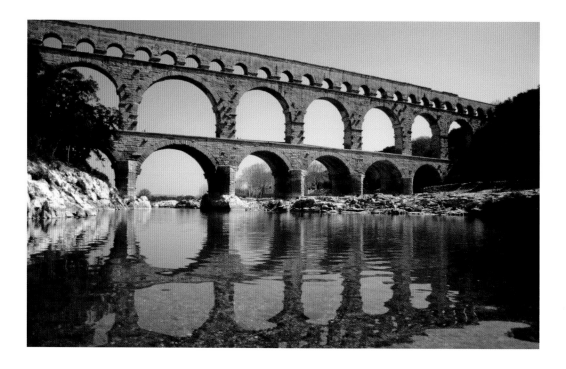

traditions fused. But even this is questionable: the material culture of the Roman provinces seems to suggest that the periphery served as a middle ground in which numerous traditions met and made contact with each other, thus resembling perhaps the creole world of the Spanish Caribbean where something completely new emerged, than the proposed model of hybridization.

As a result, the empire became romanized, but not necessarily more homogenous than before. This was particularly apparent in the frontier zones in western Europe and the Near East. In general, the power and cultural appeal of empires do not simply finish at a boundary – though the Roman empire had a clear-cut border, the *limes* – but gradually fade out towards the periphery. One of the cultural mainstreams of the ancient Mediterranean, Hellenism, had struck roots throughout the Near East long before the Romans arrived: uncounted Greeks and Macedonians had settled in the vast area between the Mediterranean and the Indus since Alexander had subjugated the Achaemenid empire (Chapter 6); still more locals had adopted the conquerors' lifestyle. In the twilight zone between east and west the various traditions existed side by side. Greek *poleis* – the *polis*

was the fundamental model of an urban settlement governed by its own citizens, which the Greeks of the Archaic period (7th–6th centuries BC) had spread all over the Mediterranean – were built next to indigenous settlements, Greek was spoken along with Aramaic, western gods were worshipped along with eastern deities, Greek-style artifacts were produced together with native ones. From this, eastern Hellenism emerged, an idiosyncratic creole culture, neither 'western' nor 'eastern', but distinct and – despite obvious local variations – strikingly uniform in its appearance. This sphere of close interaction did not cease when the Romans arrived. Cross-border ties remained strong in the Partho-Roman Near East and they did not weaken when the Sasanians took over from the Parthians. Phenomena such as the wall paintings from Dura-Europos, the stunning rise of the city of Palmyra – which made a short, but decisive appearance on the stage of world politics during the power vacuum that resulted from Valerian's defeat in 260 (see p. 220) – and the puzzling religious complexity of places like Hatra can only be fully understood if the cultural ambiguity of the Syro-Mesopotamian steppe frontier is taken into account.

FAR LEFT: The so-called Fresco of Konon, a wall painting from the Temple of Palmyrene Gods in Dura-Europos (late 1st century AD). The painting probably depicts the man who sponsored the sanctuary's wall paintings: Konon, wearing conical headgear, is shown in an act of sacrifice.

LEFT: Tomb of Es-Senama in Tripolitania, Libya, from the early Roman imperial period.

FOLLOWING PAGES: Hadrian's Wall in winter.

Palmyra: Oasis City

Hardly any place reveals better the complexities of Roman imperial rule than Palmyra, though – or perhaps because – the city in the Syrian desert was exceptional in the Roman world by any standard. Of ancient origin, but probably re-established in the Hellenistic period, the oasis city accumulated enormous wealth by getting involved in the expanding long-distance trade between Rome on the one hand, South and East Asia on the other. Palmyra became part of the Roman province of Syria, but maintained an unusual degree of autonomy. Politically and economically the most active parts of the population were tribal elites who shuttled between steppe and city. Their influence reached far into the Parthian realm. In the 3rd century, Septimius Odaenathus, a Roman citizen, achieved a quasi-monarchic position. When the emperor Valerian was defeated at Carrhae, he remained loyal to Valerian's son Gallienus, re-organized resistance, warded off the Persian attack and pursued the Sasanians deep into their own territory. When Odaenathus was killed under mysterious circumstances, his widow Zenobia succeeded him. Though this was consistent from a Palmyrene point of view, the Roman emperors regarded Zenobia as a usurper. Anticipating their reaction, Zenobia subdued large portions of the Roman Near East, before she was finally defeated and taken prisoner by Aurelian (272).

LEFT: Palmyra, the colonnaded road. The central axis of Palmyra, 1,200 metres long, was built in the 2nd century AD. Despite their distinctively 'classical' look, colonnaded roads were a feature exclusive to the eastern Roman provinces.

ABOVE: The Temple of Bel in Palmyra, another building giving a deceptively classical impression: the temple was dedicated in AD 32 and looked, with its Corinthian columns, western. However, a number of features, like the flat roof and the pinnacles, suggest that the sanctuary actually housed a cult strongly influenced by Near Eastern traditions.

The frontiers seemed distant from Rome, but the inhabitants of the capital got a notion of what was happening on the periphery when Varius Bassianus Avitus, a youth from the Syrian town of Emesa, became emperor in 218. Avitus, an offspring of a local priestly dynasty, later became notorious under the name of his ancestral god: Elagabalus. Educated as a priest himself, he tried to introduce worship of the Syrian sun-god in Rome, where he met fierce resistance. His reign polarized the capital and provoked a cultural war which even divided the imperial palace. Elagabalus' attempt to turn Roman religion upside down was abortive, and the emperor was murdered after four years in power. But whereas most contemporaries tried to dismiss the revolution as just another mad emperor's fury, some observed the cultural rifts that had begun to split the empire. Elagabalus was unsuccessful, but he was the writing on the wall announcing that the great tradition of Greco-Roman, 'classical' elite culture was not the only expression of Roman imperial identity in these times. The Roman world was perhaps more than ever 'common to all', but it was no longer the 'single household' invoked by Aelius Aristides.

LATE ANTIQUITY: THE END OF ROME?

The empire had begun to drift apart at specific points on the frontiers, where weaknesses were apparent and schisms inevitable: the imperial population was increasingly divided by religious, ethnic and cultural contrasts, and various parts of the empire slipped away from the central government's control for substantial periods of time. At first, however, this process was hardly visible. Aurelian had succeeded in eliminating the two renegade empires that had emerged at the empire's Gallic and Near Eastern fringes. When Diocletian came to power in 284, his first action was to change the Roman state's political and administrative layout. He appointed his fellow officer Maximian as 'Augustus' – now the title of the senior rulers – in 285, thus

making him formally his co-emperor. In 293 two more emperors, Galerius and Constantius, were appointed, but remained inferior in rank. As 'Caesares' they were the designated successors of the two Augusti, who announced their abdication after their 20th year of rule, in 305. No matter whether the resulting tetrarchy (leadership of four men) was a master plan designed by Diocletian from the beginning or an ingenious piece of improvisation, the new array resolved two of Rome's most pressing problems: it integrated potential adversaries into Diocletian's camp and thus gave back urgently needed political stability to the empire, and it quadrupled the empire's military and administrative leadership, allowing emperors to be present where they were needed. Although laws issued by the tetrarchs were in principle still effective for all provinces, each emperor was in practice responsible for his own part.

Diocletian and his colleagues all shared the widespread belief that the problems of the empire were due to the deteriorating relationship between the Romans and their ancestral gods. In order to rectify this, the Augusti closely associated themselves with the Olympian gods by adopting the titles of *Iovius* (Diocletian) and *Herculius* (Maximian). It was their firm belief that common well-being could be restored by their subjects honouring the right gods. While religion had hardly been an imperial affair – it had traditionally been the business of the individual cities – faith now moved into the focus of the state's attention. For the first time in Roman history, Christians were systematically persecuted because of their faith.

Although the tetrarchs were successful in stabilizing the empire, their achievements did not survive long. After the abdication of Diocletian and Maximian and Constantius' death, the personal ambition of various pretenders overwhelmed the tetrarchy's sophisticated structure, causing the system to collapse and leading to another civil war. Furthermore, the traditional cults on which Diocletian and his co-emperors intended to base their rule were in rapid decline. The attempt to restore them through force was doomed to failure. Constantine, one of the

The tetrarchs, from St Mark's Basilica, Venice. The porphyry sculpture shows the four emperors Diocletian, Maximian, Galerius and Constantius I, embracing each other in a symbolic gesture of mutual solidarity.

The Battle of the Milvian Bridge, as painted by Pieter Lastmann, oil on canvas (1613, Kunsthalle Bremen). The painting shows the collapse of the bridge and, to the left, crosses as Constantine's standards.

pretenders, was acutely aware of that when he met his rival Maxentius, Maximian's son, at the Milvian Bridge, a few miles to the north of Rome, in 312. He reportedly received a vision before the battle – a message saying *in hoc signo vinces* ('in this sign, you shall conquer'). He saw the monogram of Christ (the Greek letters *chi* and *rho*) in the sky and immediately adopted it for his soldiers' legionary standards. This was politically a very opportune omen, as Christianity, which had gained numerous supporters during the preceding century, was now a force to be reckoned with. The battle was a triumph for Constantine, and Christianity turned from illegality to state religion almost overnight.

Constantine's move was shrewd. He re-integrated the Christians into Roman society and finally solved the problem of the Principate's inherent illegitimacy. By associating his fate with the Christians' almighty God he created a powerful, nearly inexhaustible source

of authority for the ruling monarch. The emperor was now God's chief representative on earth. But Constantine and his successors were forced to realize that getting involved in the Church's affairs had its drawbacks. The early Church was divided over such theological issues as the relationship between God, his son and the Holy Spirit; to modern observers such niceties may appear trivial, but for contemporaries they were worth going to war for. Not accidentally, the trenches of the sectarian divide roughly resembled cultural schisms already visible in the 3rd century: the breaking away of various regional churches, mainly in the eastern provinces, became a major burden for the empire and prepared, indirectly and in the long run, for the defection of Syria and Mesopotamia – the sphere of eastern Hellenism – to the Muslim Arabs in the 7th century.

Under Constantine, the empire's centre of gravity moved irreversibly eastwards. In 326, a new capital was inaugurated which bore the emperor's name: Constantinople, ancient Byzantium, a Christian capital from the very beginning, home to its own Senate and magistrates. Here, the emperor and his court were closer to the resources of the wealthy East, and the city controlled the strategically important straits of the Dardanelles. After more than a millennium, Rome was rejected as the empire's political nerve centre. And so were the ancient traditions it stood for: the triumph of Christianity in its various denominations was almost complete, and paganism – even though there were few minor pockets of resistance, most notably the old capital's senatorial aristocracy – was in agony. When he became sole emperor in 361 Constantine's nephew Julian tried to reform and restore paganism by overlaying it with the hierarchic structures of the Christian church, but soon he had to realize that he had tried to resuscitate a corpse. As a consequence, his attempt to roll back the wheel of history remained just a minor episode: the emperor was killed on a Persian campaign in 363, his pagan 'Church' died with him. The over-hasty retreat from military action prompted by his successor led to a disgraceful defeat, and the Sasanians occupied the strategically important town of Nisibis in Mesopotamia.

The Persians, however, were not to remain the emperors' main concern for long. The menace of migrating tribes returned suddenly when a large group of Goths, fleeing the Huns, appeared on the Lower Danube and asked for permission to settle as Roman allies (foederati). Although the Romans usually turned down such requests when brought forward by entire tribal groups, they made an exception in this case. Soon, however, the situation spun out of control, not least because of the mismanagement of Roman officials. The Goths clashed with a numerically superior Roman army under the command of the emperor Valens near Adrianople in Thrace. For the empire, the battle ended in disaster: Valens was killed, an army of 20,000 men annihilated. The Roman legions never recovered fully from Adrianople; their ranks were filled with

an increasing number of tribesmen who maintained, even as Roman soldiers, their allegiance to their leaders. Henceforth, Roman armies and migrating Germanic tribes in arms were often hard to distinguish.

Following the death of the emperor Theodosius (379–395), the empire was divided between his two sons: Arcadius received the Greek East, Honorius the Latin West. The two sections irreversibly drifted apart. The stronger East managed to divert the bulk of the migrating tribes to the West, where their impact was devastating. Scholars are divided on the question whether the tribes encountered an empire in agony, crippled by internal strife and economic crisis, or whether Rome was, even at the turn from the 4th to the 5th century, a thriving polity, just accidentally swept away by hordes of marauding barbarians. Either way, the sheer facts are daunting: the Visigoths entered Italy (401); the Vandals, Suebi and Alans crossed the Rhine (406), from where Roman troops had been transferred to Italy the year before; Rome was captured and looted by the Visigoths (410); the Suebi, Burgunds, Visigoths and Vandals established de facto autonomous kingdoms in Gaul, Spain and North Africa (411–429); the Vandals captured and looted Rome (455). The long decline of the western empire ended in 476, when the Roman general Odoacer, of Germanic origin himself, deposed the last emperor Romulus ('Augustulus'), who, ironically, was named after the mythic founder of Rome.

Was this the end of Rome? In one sense, it was; in many other senses, clearly not. The western monarchy ceased in 476, but many of the institutions that made Rome did not. There were still the Senate, the consuls, praetorian prefects and numerous other officials. There was, physically, the city of Rome, the Eternal City which stands, manifold menaces notwithstanding, including various enemy attacks, traffic problems and incapable politicians, till the present day. There was also the Church, which had taken over many of the administrative duties in the towns and cities and which stood, with its learned higher clergy, for cultural and spiritual continuity. There was, of course, the second Rome, Constantinople, which became increasingly Greek in language and style, but strongly maintained the awareness of its Roman origin. The eastern emperors, the rulers of the empire of the *rhomaioi*, as it was called in Greek, never really abandoned their claim to supremacy over the West, until Byzantium finally fell in 1453.

And there was, first and foremost, the idea into which the Roman empire had gradually been transformed. When Europe became fragmented, once more, into petty tribal kingdoms, the idea of empire proved powerful enough to survive and inspire the minds of ambitious rulers. The empire-turned-idea implied that empire was transferrable: *translatio imperii* was one of the dominant political ideologies in medieval and early modern Europe. It meant that the crown of empire was handed down from the Assyrians to the Babylonians and from them to the Persians, Greeks and finally Romans. The course of its onward journey depended on the observer's point of view: Otto of Freising, a German bishop of the 12th century, regarded Longobards, Franks and the Holy Roman empire as the Romans' natural heirs; the French poet Chrétien de Tours, a contemporary of

Otto's, saw in France the logical continuation of the Roman empire; and Richard de Bury, an English intellectual, politician and cleric of the 14th century, believed that the English were the predestined caretakers for Rome's legacy. Constantinople was the 'second Rome', Moscow, its cultural and religious offspring, the 'third Rome' and Washington was – in the eyes of the founding fathers of God's chosen country – a 'fourth Rome'. Napoleon styled himself as a reincarnation of the Roman Caesars. And British thinkers, such as John Robert Seeley and Charles Dilke, the reformist politician, took Rome as a model for the British empire, which they emphatically advocated. The fascination with the Roman empire endures: is its fate the writing on the wall for imperial powers of later epochs, not least the United States? Its apparent relevance to the current situation may explain the persistent presence of ancient Rome in modern popular culture.

Did the year 476 then mean an end to Rome? Rather, when considering the enormous impact the empire had on European history since then, one is inclined to believe that it instead marked a new beginning.

ABOVE LEFT: The 'second Rome', Constantinople, became the capital of the eastern emperors who (known today as the Byzantines) ruled until their defeat by the Ottoman Turks in 1453. Their greatest church, the Hagia Sophia, built by the emperor Justinian I (527–565), was turned into a mosque by the Ottomans.

ABOVE: The 'fourth Rome', the United States, had its seat of power in the Capitol in Washington, completed in 1811. Its dome harks back to antecedents in the Pantheon in Rome and the Hagia Sophia.

It is tempting, in the light of the modern history of India, to see the various empires of ancient South Asia as following the same narrative – each contributing to the gradual task of establishing a uniform rule (and culture) over the vast and disparate subcontinent, each building on its predecessor's achievements. The most striking fact about the Mauryan, Kushan and Gupta empires, however, is their diversity – a diversity not only between empires but between kings of the same dynasty. Each empire had different origins. Each employed different methods (more or less centralized) in establishing and maintaining rule. And each expressed their rule in markedly different ideologies; with some kings using force, and others Buddhism, as the main means of the expansion of their influence.

King List

MAURYAN RULERS

321–297 BC	Chandragupta Maurya
297–272 BC	Bindusara
272–235 BC	Asoka
235–221 BC	Dasaratha
221–185 BC	Brihadratha

KUSHAN EMPERORS

30–80	Kujula Kadphises
80–105	Vima Taktu
105–127	Vima Kadphises
127–147	Kanishka
140–183	Huvishka
191–225	Vasudeva

GUPTA EMPERORS

319–335	Chandragupta
335–375	Samudragupta
380–413	Chandragupta II
414–454	Kumaragupta
455–467	Skandagupta

PREVIOUS PAGES: A hunting scene carved in ivory recovered from Begram in Afghanistan. It depicts two men armed with bows sitting on a long platform hunting two winged creatures. The men wear a cross-belt to indicate valour and war-like qualities. These remarkable scenes give us an invaluable insight into the mythologies of ancient India, from the mythical beasts to the seemingly flying platform. It marks a significant change in the dissemination of religious and imperial doctrine from the textual edicts of Asoka.

LEFT: 'Buddha preaching the law.' This 5th-century AD masterpiece from Sarnath depicts the seated Buddha preaching to his followers. The sculpture is carved from Chunar sandstone – the very same material used 800 years earlier by Asoka. Sarnath was the site of the Buddha's first sermon, and remains an important pilgrimage centre.

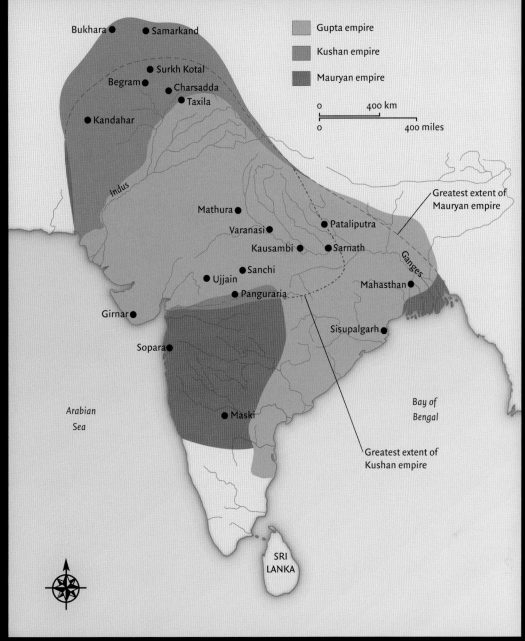

Gupta empire

Kushan empire

Mauryan empire

0   400 km
0   400 miles

Bukhara ●   ● Samarkand

● Surkh Kotal
Begram ●   ● Charsadda
     ● Taxila
● Kandahar

Indus

Mathura ●

Varanasi ●
   Kausambi ●   ● Sarnath
      ● Sanchi
Ujjain ●
   ● Panguraria

● Pataliputra

Ganges

Mahasthan ●

Girnar ●

● Sisupalgarh

Sopara ●

Greatest extent of
Mauryan empire

Greatest extent of
Kushan empire

Arabian
Sea

Bay of
Bengal

● Maski

SRI
LANKA

Chandragupta Maurya founds
the Mauryan dynasty
321 BC

Kushan empire expands
into Ganges basin under
Vima Kadphises
105–127

Annexation of
Gandhara by
Achaemenid empire
c. 550 BC

Collapse of Mauryan
empire and emergence
of Sunga dynasty
185 BC

Kushan empire
collapses due to
Sasanid pressure
225

Unifying campaigns
of Chandragupta II
409

| 500 BC | 400 BC | 300 BC | 200 BC | 100 BC | 0 | AD 100 | AD 200 | AD 300 | AD 400 | AD 500 |

Conquest of
Alexander the
Great
326 BC

Conquest of Kalinga,
and Asoka's subsequent
conversion to Buddhism
265 BC

Kushan empire
emerges in Bactria
and Sogdiana
AD 60

Rise of the
Gupta empire
280

Asoka ascends to
the Mauryan throne
272 BC

Invasions of north India by the
Heptholites and demise of
Gupta's empire
530

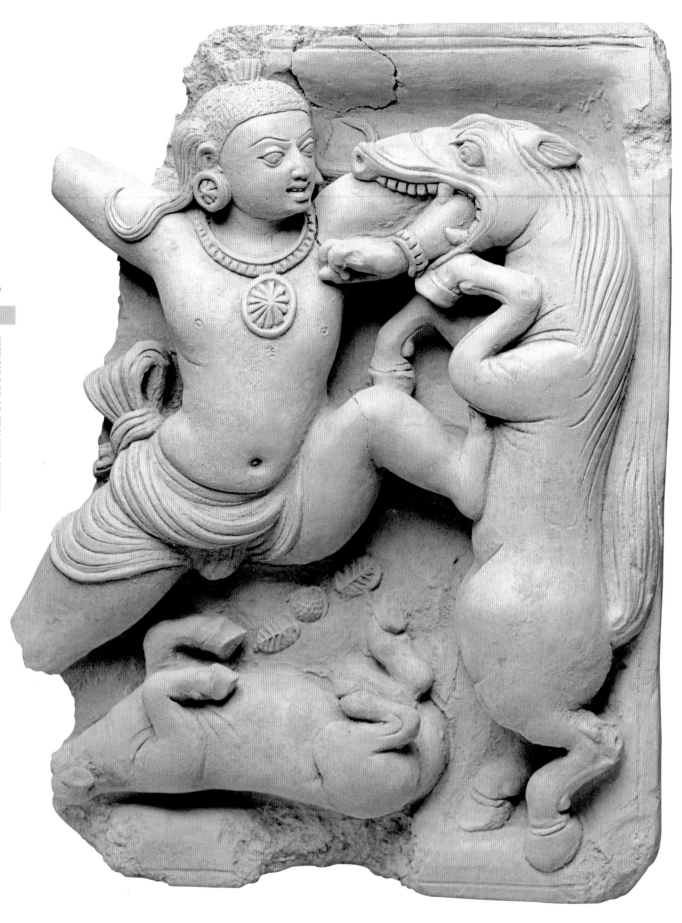

When thinking of the mechanisms behind the term 'empire' in an Indian context, many consider the Anglo-Indian civil and military hierarchies which underpinned Britain's 'jewel in the crown' – the Raj – the exemplar. The nature of these hierarchies was reinforced at the coronation of each British ruler, none more explicitly so than when George V was proclaimed King-Emperor in the gateway of Delhi's Mughal fortress in front of an audience of 80,000 on 12 December 1911. As Kaisar-i-Hind, George became the master of 315 million subjects and over 5 million sq. km (1.9 million sq. miles), stretching from Persia in the west and China in the north to the eastern borders of Burma.

For all its apparent uniformity, the Raj was subdivided into a mosaic of directly administered provinces, tribal agencies largely run by elders, and over 500 princely states. Viceroys therefore had not only to contend with governors and nawabs, maharajas, nizams, mehtars, rajas, badshahs and a wali within each domain, but also with indistinct borders shared with a variety of other figures ranging from the Shah of Persia and the Emir of Afghanistan to the theocratic Dalai Lama of Tibet. The complexities of late 19th-century and early 20th-century India provide an extremely useful guide to the complexities of the region's first empires, which emerged at a time when historical records and inscriptions offer only partial coverage and need to be understood with reference to archaeology. The comparisons also display the difficulties of imposing imperial control over communities that inhabit different environmental settings, and that enjoy very different levels of social, economic and ideological integration with the centre.

The Raj's cadre of archaeologists and historians were keen to investigate their imperial antecedents, and viewed the earliest emergence of states in the Ganges valley and the northwest Indus region as the direct result of earlier waves of soldiers and administrators bringing imperial ideas and technology from the west. Sir John Marshall, Director-General of the Archaeological Survey of India between 1902 and 1928, saw clear evidence of Persian and Hellenistic imperial connections during his excavations of the city of Taxila in the Punjab. Sir Mortimer Wheeler, one of his successors as Director-General, sought and found similar evidence of an initial Persian foundation at the Bala Hisar or 'High Fort' of Charsadda in the vale of Peshawar. Not only did Wheeler suggest that such settlements were originally outposts of the Persian empire, he also suggested that the collapse of that empire under the onslaught of Alexander resulted in a migration of craftsmen to the east, providing the nascent states of the Ganges with the crafts of empire.

More recent scholars highlight the uniquely South Asian character of the region's states and empires and view the writings of Wheeler, and other earlier European scholars, as deliberately downplaying the region's indigenous achievements. Indeed, they suggest that ancient India and its early communities were classified as culturally stagnant in order to legitimize British rule. Whichever perception is correct, it is undeniable that two powerful forces have influenced South Asia's development – fusion and fission. This chapter will examine three of the earliest attempts to fuse distinct geo-political entities over large expanses of South Asia during its Early Historic period. Acknowledged by many as representing India's 'golden age', the successive Mauryan, Kushan and Gupta empires introduced key imperial characteristics which shaped the course of South Asian history for 2,000 years.

THE MAURYAN EMPIRE

The Mauryan empire is frequently identified as the first example of a unified India, rising as it did from internecine fighting between kingdoms in the Ganges valley in the 4th century BC. Its founder, Chandragupta Maurya, exploited the power vacuum resulting from Alexander the Great's excursions into northwest India and seized control of the kingdom of Magadha, proclaiming himself king in 321 BC. Imposing hegemony from the Hindu Kush mountain range in the west to the Brahmaputra delta in the east, and from the foothills of the Himalayas in the north to the Deccan plateau in the south, Chandragupta Maurya fused together

OPPOSITE: This terracotta plaque from an unknown temple in Uttar Pradesh depicts Krishna fighting the demon Keshi, who has taken the form of a horse. Dating to the Gupta period, it demonstrates the focus upon Hindu literature and story telling. The corpse at the base of the plaque reveals the eventual winner in this battle. It represents the growing importance of Hinduism within what was a previously Buddhist landscape.

BELOW: The Didarganj Yaksi is a free-standing sculpture of a spirit holding a fly whisk. Discovered on the banks of the Ganges in 1917, it is dated to the Mauryan period as it is carved from Chunar sandstone, the same source as Asoka's pillars. As she was recovered out of context, it is difficult to establish whether she was the focus of a shrine or merely an attendant of a more powerful deity.

Voices of Empire

The identification of Sanskrit as an Indo-European language during the 18th century led to a proliferation of translations of early Indian texts, as scholars sought to identify links between ancient Europe and India. These translations have often formed the basis of our understanding of the social and political organization of these early empires – most notably through Asoka's edicts and the plethora of Gupta literature. This corpus of knowledge has been supplemented by Greek, Roman and Chinese accounts of diplomats, soldiers and pilgrims who journeyed through the region. The archaeological record has often been demonstrated to be at odds with the texts, which now appear to be idealized notions of ancient life in India. However, this has not dampened modern India's enthusiasm to recall this time period as the Golden Age of India.

'The welfare of the state depends upon adopting a foreign policy of non-intervention or overt action… A king makes progress by building forts, irrigation works or trade routes, creating new settlements, elephant forests or productive forests, or opening new mines. Any activity which harms the progress of the enemy engaged in similar undertakings is also progress.'

From the *Arthasastra* (6.2.1–3…7.1.20–22), a political treatise on the duties of the king, written by Chandragupta Maurya's chief minister, Kautilya

The Roman philosopher Arrian, the author of *Indica* in the 1st century AD, records the scale of the Mauryan capital Pataliputra. The majority of Arrian's writings are compiled from earlier works, most notably those of Megasthenes, the Seleucid ambassador to Chandragupta Maurya's court

'The greatest city in India is that which is called Palimbothra [Pataliputra] in the dominions of the Prasians, where the streams of the Erannoboas [Son] and the Ganges unite … Megasthenes says further of this city that the inhabited part of it stretched on either side to an extreme length of 80 stadia, and that its breadth was 15 stadia, and that a ditch encompassed it all round which was 6 plethra in breadth and 60 cubits in depth and that the wall was crowned with 570 towers and had 64 gates.'

13th Major Rock Edict

'When he had been consecrated eight years the Beloved of the Gods, the king Piyadass [Asoka]i conquered Kalinga. 150,000 people were deported, and 100,000 were killed and many times that number perished … On conquering Kalinga the Beloved of the Gods felt remorse, for, when an independent country is conquered the slaughter, death and deportation of the people is extremely grievous to the Beloved of the Gods, and weighs heavily on his mind… The Beloved of the Gods considers victory by Dhamma to be the foremost victory… [He] has gained this victory on all his frontiers to a distance of 600 yojanas [c. 1500 miles] where reigns the Greek king named Antiochus and beyond … in the lands of the four kings named Ptolemy, Antigonus Magas and Alexander.'

Xuanzang, a Chinese pilgrim travelling through northern India in AD 650, discusses the Indian caste system

'With respect to the divisions of caste, there are four classes. The first is called the Brahman, men of pure lives. They adhere to the teachings of the religion. Live clean lives, and observe the most correct principles. The second is called Kshatriya, the royal caste. For ages they have been the ruling class: they apply themselves to benevolence and mercy. The third is called Vaisyas, the merchant class; they engage in commercial transactions and seek profit at home and abroad. The fourth is called Sudra, the agricultural class; they engage in cultivating the soil and occupy themselves with sowing and reaping.'

'Thus speaks the Beloved of the Gods, the king Piyadassi [Asoka]: Dharma is good. And what is Dharma? It is having few faults and many good deeds, mercy, charity, truthfulness and purity.'

Chandragupta's grandson, Asoka, promulgated his philosophy through edicts carved either into natural rock-faces or onto ashlar pillars erected throughout the Mauryan empire

The Asokan pillar at Lauriya-Nandangarh stands 12 m tall and is topped by a seated lion. Erected in 244 BC there are six Asokan edicts carved onto the side of the pillar. The tree in the background is a sacred *pipal*.

one of the largest empires witnessed in early South Asia.

MAURYAN LITERATURE, ART AND ARCHITECTURE

Our knowledge of the Mauryan empire comes from a limited number of textual sources – namely the *Arthasastra*, the writings of Megasthenes and the inscriptions of Asoka Maurya. The *Arthasastra* is a political treatise widely believed to have been compiled by Kautilya, Chandragupta Maurya's chief minister. Dating to the formative years of the Mauryan empire during the 4th century BC, it was never intended to be theoretical and the records of Megasthenes, Seleucid ambassador to Chandragupta Maurya's court, frequently corroborate its advice. Finally, many aspects of the empire's spatial, ethnic and administrative characteristics have been reconstructed from the rock and pillar edicts of Chandragupta's grandson, Asoka.

The *Arthasastra* details the idealized structure of a kingdom, providing us with an unparalleled insight into the philosophy of Mauryan political, military and economic strategy during the 4th century. Kautilya advised that all neighbouring kingdoms were enemies, but that distant lands were potential allies. Taking this categorization further, he considered strong kingdoms to be 'foes', weak kingdoms fit only to be 'exterminated' and kingdoms facing internal problems to be 'vulnerable'. This formative Mauryan philosophy dictated that it was the duty of prosperous kingdoms (like themselves) to extend their control over the weak through a combination of military campaigns and covert

operations. Considering the rapid expansion of the Mauryans through northern India, it would appear that this was not merely a theoretical approach, but one which was actually realized. Once conquered, the *Arthasastra* also provided advice as to the organization and administration of a new province. It advocated the appointment of a prince or member of the royal family as governor but warned that princes may be a source of danger, and that competition between them could lead to wars of succession and the use of provincial forces against one another, as occurred with the bloody accession of Asoka in 272 BC.

Having removed fraternal threats to his new throne, Asoka planned the annexation of the last independent state of northern India, Kalinga. Trained for this task by governing Taxila as viceroy, Asoka led a brutal campaign and caused 100,000 deaths and 150,000 deportations. Appalled at the suffering that he had caused, Asoka revoked Kautilya's guidance and pursued a Buddhist-aligned philosophy of Dharma, which forsook violence. Far from being politically naive, the success of Asoka's new campaigns is illustrated by his bloodless expansion of hegemony over Sri Lanka, where his son converted the court to Buddhism. Asoka's edicts also record that he sent missionaries to his Hellenistic neighbours, but the spread of Buddhism into central and eastern Asia was only to occur later during Kushan times.

There is little extant Mauryan art or architecture, such monuments having been remodelled in later times, but the remnants suggest a centralized monumental style. Mirroring the iconoclasm of contemporary heterodoxical traditions, we have no images of the Mauryans themselves and the most striking survivals are Asoka's pillars which carried the emperor's edicts. Encapsulating his philosophy, these highly polished sandstone pillars were mostly quarried at Chunar on the Ganges and were surmounted by capitals bearing elephants, bulls, lions and horses. Reminiscent of Persian pillar styles, similarities may also be drawn between the Persian *apadana* (a pillared throne-room) and a rectangular pillared hall excavated

The Asokan rock edicts at Shahbaz Gahri are carved on two large boulders on the side of a rocky outcrop, and displayed edicts of the Mauryan empire to passing traders, pilgrims and armies, projecting the emperor's Dharma, or philosophy, and exerted a 'Mauryanization' effect by drawing local communities into a network of shared social, cultural and ritual relationships.

The Dharmarajika stupa at Taxila was first constructed by the Mauryan emperor Asoka in the 3rd century BC. A solid mound of limestone blocks built over Buddhist relics, it was located 3 km (1.9 miles) outside the Mauryan provincial capital in order to offer the monks relief from the temporal nature of city. Established as an imperial monument, within 100 years it had become hemmed in by a ring of private votive stupas, demonstrating the temporary nature of authority in the borderlands of the empire.

in the precincts of the Mauryan capital, Pataliputra. This elite construction dwarfs the rectangular brick-built merchant houses of Bhita which comprised simple ranges of rooms set around a central courtyard. Much more remains of Mauryan Buddhist monuments, including Asoka's great stone stupas at Sanchi and Taxila. Built over relics of the Buddha and his disciples or at the scene of notable events, these solid 10-m (33-ft) high mounds represent clear imperial investment. Less well preserved are the smaller apsidal constructions that frequently accompany them, such as the shrine at Sarnath, where the Buddha first preached.

MAURYAN SOCIAL AND POLITICAL STRUCTURE

Asoka's rule witnessed the Mauryan empire at its zenith, as it fused much of the Indian subcontinent under a single political entity. Ancient historians have used the scant sources to suggest the presence of a highly centralized empire ruled from Pataliputra, modern Patna, through a council of ministers and imperially appointed provincial governors. Physically, this division is supported by the pre-eminent size of the capital Pataliputra (1350 ha, 336 acres) and the monumental nature of its timber defences. There was a second tier of fortified provincial capitals at Taxila, Ujjain, Tosali, Sisupulgarh, Maski, Mahasthan and Suvarnagiri, with further categories of sub-provincial cities like Bhita and then towns and villages. Administrative activities, such as markets and mints, may have been reserved for higher-order centres, while the lower-order settlements were purely agricultural.

Despite apparent corroboration between archaeology and the *Arthasastra*, a number of recent scholars have argued that Mauryan centralization is over-emphasized and note that there was little state investment in communication networks and that the provincial capitals were all already established before Mauryan hegemony. This is not to suggest that the Mauryans did not exercise control over large areas, but that their empire was not necessarily uniformly administered or that it was fully centralized. One scholar, for example, has suggested that the distribution of Asokan edicts indicates an ideological, rather than political, claim over the landscape and that the Mauryans co-ordinated a network of shared social, ritual and cultural ties rather than a centralized empire.

THE DECLINE OF THE MAURYANS AND THEIR LEGACY

The integration imposed by the Mauryan dynasty weakened in the 2nd century BC. Kingdoms that had succumbed to Mauryan

The Great Stupa of Sanchi

In Sanchi, a small village in central north India, lies one of the greatest treasures of the Mauryan dynasty, the 'Great Stupa'. This is one of the 84,000 stupas (mound-like monuments that hold Buddhist relics) commissioned by the emperor Asoka in the 3rd century BC, measuring 20 m (65 ft) in diameter and 8 m (26 ft) high. After being vandalized in the 2nd century BC the stupa was rebuilt to double its size, and a three-tiered umbrella, known as a *chattra*, was placed on its flattened top, representing the Three Jewels of Buddhism: the Buddha, the Law and the community of monks.

In the 1st century BC, a stone balustrade with four monumental gateways that faced the cardinal directions was added. These gateways were known as 'toranas' and reach a height of 10 m (33 ft). They are intricately carved with symbols that represent the presence of the Buddha, such as empty thrones, footprints and umbrellas, and by narrative sculptures that show scenes from the life of the Buddha, integrated with everyday events to show how relevant the Buddha was to people's lives. These carvings were paid for by donations to the stupa that could be exchanged for spiritual merit. A devotee's favourite story could be engraved along with their name, though the Buddha was never shown as a person, the human form being too confining for his spirit.

By the end of the 1st century BC, the Great Stupa was the greatest Buddhist monument to be found in India.

BELOW AND OPPOSITE: The northern gateway of the Great Stupa.

ABOVE: Asoka's famous lion capital, erected at Sarnath, the scene of Gautama Buddha's first sermon. The four lions proclaim the Buddha's sermon to the universe, reinforced by the presence of the elephant, lion, horse and bull on the drum below and illustrating the wheel of Dharma in motion. The inverted lotus base of the capital is very reminiscent of Achaemenid pillar capitals.

BELOW: Gold double stater of Vima Kadphises depicting the emperor sitting on a stool. His portrait is surrounded by a Greek legend giving him the title *basileus*, or king. The reverse of the coin reflects the nature of his other subjects and depicts the Indian god Siva, and a bull with a legend declaring Vima Kadphises to be the lord of the world, as well as an avatar of Siva himself.

domination began to reassert their identities and the Hellenistic rulers of Afghanistan expanded southwards. Events came to a climax when Pushyamitra Sunga, commander-in-chief of the Mauryan army, murdered Asoka's grandson and proclaimed himself the founder of a new dynasty. Cultural and ideological ties broken, the newly emergent Sunga state became increasingly restricted to the Gangetic heartland.

The Mauryan empire was the first recorded attempt to fuse the disparate populations of localized kingdoms into a conglomeration of kingdoms, chiefdoms and dynasties within a centralized polity. Whether the Mauryans developed an empire in the modern sense of the term is debatable, but their cultural influence was widely spread, particularly along key trade routes. Kautilya's formative strategy of brutal conquest was replaced in the 3rd century BC by Asoka who undertook conquest by Dharma. By twining central Mauryan hegemony with Buddhist proselytization of the peripheries, Asoka achieved a far greater influence in the region than his grandfather. His method of fusing disparate religions, languages and ethnic identities into a unity remains an ideal for South Asia's rulers, and it is no coincidence that when India achieved independence from the British empire, the new state chose one of Asoka's pillars as its national emblem.

THE KUSHAN EMPIRE

The rise of the Kushan empire marks a distinct shift in power from the Ganges valley to the Northwest. Central Asia and the Indian subcontinent were bound into a single political entity. This movement is also reflected in the emergence of a very different social, political and economic system. From territorial holdings in Central Asia in the 2nd century BC, the Kushan dynasty first asserted regional hegemony under Vima Kadphises in the 2nd century AD and remained in power until 375. A nomadic tribe, the Kushans were driven from their homelands and settled in Bactria in modern Afghanistan. Expanding into Kashmir, they found themselves acting as a buffer between the two ancient superpowers of the

Romans (Chapter 8) and the Han (Chapter 10) by the 2nd century BC.

It was this unique vacuum between the ancient world's most powerful empires that allowed the Kushans to expand as they established control of the key trade route between the two states – the famed Silk Road. Constructing fortified strong-points at Dalverzin-tepe in Uzbekistan and Begram in Afghanistan, the Kushans were able to extract revenue from passing traders as reflected in the horde of Roman glass and metal and Chinese lacquer work recovered from a storeroom in the latter city. The presence of carved ivories from the Ganges in the hoard (pp. 240–41) indicates the Kushan grip on the branch routes into South Asia, controlled from Mathura on the Jamuna river, Sirsukh in the Taxila valley and Peshawar at the gates of the Khyber pass.

KUSHAN ART, ARCHITECTURE AND LITERATURE

For many years the chronology of the Kushan empire had been constructed from coins or oblique references within Chinese literature. This changed with the discovery of an inscription at Rabatak in Afghanistan in 1993, which revolutionized our knowledge. Written in the Bactrian language, the inscription provides a definitive king-list, as well as a list of the Kushans' provincial cities in northern India, including Kausambi and Pataliputra. The inscription is now supported by a number of documents and letters, discovered through the illegal looting of sites, which detail records of land-ownership across a large swath of the Silk Road from northern Pakistan to the Turfan Oasis in the west of China. This broad distribution and the common use of Bactrian script indicate the influence of the language which flourished under Kushan rule and provided a lingua franca for administrators and travelling traders alike.

Unlike the Mauryan use of existing cities, many of the Kushan strongholds had fresh foundations, such as the examples in the Taxila valley. Here, the old Hellenistic city of Sirkap was abandoned and a new site, Sirsukh, was created nearby. It enclosed an area of 1,370 x 1,000 m (4,511 x 3,280 ft) within a 5.5-m (18-ft)

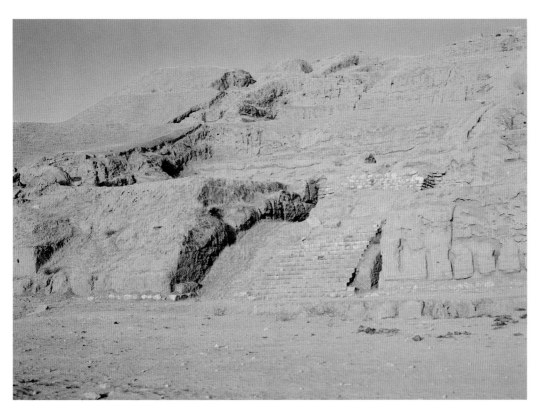

The Kushan ceremonial complex at Surkh Kotal in Afghanistan was built on a rocky hillside by Kanishka in the middle of the 2nd century AD. The hillside was graded by the cutting of huge terraces before a central brick and stone staircase was constructed leading from a well at the base of the slope to its summit. As the devotee ascended the staircase, they would have passed through terrace walls faced with inscriptions commemorating the dedication of the complex before reaching a columned fire-temple complete with life-size dynastic sculptures.

thick wall strengthened by a rounded berm. The layout of the city and the rounded stirrup bastions that punctuated the wall demonstrate strong links with the military architecture of Central Asia. The absence of thick occupation deposits within the enclosure suggests that Sirsukh may have housed a mobile force who could maintain control over a wide area, and similar plans have been identified at Begram and Dalverzin-tepe.

This investment in fortified strong-points reflects Kushan domination of a potentially hostile landscape and it can be assumed that speed and mobility allowed them to control key access points and regulate the trade networks that flowed along the Silk Road. There was a constant struggle between the Han, Central Asian princes, Romans and Parthians to establish control over this route. The Kushans established themselves as the dominant middle-men and this intercontinental trade network not only facilitated the movement of goods, but also the exchange of art, architecture, religion and philosophy.

Although the Kushans had a favoured style of military architecture, it is clear that they did not attempt to impose a single religious tradition on their empire but rather patronized key regional cults. Vima Kadphises' son, Kanishka (127–147), thus dedicated a major ceremonial complex at Surkh Kotal in Afghanistan which combined dynastic statues with a fire-temple but also established a major Buddhist stupa at Shahji-Dheri, in Peshawar to the south. His coinage demonstrates similar plurality, and he was equally happy to be portrayed with the Hellenistic deity Helios, the Iranian divinity Adsho and the Buddha, whose identities were confirmed in Greek script. In particular, the reign of Kanishka is associated with a dramatic rise in the number of Buddhist monasteries, some newly established and some constructed at already significant sites.

This plurality of religious devotion and patronage is also evident in Kushan art. While the Mauryans were largely iconoclastic, Kushan art focused on the individual, and it is no coincidence that the Gandhara and Mathura schools of sculpture emerged at this time. Originally an important centre of Jainism, the Kushans established Buddhist shrines and stupas at Mathura when it became their

The Begram Ivories

ABOVE: An ivory depicting four women. A large number of the ivory carvings from Begram depict women, often in groups of pairs, in scenes of leisure or relaxation. Scholars have suggested that these are scenes from the women's quarters, reflected by the lack of male figures.

OPPOSITE: Ivory depicting two women standing below a balustrade, adorned with striped *dhotis* and wearing elaborate headdresses and jewelry. The carving is indicative of the Mathura school of Gandharan art, and highlights the importance of the South Asian as opposed to Hellenistic influences of the Kushan empire.

In 1937 Joseph Hackin led an expedition to Begram, one of the ancient cities astride the Afghan portion of the Silk Road. While excavating two walled-up storerooms, Hackin was amazed to find a hoard of artefacts whose origins stretched from one end of the Silk Road to the other. Demonstrating the economic power of Begram, the hoard yielded Greco-Roman bronzes including a mask of Silenus, painted glass vessels from Egypt, Chinese lacquered vessels as well as Indian ivory brackets, figures and plaques.

Once thought to represent a hidden treasure of a Kushan king, it is now thought to represent a merchant or official's hoard demonstrating the wealth of goods flowing through the Kushan domain as their position at the centre of trade between east and west. Excavations suggest that the city was founded during the 1st millennium BC. It was captured by the Achaemenids during the 5th century BC and by Alexander the Great in 323 BC, and was later traded to the Mauryan

empire in 305 BC. After the collapse of the empire the city was absorbed into a number of Indo-Greek kingdoms, before becoming the summer capital of the Kushan empire. The city was finally abandoned after Sasanian incursions in AD 241.

The carvings found at Begram are unparalleled throughout the world, providing a unique insight into the ancient craft. Ivory working has a rich history within Early Historic South Asia, with examples found from archaeological excavations at Begram and Taxila in the northwest, at Patna, Kasuambi and Hastinapura in the Ganges valley, and from Anuradhapura in Sri Lanka. Textual evidence also suggests that the ancient city of Benares (Varanasi) had an entire street dedicated to ivory-carvers. Furthermore, an carved ivory figurine has been found as far away as Pompeii, complete with an inscription suggesting it was manufactured in or around Begram or Taxila. Buried in the eruption of AD 79, it provides proof of the far-flung trading networks of the Kushan empire.

BELOW: Gold coin of Kanishka depicting the emperor standing beside an altar. Crowned with an imperial tiara or helmet, he wears a long cloak and holds a standard in his left hand while sacrificing with his right. His portrait is surrounded by a Greek legend giving his name and the title 'King of Kings'.

BELOW: This freestanding image of Kanishka wears the characteristic long Kushan robe but it is strange that this ruler, so closely identified as a patron of Buddhism, is in a distinctly martial pose with legs apart. Closely grasping a mace and sword, though it is missing its head, the figure exudes imperial authority and presence and it barely needs the short inscription which states that the figure is the 'Great King, King of Kings, Son of God'.

southern capital. Well known for its production of Buddhas and Bodhisattvas, the Kushans commissioned their own images, including an outstanding life-size image of Kanishka carrying a sword and ceremonial mace. Even in the Buddhist heartland, however, the Kushans patronized less mainstream cults as indicated by the presence of a monumental naga, or snake shrine, at Sonkh, 22.5 km (14 miles) south of Mathura. Representing an attempt to incorporate a less centralized cult into their pantheon, it epitomizes the methods by which Kushan elites incorporated disparate regional populations into their empire.

KUSHAN SOCIAL AND POLITICAL STRUCTURE

Although the Kushan were masters at utilizing regional cults and traditions, as in the case of Kajula Kadphises who depicted himself as Augustus on a curule chair, this makes our understanding of their social and political structure more difficult. The Mathura statue of his son, Kanishka, is inscribed with the title 'Great King, King of Kings, Son of God', and it has been suggested that this indicates the Kushans adopted the South Asian concept of a universal ruler or Chakravartin. Son of God by title, the Rabatak inscription suggests that imperial administration was enforced by local officials, such as Nukunzuk the Ashtwalg and Shafar the Karalrang. It is also clear from Chinese records that client rulers were installed in peripheral areas like Kashgar, and that treaties were signed with petty rulers close to vulnerable passes such as with the rajas of Odi or Swat. Unlike the Mauryan system of a single imperial capital, the Kushan response to ruling an empire containing many different ethnicities, religions and languages stretching across two distinct regions was to operate from multiple capitals. With a summer capital in Begram, a winter capital in Mathura and a transitional capital in Peshawar, Kushan rulers were able to move annually between Central and South Asia. Moving the imperial powerbase from north to south ensured that the disparate parts of the empire were unified, and individual cities were governed by a mixture of princely viceroys and governors. Combining earlier Persian and

Hellenistic traditions with concepts of divine kingship reinforced the operational flexibility of the Kushan emperors.

THE DECLINE OF THE KUSHANS AND THEIR LEGACY

After the death of Vasudeva (191–225), the last of the Great Kushans, the empire was divided into eastern and western halves. At the same time as the rise of Ardashir, who had defeated the Parthian king and established the Sasanian dynasty in Persia, within 15 years the Sasanians had captured much of the western half of the Kushan empire. The major cities of Peshawar and Taxila were to fall to Ardashir's son Shapur I by 270 and their Gangetic territory was lost in the late 3rd century. The Kushan kings were left with a small territory in Central Asia, but were practically now no more than vassals of the newly emergent state. The dynasty held on until the 5th century when they were defeated by the Hephthalites who were to wreak havoc across much of northern India.

The Kushan empire successfully fused southern and Central Asia by respecting and patronizing regional traditions, while creating a central fortified line communication from the Oxus to the Ganges. The Kushan methods of imperial rule were not revolutionary, indeed they copied and imitated pervious Persian, Hellenistic and Indian rulers, but their choice of combinations was unique. Their coinage and religious patronage demonstrate these combinations, as does their ability to harness the newly emerged genre of iconic sculpture and to produce some of southern Asia's first imperial portraits. Fuelled by the luxury trade between east and west, they were also the first to establish formal winter and summer capitals, a feature which was to become an annual characteristic of later empires struggling to fuse the disparate communities of South Asia and its mountainous barriers to the north. Other than a distinct military and monastic architecture and iconic coinage, the Kushans' strategy of adopting regional customs and traditions had resulted in there being little linkage between the Kushans and modern South Asian communities who are greatly indebted to the Mauryans and Guptas. However, it was during Kushan hegemony that Buddhism began to spread along the Silk Road to Central Asia, China and beyond. This new branch of Buddhism, Mahayana, differed from the traditional Theravada Buddhism of South Asia, and was heavily influenced by Hellenistic and Persian ideas. The spread of Mahayana Buddhism was to have a huge impact upon the later development of east Asian ruling dynasties, which outlasted and superseded the Kushan empire from which it emerged.

THE GUPTA EMPIRE

With the decline of Kushan power in the northwest, their Indian empire was fragmented into petty domains run by individuals who termed themselves maharajas and rajas. One such princeling was Chandragupta, who married a daughter of the Licchavi clan, and received the kingdom of Magadha as dowry. Reviving the Kushan title of 'Great King of Kings' or 'maharajadhiraja', Chandragupta and his son, Samudragupta (335–75), in the 4th century mounted a series of military campaigns and extended hegemony over the old kingdoms of the Ganges, exacting tribute or suzerainty from states to the south. Described by a descendant as 'the exterminator of all kings … whose fame was tasted by the waters of the four oceans', Samudragupta's direct control was restricted to the Ganges basin with a series of client-kingdoms extending down the eastern coast of India.

It was during the reign of Chandragupta II that the Gupta empire consolidated control of northern India from the Arabian Sea to the Bay of Bengal during a series of campaigns between 388 and 409. This military strategy was paralleled by a political one, when Chandragupta II's daughter married Rudrasena II, king of the Vakataka tribe, in a move that secured the southern borders. In order to consolidate his power in the west, Chandragupta II established a second capital at Ujjain and secured trade routes to the newly annexed Indian Ocean ports on the west coast. These

BELOW: Gold coin depicting Chandragupta, who achieved power by marrying into the Licchavi clan and revived the title of 'Great King of Kings'.

LEFT: The façade and plan of Cave 26 at Ajanta. The rock-cut cave forms a *chaitya-griha*, or stupa chapel, and was entered through an entrance hall faced with square pillars, now broken. Three doorways led from this hall into a horseshoe-shaped central chamber. Lit by the great central *chaitya*, or window, the vaulted ceiling and pillared sanctuary was focused on a stupa at the end of the chamber. The pilgrims and attendants circumambulating the stupa must have drawn strength from the carvings on the walls depicting the Buddha's meditations continuing unaffected by the assault of the armies of Mara, the tempter.

OPPOSITE: This sandstone relief shows Vishnu asleep on the serpent Shesha, during the periodic annihilation and renewal of the world. Above are the gods Karttikeya, Indra, Shiva and Parvati, while he is surrounded by courtiers. It was found at the Vishnu Temple in Deogarh in Madhya Pradesh, one of the earliest surviving stone-built temples in India. Constructed during the Gupta period, it follows the trend of devoting religious structures to individual deities, rather than the wider pantheon.

OVERLEAF: This 5th-century fresco from Cave 17 at Ajanta depicts a scene from one of the former lives of the Buddha when, as Prince Visvantara, he and his family renounce their privileged life in the palace in order to alleviate the suffering of his father and people. Commissioned by a noble under the patronage of one of Gupta's vassals, King Harisena, it depicts the splendour and order of courtly life, as well as the complex web of relationships between Brahmins, Buddhists and their patrons.

ports, Broach, Chaul, Kalyan and Cambay, traded with the Mediterranean and western Asia and exported spices, peppers, sandalwood, pearls, semi-precious stone, indigo and herbs. In exchange they imported horses from Arabia, ivory from Ethiopia and goods from as far away as Madagascar and Zanzibar. On the east coast, ports such as Tamralipti, Ghantashala and Kadura were engaged in equally extensive trade with China and southeast Asia, allowing the Guptas access to the maritime Silk Road.

GUPTA ART, ARCHITECTURE AND LITERATURE

Ending the quest for the centralized socio-economic and religious integration of the Asokan ideal, the Gupta era is also referred to as the 'Classical Age of India' and is renowned for its commitment to art, architecture and Sanskrit poetry. Based at the old Mauryan imperial capital of Pataliputra, by the end of the Gupta reign northern India was transformed from a predominantly Buddhist landscape into one where Hindu cults were revived and where feudal land holdings were embedded. This revival was quite unlike that of the Kushan's use of Hindu gods on their coinage, as the Guptas established temples and patronized Brahmans by awarding them landholdings as well as re-establishing pre-Buddhist Vedic sacrifices, such as the Ashvamedha. This ancient rite allowed the king to release a sacrificial horse to wander for a year and then claim all the land through which it had travelled. Unifying imperial territory with Vedic sacrifices re-established the presence of a king of kings within South Asia and the court reinforced its precedence. The Vedic revival was paralleled by a revival in Sanskrit literature, and Chandragupta's court was revered for the presence of nine 'gems', or court poets. These included the dramatist Kalidasa, though another production of the era, the *Kama Sutra*, is rather more widely read today. Representing far more than simple titillation, it embodies the rigid norms of behaviour which governed the Gupta court. Finally, while textual sources record the establishment of Hindu temples throughout Gupta territories, few have survived though many of their Buddhist monuments

still stand. The monuments range from the cave shrines and monasteries of their Vakataka sub-rulers at Ajanta, whose frescoes detail the lives of princes and paupers, to the great stupa at Sarnath and the state-sponsored University at Nalanda.

GUPTA SOCIAL STRUCTURE AND DECLINE

The Gupta emperors, or rather Maharajadhirajas, ruled from their capital at Pataliputra and were surrounded by the members of their imperial court. Monumental inscriptions record the close presence of military and security advisers as well as court Brahmans and poets. Details concerning the social and political structure of the kingdom have survived in greater numbers. These records are not state archives but rather individual land-grants inscribed for prosperity on copper plates. From them it is possible to deduce that the core empire was divided into a number of territorial and administrative units, of which the largest was a *bhukti*, or province. The province was in turn subdivided into districts, or *pradesha*, and districts into villages and towns, where representative councils were involved in decision-making. As each copper plate represents the transfer of land from royal ownership to individual ownership, it is clear that the Guptas developed a strategy of permanent land alienation in return for religious, military and administrative services creating a feudal link between crown and landlords.

Kumaragupta (414–454) was the last undisputed Gupta ruler, but even in his final years internal instability was apparent with the growing strength of the Pushyamitra clan. Such was their threat to the Ganges heartland that Kumaragupta's son, Skandagupta, was given the task of pacifying them. As recorded in his Bhitari inscription, Skandagupta undertook to 'restore the fallen fortunes of his family' and returned to Pataliputra victorious having used the vanquished king as his 'footstool'. On the death of his father, Skandagupta's accession was contested by his older brothers and, though victorious in 455, his authority was continually threatened. While his inscription on the Bhitari pillar

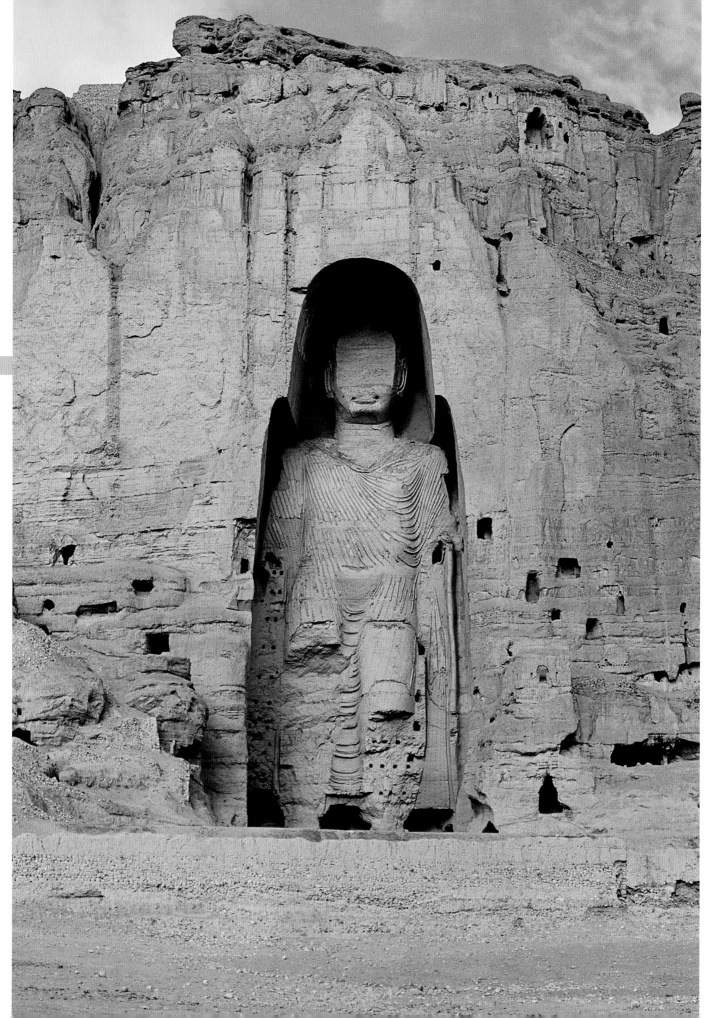

merely relates that he 'joined in close conflict with the Huns', the Hephthalite threat to the stability of the Gupta state was very real. The protective ring of client rulers quickly capitulated within 30 years of Skandagupta's death in 467, and the Hephthalites penetrated into the Ganges basin itself. With collection of imperial revenues seriously disrupted and overland trade destabilized, the Gupta empire had collapsed by the middle of the 6th century and a mosaic of petty rulers rose to fill the vacuum. Chinese Buddhist pilgrims witnessed the resulting chaos, and the monk Xuanzang recorded that 'the towns and villages are deserted … and in ruins … They are filled with wild shrubs and solitary to the last degree'. It would take the advent of Islam before the subcontinent would be united again.

While not as territorially expansive as the Mauryan or Kushan empires, the Gupta era represents a major shift in policy. When the Mauryan and Kushan attempts at centralization ended, a new model of client-kingdoms surrounding the imperial core run by governors was developed. As with the Kushans, they capitalized on the growing international trade routes and sought to maintain and revive earlier traditions by supporting not only Hindu institutions, but also Buddhist, Jain and other local traditions. This delicate political balance and freedom of religion ensured that art and literature from a wide variety of regions and backgrounds was able to prosper. While the Mauryan empire is seen as the first unified empire of India and the origins of the modern state of India, the Gupta empire is portrayed as its zenith. Often referred to as a 'Golden Age', to many modern Indians the Gupta period was an era during which arts, literature, architecture, religion, music and poetry flourished under a single unified state, ruled by Hindus.

THE NATURE OF EARLY INDIAN EMPIRES

Here we have highlighted the unique nature of 'empires' within India. The phases of fusion and fission evident from the archaeological record testify to the continual quest for a uniform but sustainable pattern of political rule and religious patronage. The Mauryan empire was a decentralized one, its ideology of Dharma disseminated from a series of regional strongholds. The Kushans, remarkably tolerant of regional diversity, were adept at adopting pre-existing religious traditions within their borders. This tolerance, or perhaps astute political strategy, is best demonstrated on Kushan coinage where depictions of Hellenistic, Persian and South Asian deities can be found, often on opposing sides of the same coin. Finally, the Gupta empire is probably the closest of all three ancient dynasties to the modern definition of an empire. It was firmly built around a relationship between an imperial core and vassal states – a solution also followed by the Mughals. Yet it was not until the arrival of the British in the 18th century that the entirety of the subcontinent was brought under the rule of a single polity – and even then this was only brought about by the maintenance of a tenuous web of political alliances between maharajas, nawabs and tribal elders, and the occasional brutal repression of uncooperative elements.

The desire of early British scholars to portray the Raj as the natural successor to earlier Indian empires and post-Independence scholars to portray Indian history as one of unity and cohesion has created Indian empires with pervasive static or retrogressive characteristics. This chapter has demonstrated that the opposite is the case, and that the Early Historic empires of South Asia continually experimented with different combinations of ideology, religious practice and administrative organization to reach a point of territorial sustainability.

OPPOSITE: The valley of Bamiyan is located 150 km (90 miles) northwest of Kabul in Afghanistan, and contained – until they were destroyed by the Taliban in 2001 – two of the largest Buddha images of the ancient world. The tallest, 53-m (174 ft) high, was cut out of the cliff and was accompanied by a smaller, 35-m (115-ft) high, image. Situated on the Silk Road between Balkh and Taxila, they represent the impact of Kushan patronage on the spread of Buddhism into Central Asia.

The Qin and Han empires of China rivalled those of Rome and Persia. At its greatest, Han power stretched over 3,000 km (2,000 miles) from Korea to Central Asia, and 2,500 km (1,500 miles) from Inner Mongolia to the tropics. Qin's ambition was boundless: control over its subjects' lives was exercised through an army of officials, who applied a strict code of laws and regulations, relying on constantly updated records of everyone and everything. All this depended on a single official language written in a standard script throughout the empire. But the harsh Qin dictatorship was self-defeating: its subjects were driven to rise up and destroy it soon after the First Emperor's death. Han inherited many aspects of the Qin bureaucratic state, but never could or would apply Qin's absolute dictatorship to the whole empire. Most emperors were ineffectual, and the bureaucracy tended to run itself. Yet by muddling through Han lasted 400 years, and left as a legacy the assumption that the Chinese world should be under a single supreme authority.

PREVIOUS PAGES: These terracotta armoured infantrymen drawn up in columns of four were the main force of the army to guard the First Qin Emperor after death. They were found buried east of the emperor's tomb near modern Xi'an, and were modelled on the men who made up the brutally efficient war machine that conquered China for him.

The Qin and Han Emperors

This table follows the Chinese convention of dating reigns from the first new year after the death of the previous emperor. Very short reigns have been omitted.

QIN
221–210 BC	Qin Shi Huang di, First Qin Emperor
209–207 BC	Qin Er Huang di, Second Qin Emperor

WESTERN OR EARLIER HAN
206/2–195 BC	Gaozu or Gaodi (Liu Bang)
194–188 BC	Huidi
187–180 BC	Empress Lü
179–157 BC	Wendi
156–141 BC	Jingdi
140–87 BC	Wudi
86–74 BC	Zhaodi
73–49 BC	Xuandi
48–33 BC	Yuandi
32–7 BC	Chengdi
6–1 BC	Aidi
AD 1–5	Pingdi

XIN
9–23	Wang Mang

EASTERN OR LATER HAN
25–57	Guangwudi
58–75	Mingdi
76–88	Zhangdi
89–105	Hedi
107–125	Andi
126–144	Shundi
147–167	Huandi
168–189	Lingdi
190–220	Xiandi

LEFT: A kneeling crossbowman with some of the pigment with which he was once brightly painted. He was from a smaller, more mobile unit of the buried army consisting mainly of chariots and cavalry. In Qin law a coat of armour was the fine for many minor offences.

Additional Han territory

Loosely held Han territory

Qin territory, later taken over by Han

Loosely held Qin territory

Ferghana

Xiongnu

Jiaohe

Wuhuan

Dunhuang

Zhongshan

Xianyang

Chang'an
(Xi'an)

Luoyang

Yellow

Yangtze

Changsha

Lingqu Canal

Bay of Bengal

South China Sea

0 400 km

0 400 miles

▶ Ying Zheng, future First Emperor, becomes king of Qin
247 BC

▶ Widespread rebellions in conquered states end Qin
209–206 BC

◀ Massive Han offensives against Xiongnu on northern frontier
127–119 BC

▶ Han conquests in today's Xinjiang and Central Asia
108–90 BC

◀ End of Western Han. Wang Mang makes himself emperor of Xin (New) dynasty
AD 8

◀ Bitter struggles between court eunuchs and regular officials
AD 166 onwards

▶ Definitive texts of five Confucian classics inscribed on stone in Luoyang
AD 175

◀ Beginning of resistance wars by Qiang people in west of empire
AD 107

▶ Yellow Turbans rebellion
AD 184

200 BC   100 BC   0   AD 100   AD 200

▶ Han vassal kings lose much power after failed rising
154 BC

▶ Han power in parts of Xinjiang restored
AD 91–101

◀ Warlord Dong Zhuo destroys capital Luoyang
AD 190

◀ Xiongnu shanyu (khan) accepts Han suzerainty
51 BC

▶ Liu Bang wins post-Qin civil wars, becomes Han emperor
202 BC

▶ Liu Xiu (Emperor Guangwudi) reestablishes Han dynasty (Eastern Han)
AD 25

▶ Shi Huang di proclaims himself First Qin Emperor after conquering other Chinese states
221 BC

◀ Risings bring down Wang Mang regime
AD 17–23

◀ Last Han emperor deposed
AD 220

The Qin and Han empires were big. Although their territories varied and were in places ill defined, they never covered less than 1,600 km (1,000 miles) from east to west and from north to south. They were populous: in AD 2 the Han government had nearly 60 million subjects on its books. With the exception of a few frontiers and inaccessible regions, these millions were closely governed by a centralized bureaucracy that imposed a single written language and a high culture and had more control over people's lives than any large state in Europe before the 18th century. In many areas of technology they were ahead of the Roman world. Qin and Han between them set the pattern for Chinese regimes for the next 2,000 years.

The Qin empire, founded in 221 BC, was meant to endure for ever, but actually lasted only 15 years, not long enough to impose any

lasting changes on those parts of China that had not long been part of the kingdom of Qin. But the totalitarian bureaucratic dictatorship that had made the state of Qin so effective as a warfare state since the middle of the 4th century BC long survived the Qin empire. It gave Han, the regime that emerged from Qin's wreckage, the tools with which to make an empire that lasted for so long that, by the time it ended in AD 220, the pre-Han world was ancient history.

In 221 BC the king of Qin believed he had transformed the Chinese world. Over the previous nine years his armies – the real-life equivalents of the brigade of imposing terracotta soldiers buried to guard his tomb – had destroyed all the other states of China in a series of blitzkrieg wars. He had imposed unity after a period of over 500 years in which war and the threat of war between rival Chinese states were endemic, and now he wanted a more splendid title for himself than any Chinese ruler before him. He chose *huang di*, a term which implies not just 'emperor', its usual English translation, but also 'god'. He was the First Emperor, his successor would be the Second Emperor, and so it would go on till the Ten Thousandth Emperor. His permanent new order soon turned out to be as much of a delusion as the personal immortality to which he devoted his last years. Eleven years later he was dead, and after four more the Qin empire was gone.

Liu Bang, the Han dynasty's founder, joined the rebellions against Qin after the First Emperor's death as a minor local government official on the run. By skill and luck, he came out on top in the civil wars that followed the fall of Qin, becoming emperor in 202 BC. Far from having a grand plan to change the world, his whole career was one of improvising quick solutions to immediate problems. Yet he and his heirs managed in time to turn a precarious regime into a stable one. The Han empire, which both rejected and continued the Qin model of rule, lasted. After Wang Mang, an imperial in-law, replaced the Han with his own Xin (New) dynasty in AD 8 the most effective resistance to his rule came from peasant rebels; but those who put a new regime in place did so under the banner of Han. A new Han dynasty was created that continued for another 200 years.

THE RISE AND FALL OF QIN

Qin began as a poor and backward state on the edge of the Chinese world. Its chiefs had covered the flight from the Wei valley in 771 BC of the former supreme Chinese rulers, known as the Western Zhou, then taken most of the valley for themselves and been recognized as a Chinese state. The Wei valley was well protected by natural defences from rivals to the east, but for over 400 years Qin was a second-rank player in the wars to control China's core area, the north China plain, as it had no direct access to it. It lagged behind the transformation of the central Chinese states.

All this changed in the middle of the 4th century BC. Between 356 and 340 BC Duke Xiao of Qin enforced drastic reforms to strengthen his state and weaken society. These reforms were proposed and implemented by Shang Yang, a political consultant who had come to Qin from the east. Households were organized into groups of five and ten, with each member liable for crimes committed by any other member. Hereditary aristocracy was replaced by a system in which rank could be won only by serving the state in agriculture and war. Feudal relations gave way to direct rule by state officials. Idlers and traders would have their wives and children enslaved. Any comment on the reforms, even praise, was punished.

These and other changes gave the state direct control over its whole population and set it on the way to being a formidable military power. Qin used deliberately harsh measures to compel its subjects to obey it and serve its interests. Although Shang Yang's methods were somewhat relaxed after his death, the essentials were maintained. They worked. Qin grew stronger, pushing back its eastern neighbours and making bold moves to the south. In 316 BC Qin took the Sichuan basin, and in 278 BC the capital of the main Yangtze power, Chu. Diplomatic and military ruthlessness gave Qin strategic

ABOVE: The watchtowers along the Qin and Han northern frontiers were key components in the defence system. These Han towers in Gansu have outlasted the wall itself. Such strongpoints were all in sight of others and could report Xiongnu activity with beacon fires by night and smoke by day. Some have yielded detailed records of Han soldiers' lives.

OPPOSITE: These model spearmen from a Western Han tomb are much smaller and cruder than the First Emperor's larger-than-life warriors. These painted clay figurines probably held wooden shields in their left hands.

OPPOSITE: This infantryman in his coat of iron-plate armour was one of some 6,000 terracotta soldiers, all slightly larger than life-sized, found in a huge pit to the east of the mausoleum. The soldiers were armed with crossbows, light halberds, pikes and swords. Their officers rode chariots. A nearby pit held about 90 battle chariots and over 100 cavalrymen together with crossbowmen, and a third one a command centre.

LEFT: In 1980 archaeologists found exquisitely made half-sized gilt bronze models of two of the emperor's personal vehicles near the mausoleum. One was this light, fast chariot with crossbows and arrows by the driver that may have been for the emperor to use on his posthumous hunting trips. The other was a larger, enclosed carriage in which he could travel unseen.

BELOW: A pit near the tomb contained terracotta jugglers and this strong man, who may have supported several of them as they performed aloft. Another pit contained elegant bronze water birds and terracotta musicians.

The First Emperor's Buried World

After the First Qin Emperor achieved greater control over the living than any Chinese ruler before him, he squandered lives and resources pursuing immortality. When that failed and he died at the age of 49 he already had a vast underground palace complex of an unprecedented size (some estimates say it covers more than 50 sq. km) in which to enjoy and dominate the spirit world after death. Its construction had begun when he became king of Qin as a 12-year-old, and after the conquest 700,000 labourers were forced to work on it. Though the man-made hill near Xi'an in which he was buried (below) has yet to be excavated, some of the pits around it have revealed a life-size clay army as well as full-scale models of civilian officials and servants. When the mausoleum is opened we will know whether there really are the rivers of mercury representing the rivers of China in it of which the Han historian Sima Qian tells us.

The writing brushes of Qin civil officials were as essential to the Qin dictatorship as the swords and crossbows of the army. Written records and a constant flow of information kept everyone under the state's control. This bureaucrat, whose rank is shown by his hat and clothes, was in a pit closer to the emperor's underground palace than the buried army.

domination over the rich north China plain. In 260 BC the Qin army reportedly buried alive 400,000 soldiers who had surrendered. However, Qin ruthlessness was not reckless: it did not devour territory faster than the Qin dictatorship could absorb it.

This step-by-step approach changed after the future First Emperor came of age as king of Qin and took full power in 238 BC. Seventeen years later he had conquered the whole Chinese world and made himself emperor. His ambitions and his vanity knew no limits, as is clear from the inscriptions full of extravagant praise for his own achievements he had carved around the empire. After the conquests the harsh Qin dictatorship was forced upon a huge new population that resented it. The First Emperor used his power not just to impose unified laws, regulations, script, weights and measures on the whole empire, but also to make his new subjects work on vast projects. The biggest were war on the northern frontier and building, manning and supplying the Great Wall. This required huge numbers of conscripts from all over the empire. A network of highways was built from the capital Xianyang. Hundreds of thousands of families were forcibly resettled. Seven hundred thousand labourers were made to build his vast palaces and mausoleum. The severity of Qin rule eventually became self-defeating. In 209 BC rebellions spread all across the newly conquered territories, with locally recruited petty officials using their knowledge of the system to bring it down.

The Qin dictatorship had depended on an extraordinarily effective bureaucracy in which every post had its job description that the holder had to fulfil to the letter. No official, no matter how high or how low, had any security of tenure. He could be dismissed or punished for failure. Among the terracotta figures found in the First Emperor's huge burial complex are a few civilian officials. They do not look as impressive as the soldiers, but with their writing brushes they were as essential to state power within Qin as the armies were for dealing with external enemies. The officials

kept detailed information on everyone so that no one could escape the demands of the state. They even reported how the rainfall was affecting the crops place by place and kept records of the girth of each draught ox each year so that their keepers could be rewarded or punished. The Qin information dictatorship was continued by Han.

A web of laws and regulations spelled out what officials and commoners must and must not do. If a criminal offence was committed legal officials had to find out exactly what had happened and then apply the correct punishments as specified in the code. There were regulations on how to investigate a crime, interrogate suspects, and write up the investigation. Oral statements had to be written down and put into the case file. If something in a statement seemed wrong the suspect had to be questioned again, and asked to explain any discrepancies. Torture was only to be used as a last resort because statements made under duress were unreliable, and its use had to be minuted in the file. Investigating officers could be punished for failing to get the truth. Qin legal culture was a formidable assertion of the state's determination to know everything. With modifications, Han continued to use Qin law.

IMPROVISING HAN

Liu Bang joined the rebellions against Qin as a minor official and emerged from the seven years of chaos and civil war that followed to become the first emperor of a new dynasty, Han, in 202 BC. He rose from nowhere to obtain supreme power by knowing how to find a quick solution in a crisis. He was a fixer, even something of a trickster, and a clear-sighted political realist who knew how to get out of trouble and build coalitions. Although no soldier himself, he could use generals. When his armies took over the former Qin heartlands in 206 BC, he kept them in working order. His people seized Qin's military maps and central databases, and put the local bureaucracy into the service of his new local regime. The state machinery of pre-imperial Qin gave him a firm power base that enabled him to win the civil wars that followed the end of Qin and become Han emperor.

In 227 BC the state of Yan sent Jing Ke to the Qin capital with the freely given head of a top Qin defector in a box (bottom centre) and a map of some Yan territory. This was bait to get Jing Ke close enough to the king of Qin, the future First Emperor, to kill him with a poisoned dagger. When the king broke free (right) Jing Ke, obstructed by the royal doctor (left), threw his dagger, only for it to stick in a pillar. The heroic failure was illustrated over 260 years later in this rubbing of a bas-relief.

Beyond the firmly controlled Qin heartlands his empire was shaky from the outset. He did not have the resources to impose direct rule over the whole of China. He kept promises to allies in the civil wars to recognize them as vassal kings outside the Qin core area, and when they rose against him this justified crushing them. Replacing them as vassal kings with members of the Liu family also led to troubles for his successors when they in turn rebelled, but it bought time for Han to consolidate itself. None of the rebellions succeeded. Under his successors direct rule was extended over more of the empire and vassal kings and marquises lost most of their powers. One problem, however, that was never solved was that of the northern frontier.

EMPERORS AND OFFICIALS

In theory the Han system was run by an all-powerful emperor. The founders of both Han dynasties understood the real world and could use power. They rose from obscurity in times of chaos and had to be realists to take the throne by force. Liu Bang's widow, Lü Zhi, had been his active and tough-minded partner throughout his dangerous career. From his death in 195 BC until her own 15 years later she ruled alone, first as regent for her son then, after his death, as reigning empress. This offended traditional views about a woman's place, but as a co-founder of the Han dynasty she was able to defy them. However, by trying to arrange a takeover of the Liu family regime by her own Lü family, she went too far. She made too many enemies, and the Lü were slaughtered

once she died. After the founders few emperors made any impact. Many of them were chosen precisely because they were young children whose powers would be handled by regents.

Nearly all premodern Chinese historians of Qin and Han have given most of their attention to court politics, central government and the most powerful regional leaders. Their accounts show weaknesses in the dynastic system that one might think would have been fatal to it. There was no fixed rule, such as that of primogeniture, to determine succession. Another related weakness was that an emperor's wife did not necessarily have the same interests as the ruling house until he was dead and her son succeeded him. The higher-ranking wives of an adult emperor all wanted to produce a son and potential heir. This made for vicious struggles. There are plenty of stories of empresses trying to do away with rivals and their sons. Once a palace woman was mother of an emperor or potential emperor she would often use her position to advance her own blood relatives. An empress dowager could work with male relatives and trusted officials to have a son or a malleable young boy of the imperial clan chosen as emperor so as to allow them a long period of regency. The families and factions of rival palace women sometimes fought to the death in the streets or in the law courts. The highest point of imperial in-law power came in AD 8 when one of them, Wang Mang (45 BC–AD 23), replaced the Western Han dynasty with his own Xin (New) dynasty. His life and his regime both ended amid mass uprisings 15 years later. Yet despite all these problems at the centre the

Voices of Empire

We know the Qin and Han worlds largely from the work of historians, who drew mainly on official and family records. The most influential of these was Sima Qian, who also used any other spoken and written evidence he could find. He records both the Qin propaganda and the business thinking quoted here. We also have a probably fictionalized account of a court conference in 81 BC that lets us listen in on great and fundamental debates on Han foreign and domestic policy. In the 11th century a research team led by Sima Guang cut and pasted many Qin and Han sources with meticulous care into the relevant parts of *Zi zhi tong jian* (The Universal Mirror to Aid Government), a huge, reliable and invaluable annalistic history of the Chinese world from 403 BC to AD 957. From the middle of the 20th century onwards some original Qin and Han documents have been found, including the legal manuals excerpted here.

'Everywhere under heaven minds and wills are one. Arms and armour are standardized; all write in the same script … The August Emperor's spirit power preserves the four quarters, smites rebellion and uproots evil, brings benefits and prosperity. Everything comes forth in abundance because he rules in accordance with the seasons.' An excerpt from the Qin regime's self-praise in an inscription carved in 219 BC

A manual on criminal procedure was buried in the coffin of a Qin law officer in 217 BC. All interviews had to be written down. Torture could be used, but was best avoided because it yielded unreliable evidence

'In handling cases be able to use written records to investigate what is said. The best way is to find out the truth about people without flogging them. Flogging is an [inferior] method. Fear [of torture] can lead to failure [to get at the truth].'

The following example of penal logic is from an early Han law code excavated in 1983

'When tattooing is the penalty for an offence, one who has already been tattooed shall have the nose cut off. One who has already had the nose cut off shall have the left foot amputated. One who has already had the left foot amputated shall have the right foot amputated. One who has already had the right foot amputated shall be castrated.'

The historian Sima Qian, writing in about 100 BC, comments on wealth

'The common people humble themselves before those who are ten times richer than themselves, fear those a hundred times richer, do labour service for those a thousand times richer, and are enslaved by those 10,000 times richer. That is the way things are. To get rich from poverty handicraft is better than farming, and trading better than handicraft. Hanging around the market gateway is better than doing fine embroidery. In other words, trading brings wealth to the poor.'

The warlord Dong Zhuo inflicted total destruction on the Eastern Han capital Luoyang in AD 190, as told in *Zi zhi tong jian* 'Dong Zhuo rounded up all the rich households, executed them on criminal charges and confiscated their property. Incalculable numbers died. The millions of surviving commoners were all forced to move to Chang'an. Driven along by foot soldiers and cavalrymen, they trampled each other underfoot, starved and were robbed. Piles of corpses filled the roads … For 200 *li* around every building was destroyed.'

Modern-day Mongolian horsemen, descendants of the Xiongnu who have kept alive the traditions of pastoral nomadism on the grasslands they once controlled.

'Every family has horses for war and good bows, and every man has the use of them. In a crisis all they have to do is string their bows and mount their horses … It takes only a wave of the command flag for all to obey.' A policy conference in 81 BC at the court of the emperor Zhaodi debated how to deal with Han's powerful northern neighbours the Xiongnu. The anti-war party maintained that the Xiongnu were unbeatable in battle machinery of government generally continued to function in the capital and in the provinces.

The one Western Han emperor who was far from ineffectual was Liu Che, known as the emperor Wudi, who came to the throne in 141 BC as a boy of about 15 and ruled until his death in 87. His reign was by far the longest in both Han dynasties, and he was an active emperor who wanted to make progress. Under him men and resources were poured into wars with the Xiongnu, in Central Asia and in the south. However, regular tax and conscription were not enough to pay for these wars. The state had to establish monopolies in iron and salt, and levy duties on alcohol. His activism put intolerable strains on state and society. Weak emperors sometimes did less harm.

The next Han dynasty, later known as Eastern Han as it made its capital in Luoyang, presented itself as a restoration of the earlier or Western Han based in Chang'an. Although it was different from Western Han in some important ways, its emperors were also rather ineffective after the founder. The problem of overpowerful families of emperors' mothers continued. Another group who were more prominent than under the Western Han were palace eunuchs. They could be very useful to emperors and empresses who had been brought up under their influence. Unlike palace ladies and intact males, they could move between the harem and the outer world. Especially in the last century of Han rule there were frequent and at times bloody conflicts between the eunuchs and the regular bureaucracy.

All these problems mask the amazing achievement of the Han state in holding together so large an empire for so long, and in creating a Chinese identity that has lasted. Here the legacy of Qin administration proved to be

Painted pottery cavalrymen, about one-third life size, from a force of over 500. They were found in pits by the tombs of two top officials at Yangjiawan near the Han founder's imperial mausoleum north of the capital of Chang'an. These horsemen still rode without stirrups.

lasting and effective. While rival cliques struggled for control of the palace and of key central government offices the provincial and local government machinery continued to function. Population registers were kept, tax and labour service levied, criminal laws enforced. The Han empire was a triumph of bureaucracy. The day-to-day administrative documents of Han frontier garrisons on the Great Wall that have been preserved in the dry sands of Gansu show government clerks keeping records of the soldiers, their performance in archery tests, their health, their movements and more. The amount of data recorded would tax a modern army's ability to process information. Until the middle of the Eastern Han men were conscripted for military service. The bureaucracy's efforts to keep records and an audit trail can be seen in the cemeteries for convicts who died when building the walls of the Eastern Han capital at Luoyang. With most bodies was a broken piece of brick on which the dead man's place of origin, criminal status, name and date of death were unceremoniously scratched, presumably so that the officials responsible could show where the men missing from their rolls had gone.

Even when magnates gained more control of local government by putting their nominees into jobs, the officials were still Han officials. Only in the final decades of the dynasty were forms of social organization outside the state's actual or nominal control allowed to develop, such as the Five Pecks of Rice cult in the southwest. And Han methods of bureaucratic rule were all continued under its successor states.

FRONTIERS

The First Qin Emperor's domains in 221 BC were rather smaller than the ones over which the Eastern Han lost control over 400 years later. At the beginning of the Qin empire China – if we use the label to refer to regions under the rule of Qin or Han – extended in the north from southern Liaoning across to northern Shanxi and Shaanxi. In the northwest it included eastern Gansu but not today's Lanzhou. In the southwest direct rule was limited to the fertile Sichuan basin between Chengdu and Chongqing. Only some areas south of the Yangtze had been absorbed into the Chinese world, notably the river plains and lakes of its southern tributaries and the Nanjing, Suzhou and Hangzhou region. Qin opened up an inland route along rivers connected by the well-named Miraculous Canal (Ling Qu) near Guilin to today's Guangdong, but was able to establish

Some of the 1,800 painted terracotta foot soldiers and 100 bandsmen from the same group of pits as the horsemen opposite. Infantry made up the bulk of Qin and Han armies. The officials they guard are thought to have been Zhou Bo and his son Zhou Yafu who served the early Han emperors well in war.

no permanent Chinese presence so far south. The great majority of the Qin population lived on and around the north China plain and in the valleys of the Wei, Fen and Luo rivers that flowed into the Yellow river.

The northern frontier was a vital concern of the Qin and Han empires as the Xiongnu, mounted peoples of the grasslands to their north, posed a military threat to the whole of north China. Nomadic pastoralism – living primarily from the animals you keep and moving with them to find pasture – had developed on steppes across Eurasia in the 1st millennium BC. Some pastoralists moved huge distances and interacted along a belt of grasslands from the Black Sea to areas north of China. Well-preserved bodies in Xiongnu and pre-Xiongnu tombs in the Mongolian Republic and southern Siberia show both 'Mongoloid' and 'Caucasian' features.

In aggressive campaigns from 214 BC Qin drove the Xiongnu from the Ordos region (the area of today's Inner Mongolia inside the great northern bend of the Yellow river), and set up garrisons and settlers on both sides of the river. It built the first Great Wall from today's eastern Gansu to the coast, joining up the northern walls of earlier Chinese states. The immense human cost of Qin's forward policy contributed much to the hatred of the Qin regime by its own subjects. The policy was also a disaster for the

This bronze flying horse with a swallow under its hoof was found in a 2nd century AD Han tomb in Gansu. Fine thoroughbreds from west of the Tianshan and Pamirs that needed much better fodder than China's own smaller, tougher horses were extremely highly valued by Han emperors, who paid high prices in lives and wealth to get them.

Xiongnu, who reacted by making themselves a military power.

Being a Xiongnu meant belonging to a political-military confederacy under a leader called the shanyu. The confederacy was made up of many different ethnic or tribal groups, and was a political rather than an ethnic label. In 209 BC, when Qin was weakened by widespread rebellions, the Xiongnu recovered the Ordos region. Under Modun, the patricidal second shanyu, they took over their eastern neighbours and drove the Yuezhi, Indo-European speakers, from western Gansu. In 200 BC the Han founder barely escaped from encirclement by the Xiongnu inside the frontier, near today's Datong in northern Shanxi.

The absence of natural barriers along most of the frontier meant that the Xiongnu could choose where to concentrate their cavalry to push far into China proper. They lived both north and south of the belt of deserts, the Gobi, that divide the grasslands of Inner Mongolia from those in the Mongolian Republic. This gave them strategic depth, and enabled them to keep their families, flocks and herds far from the frontier and Chinese counter-attacks.

The Inner Mongolian grasslands posed a dilemma for the Qin and Han. If they pushed their defence line far enough north to prevent the Xiongnu from occupying them they had to meet the astronomical cost of feeding garrisons at the end of long overland supply routes. But if Chinese defences were far enough south for convenient supply they were open to attacks by Xiongnu and others who were riding fresh horses that were well fed on the grasslands. Options open to Qin and Han included passive defence, or the Great Wall strategy; counter-attacks and pre-emptive strikes to destroy Xiongnu herds and families north of the desert belt; dividing the Xiongnu with big payments to clients; and a combination of two or more of these. All options were used, and all were expensive. The state had to be strong to make the people meet the costs.

For the first 60 years and more of the Han dynasty the Xiongnu dominated the north, raiding deep into China. Xiongnu power extended into Xinjiang and linked up with the Qiang people of what is now Qinghai, south Gansu and northwest Sichuan. Han tried and failed to buy the Xiongnu off until the reign of the emperor Wudi (140–87 BC).

Wudi launched a series of huge offensives from 127 to 117 BC. The most devastating of these campaigns in 121 BC and 119 BC were co-ordinated deep strikes from several points along the frontier into the northern heartlands of the Xiongnu, killing their people and animals. Han recreated the border defences and compelled settlers to occupy the disputed territories. These wars imposed intolerable losses on both sides. Exhaustion resulted in a comparatively peaceful period until in 101 BC Wudi began a new series of offensive wars that lasted until his death in 87 BC.

There is much first-hand evidence in documents found along the Great Wall on the organization and everyday life of frontier garrisons. With time Han developed a successful policy of dividing the Xiongnu against each other. The Eastern Han succeeded in bringing the Southern Xiongnu into supposed submission and in getting other steppe peoples to drive the Northern Xiongnu away. These policies were not quite the triumphs they seemed. The Southern Xiongnu were allowed to reoccupy the frontier grasslands, and Han power was pulled back from much of northern Shanxi and Shaanxi. The consequences were to be catastrophic. Generations of Southern Xiongnu learned how China worked from the inside. Within a century of the fall of Han they were to sack Luoyang and destroy a Chinese dynasty, the beginning of nearly three centuries in which north China was under barbarian rule. And the removal of the Northern Xiongnu only left a vacuum beyond the northern frontier into which Xianbei, Wuhuan and other steppe peoples moved, who were to cause trouble in the future.

Fears about the Xiongnu drove Han to extend its power and influence into Central Asia, Han's Western Regions. Under Wudi the first strategic move to the west against the Xiongnu was sending an envoy, Zhang Qian, on a dangerous mission far into Central Asia to

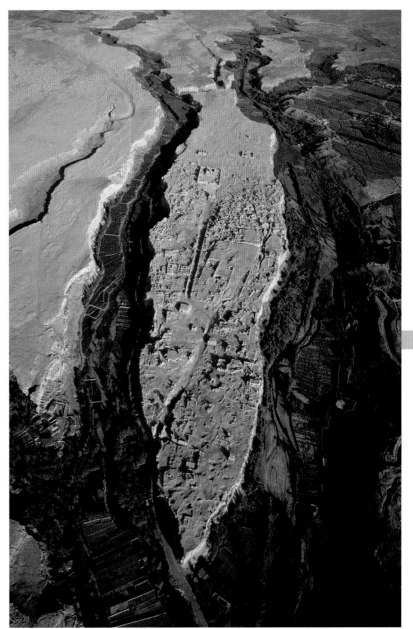

contact the Xiongnu's old victims the Yuezhi, now resettled west of the Tianshan range, and establish a strategic alliance against the common enemy. Zhang returned around 126 BC, having spent ten years as a prisoner of the Xiongnu and having failed to win the Yuezhi alliance. But he could supply a lot of detailed intelligence about the settled and nomadic peoples of what is now Xinjiang and its western neighbours from Kazakhstan to Afghanistan. This informed Han's next moves. Han settled and walled the lands the Xiongnu had taken from the Yuezhi in the Gansu corridor as far as Dunhuang to 'cut off the Xiongnu's right arm' and stop them linking up with the Qiang of the

The city known in Chinese as Jiaohe 'Joined Rivers', on a tongue of land where two rivers join. It was the capital of the non-Chinese state of Jushi (Turpan) on the only practical route between the Xiongnu grasslands north of the Tianshan range and the oases of the Tarim basin to the south. Han and Xiongnu long struggled to control it.

Great landowners in the 1st to 3rd centuries AD had their tombs decorated with images of life on their estates. Ox-drawn farm equipment, such as what can be seen in the mural, was one of the marks of wealth.

Tibet-Qinghai highlands. This gave Han access to the Tarim basin. This huge region's inhabitants were mostly 'Caucasian'-featured speakers of Indo-European languages living in widely separated oases.

For the next 200 years and more Han and Xiongnu contended for mastery in Xinjiang. Western Han achieved some spectacular but short-lived military conquests beyond the Tianshan range, including Ferghana in today's Uzbekistan. The small oasis states of the Tarim basin, which controlled movement across a region that is mostly desert, came under direct or indirect Han domination for much of this time. However, those states maintained their own identities, adding Chinese elements to their cultures in which Iranian and Indian influences were also strong. Their rulers used Han power and connections for their own purposes and were not absorbed into China. In the end the Xiongnu were beaten and Han could not sustain the costs of occupation. Contact with China did not end after Han had left the area, however, and the trade with the Western Regions that most influenced China was the importing of Buddhism.

Relations with Qiang and other peoples of the Eastern Tibet-Qinghai plateau were no better than those with the Xiongnu, especially in the Eastern Han period. The Qiang resisted Chinese rule and reoccupied large areas of the northwest. To the northeast Han extended its power into southern Liaoning and northern Korea as part of its grand strategy of containing the Xiongnu.

The southern frontier offered fertile land and far more opportunities for expansion. The mountainous terrain south of the Yangtze river divided the many peoples living in the valleys and the uplands. The southern peoples could fight fiercely in defence of their own lands, as they did right through to the 19th century, but they could not threaten the existence of the empire.

The colonization of the south was begun by Qin, which established lines of communication to Guangdong, and in the southwest to the lands south of Sichuan. Much more was done under Han. Wudi's wars of expansion south of the Yangtze river significantly increased the size of China. In some places local peoples were subdued, driven back into the hills or, if they resisted, killed. Elsewhere they were left alone. Some rulers appeared to have submitted to Han but in fact maintained their independence. There were islands of Han rule in today's southernmost provinces of China, as in parts of northern Vietnam, though large areas were not controlled. Fujian was almost untouched. Sometimes local cultures were destroyed and the people uprooted, such as when defeated Yue peoples were forcibly moved to north of the Yangtze.

By the end of Han the centre of gravity of the Chinese world had shifted south. Much of the northern and western frontier regions had in reality been lost to non-Chinese peoples. The Central Asian empire in Xinjiang and beyond, which had been repeatedly won and lost between about 110 BC and AD 150, was gone by the end of the dynasty. In the south, by contrast, the expansion of China along river valleys was to be permanent.

SOCIETY AND ECONOMY

The great majority of people lived off the land. The main food crops in the north were broomcorn and foxtail millet, which with their relatively low demand for water outside the summer rains were well suited to the unirrigated dry farming techniques that prevailed there. In the wetter climate of the south rice was the staple crop. Millets and rice had both been grown in China for at least

7,000 years before Qin and Han. Those who could afford it ate wheat.

In the 300 years before Han, farmers had swapped a largely Neolithic toolkit of wood, shell, stone and bone for iron-bladed tools, thus greatly increasing the output of food. Without that agricultural revolution there would not have been the grain to feed all the changes in the Chinese world from the 5th century BC on through the Han period, including the growth of population, state power, manufacturing, trade, cities and armies. Agricultural development continued under Han. Although it is impossible to quantify, there are signs of rising numbers of ox-drawn ploughs, seed-drills and other animal-powered equipment in the Han period, though most farming was probably still done with mattocks, hoes, sickles and other hand tools. Occasional indications of ratios of harvest to seed suggest that 10:1 was not unusual, a much higher yield than Roman farmers could expect.

Farmers also produced pulses, the main source of protein other than grain, and many kinds of fruit and vegetables. Meat was a privilege for the few. Dairy products were not part of the Chinese diet before the barbarian invasions that followed Han. While men grew the crops, women fed the silkworms with mulberry leaves, reeled the silk from the cocoons and spun it into thread. They also processed hemp, the main plant fibre for clothing in China before the later introduction of cotton, and wove hemp and silk cloth.

While some peasant families farmed their own land, others sold their labour as farm hands. There was a long-term trend through the Han period, and especially in the Eastern Han, for some families to become local magnates with large numbers of dependant tenants, serfs or slaves. The Qin and early Western Han policy of uprooting leading clans from their home districts and moving them to the area round the capital or the frontier was abandoned. Eastern Han tombs give lively images of the manorial economy and the way leading families wanted to go on living on their rural estates after death. Wall paintings and bas reliefs show all kinds of farm work as well as the pleasures of feasting, music and hunting. Ceramic models represent granaries, fishponds, grain-processing machinery and walled manor houses protected by high pagoda-like watchtowers, on some of which archers with crossbows keep guard.

More and more people farmed the fertile plains created by the silt carried down from the mountains by the Yellow and other north Chinese rivers over millions of years. Left to itself the Yellow river raises its own bed year by year until it changes course. From Han times onwards

ABOVE: The landed magnates of the Eastern Han period felt the need for multi-storeyed towers from which watch could be kept over their fortified manors. Ceramic models of towers are often found in their tombs.

LEFT: This mural from a tomb near the Eastern Han capital Luoyang shows gentlemen whose hats and long gowns mark their high socio-political rank. This was a time when the art of conversation was becoming important in winning status among the educated elite.

The woman and younger
man's innermost coffins
were each covered with a
painted silk banner. They
seem to be a guide to the
soul of the deceased as he
or she made the difficult
ascent from the mortal
world near the bottom to
heaven at the top, with the
bird in the sun and the
crescent moon. This banner
is from the man's coffin.

The Marchioness from Mawangdui

For its first 60 years the central Han government let vassals run much of the east and south of the empire. Some of the kingdoms were large and rich. The kingdom of Changsha covered most of today's south-central China. Here the king ruled through his own officials and vassals, headed by his hereditary chancellor, the Marquis of Dai. In 1972–1974 the tombs of the first marquis, his wife and a man of about 30, probably their son, were opened at Mawangdui in today's Changsha. The marchioness was the last of the three to be buried, at the age of about 50, some time after 186 BC. Sealed anaerobically inside five layers of outer and inner coffins, her body was so well preserved that the flesh was still resilient. Her burial goods, including food, textiles and lacquerware, were all in astonishingly good condition. Among the finds in the younger man's tomb were long-lost philosophical works and early texts of the *Lao zi*. All this tells much about the life and thinking of the southern aristocracy in the 2nd century BC.

ABOVE: Before it was replaced by fine porcelain after Han times lacquer was the preferred material for the eating and drinking vessels of the aristocracy. The tableware from the Mawangdui tombs includes a dish and a ewer from which water could be poured over diners' fingers.

LEFT: Apart from the massive outermost coffins all the inner coffins were lacquered, the designs growing more intricate as the coffin gets closer to the body itself. The tradition of lacquered coffins went back centuries in central China, where the lac tree was grown.

This rubbing of a bas-relief in a Han tomb combines the fanciful, such as the mythical qilin beast (bottom left), with the life of a working manor. A woman weaves at a loom, while other people look after the vats of wine or cart goods off to market. A well-filled weapon rack suggests underlying insecurity.

there were repeated efforts to contain the river within dykes, efforts that lifted the river above the plain and made the inevitable floods worse, most catastrophically in AD 11 when the river changed its route to the sea.

Except where communications were bad, agriculture was part of a commercial economy that continued to grow under Qin and Han. Walled cities and towns were primarily seats of state power, but they were also market centres linked in trade networks that enabled merchants and manufacturers to prosper when the empire was at peace. The greatest cities were Chang'an (Xi'an), the Western Han capital, and Luoyang that was rebuilt as the Eastern Han one. Most of Chang'an and much of Luoyang were taken up by huge palace complexes, but trade still flourished. A treatise on wealth creation written around 100 BC by Sima Qian celebrates the fortunes made by successful businessmen and women that enabled them to live like marquises and princes. He advocates a laissez-faire approach to the pursuit of self-interest. Although most trade was local, some high-value commodities repaid the cost of taking them to distant markets. Trade continued to let many people apart from primary

producers prosper, but not all were pleased. Some 250 years after Sima Qian, the sour Confucian Wang Fu denounces what he sees in Luoyang: hordes of dealers making money as they live off the honest toil of the peasants. He takes the common Confucian view of the economy as a zero-sum game in which merchants are parasites. Merchants were expected to accept lower social status than officials, scholars and the landed classes. They had no legitimate political voice. Throughout the Qin and Han period high office was essential to social standing, and this applied even to the great rural magnates.

Commerce encouraged many developments in technology, from iron and steel for tools and weapons to grain-processing machinery and looms that could weave intricate brocades. Medicine made great progress. Fine lacquerware cups in early Han tombs are replaced by porcelain ones in late ones.

CULTURES AND VALUES UNDER QIN AND HAN
Among the First Qin emperor's failures was his attempt to crush the open market in ideas of the 5th to 3rd centuries BC. Not content with imposing the Qin administrative order, in

214 BC he made it a criminal offence for anyone except a few state-appointed specialists to possess almost any books except practical manuals and Qin laws. The next year he also had some 460 scholars in the capital who had spoken against him buried alive. But in its few remaining years the Qin regime was not able to burn all the copies of banned books or kill all who had memorized them.

In the first century of Han rule the many pre-Qin schools of thought were revived, and there was lively competition between them. As far back as records go the main concerns of thinkers in China had been politics and the ordering of society. The political theories known as legalism that had underlain Qin rule – a strong state controlling the people through inescapable laws and taking much of their labour – continued to influence government. Although these principles were at first applied with a slightly lighter hand, the emperor Wudi reverted to harsh taxes and conscription to provide for his wars, and key ministers openly admired Legalism. The Qin system of criminal and administrative law continued to apply with only limited adjustments, and many Han officials made their careers enforcing the state's laws. Another tenet of Legalist thinking – a bureaucracy in which every official holds his job only at the ruler's pleasure and is rewarded or punished for how well he lives up to his job description – remained central to Han government.

Under the first Han rulers the methods of minimalist government associated with the mythical Yellow Emperor of remote antiquity and the more recent but shadowy Laozi were fashionable in ruling circles. Arguments that doing as little as possible was the way for the ruler to benefit the state and the people had much appeal in an empire that needed to be left alone to recover from decades of destructive war. Another approach to politics that revived for a while under Han but had no appeal to the state was that of the Mohists, a sect that had long been against the extravagance of rulers. Although they were at a court conference on frontier policy in 81 BC, they disappear from the record soon afterwards.

Great efforts were made to recover and put in order pre-Qin books of all kinds in Han times. Apart from a few early texts found by archaeologists in recent decades, all the surviving books from pre-Qin China are as handed down by Han editors. Sima Qian, whose universal history has for over 2,000 years been hugely influential in fixing our images of the pre-Qin, Qin and early Han world, was a great anthologist as well as a brilliant writer. After being penally castrated in 99 BC he devoted himself to completing the great history of China and the world known to China from remote antiquity to his own times, a project begun by his father. *Shiji, Records of the Astronomer/Historian* – the office he held combined both functions – reflects the intellectual diversity and liveliness of the early Han. In its pages he presents many different views, letting his subjects use their own words where possible. He adopts a variety of formats. One set of chapters summarizes official records of events in annalistic form. Some topics are dealt with in thematic monographs. Reference material is put in tables that can be skipped when not needed. Most of the book consists of lively accounts of representative figures of their times from sages to gangsters and of foreign nations. Where other texts of his sources survive we can see that he presents them fairly. Some of his best stories must have come by word of mouth. He does not impose a unified narrative or an overriding ideology to the book. Shiji represents Han written culture at its best. Although its form was copied by later historians, its energy and multiplicity of views was never matched.

The school of thought that triumphed under Han traced its roots back to Confucius (*c.* 551–479 BC), a Ru scholar. Ru used the texts of the Zhou past to educate the sons of the aristocracy and gentry. Confucius had been so charismatic and persuasive a teacher and interpreter of the classics that his students and their later followers made the Ru school 'Confucian'. Few Ru scholars had seemed of practical use to rulers desperate to strengthen their states in the cut-throat international competition of the 4th and 3rd centuries BC.

The Jade Queen

ABOVE: The pair of tiny bronze leopards with gilded patterning and burning eyes of semi-precious stone were among the burial goods left with Dou Wan. Real leopards lived in the hills of Zhongshan.

In 154 BC some of the Han emperor Jingdi's most powerful vassals rose against him. After the rebellion was put down the central government brought more of the empire under its direct control and cut back the powers and domains of vassal kings. The emperor installed some of his own sons to rule these much smaller kingdoms. One of these was Liu Sheng, king of Zhongshan from 154 BC till his death in 113 BC. Although Zhongshan was a small kingdom centred about 130 km (80 miles) southwest of Beijing, Liu Sheng and his queen Dou Wan (who died a little later) were buried with great splendour. Each of their tombs was cut some 50 m (165 ft) horizontally into the top of the same hillside and lavishly furnished with grave goods – his included six chariots complete with horses – both real and symbolic. At the back of each tomb was a sealed stone chamber in which the body, completely clad in jade, was placed in a single coffin.

LEFT: The gilt bronze oil lamp from Dou Wan's tomb in the form of a kneeling serving woman was as practical as it is elegant. The wide base gives it stability; the shade could be moved by the little handle to cast the light just where it was wanted; and the woman's wide right sleeve is a chimney to collect soot and reduce the risk of the flame setting hangings alight.

BELOW: The body covering of Queen Dou Wan was made of 2,156 jade plaques held together with gold cord. Inside the suit jade plugs stopped her orifices, and outside it her coffin was covered with jade discs. Her husband had an even more elaborate suit. Jade (nephrite) had long been valued above all other stone in China for its hardness and lustrous, fragile beauty. Wu Hung has argued that the jade suits were intended not to preserve the fleshly body but to replace it with an imperishable one, thus achieving immortality.

Qin had been hostile to them long before the First Emperor ruled the state of Qin, and he had persecuted them. After Qin its hostility to them became an asset to Confucians, who evidently enjoyed taking the moral high ground in denouncing Qin.

Once the Han empire was securely established Confucians had even more in their favour. Given that Han had the practical benefits of Legalist bureaucratic dictatorship and laws, an astute ruler saw advantages in cushioning this with the Confucian model of an ordered, family-based society in which everyone knew their place. Through the Han centuries education mainly meant learning the classics. The classics as interpreted by Confucians taught people how to behave. They also inculcated into future officials a sense of duty to their superiors and to those under them. A good Confucian official was not only moved by the hope of reward and the fear of punishment. He was also expected to have a conscience and do the right thing for its own sake. Being a gentleman – the goal of all good Confucians – was a matter of how one acted, not just of birth. As parvenus

the early Han emperors were also susceptible to Confucianists' advice on how to locate themselves in a great tradition of Chinese kingship going back thousands of years, even when they were really the heirs of Qin.

The emperor Wudi, who in most of his actions was a Qin-style Legalist, did more than any of his predecessors to promote Confucianism as something approaching a state ideology. Many of his officials were selected on the strength of their knowledge of the classics or their supposed Confucian behaviour. Wang Mang justified many of his policies by appealing to Confucian classics. Under the Eastern Han the classics were so important to the state that definitive texts of them all were carved in stone and displayed in Luoyang so that there could be no doubt about the authoritative wording. The text of some of the classics was deeply contested. Some scholars traced their preferred texts back to versions in old, pre-Qin, script. Others preferred texts written down from memory in the new Han script. Old-texters and new-texters accused each other of corrupting the text for political purposes. Such issues aside, the Confucian tradition served on the whole to justify a moderate conservatism that ensured social order and the basic welfare of the common people. It also discouraged original thinking.

The capital Luoyang was also the site of the Eastern Han imperial university, the successor to a smaller, Western Han university founded by Wudi. In it specialists in each of the classics taught thousands of students from across the empire who saw a classical education as the key to an official career. In the bitter struggles that pitted some career officials against imperial in-laws and eunuchs in the 2nd century

During the Han centuries the Confucian tradition became the dominant one. This rubbing from the 2nd century AD Wu family shrine in Shandong shows Zilu (centre), one of Confucius's leading disciples.

AD, students sided with Confucian-minded officials and were involved in some of the earliest mass student protests in history. The close association between the state, Confucian values and office-holding that was formed in Han times was to continue for the rest of dynastic Chinese history.

Although Confucian traditions required certain rituals which were valuable for symbolizing the social and natural order, including sacrifices to heaven and to ancestors, Confucianism was not a numinous religion; nor did it offer personal connections with a deity. Yet there were other belief systems in Han times offering the help of deities in securing a good afterlife, as can be seen from the decorations and furnishings of Han tombs in which they look after the deceased. One cult was that of the immortality-giving Queen Mother of the West. There was widespread excitement across China early in 3 BC when her devotees prepared for her coming, only to be disappointed. One group of beliefs and practices that sought to obtain magical powers, culminating in becoming an immortal, was associated with Daoism. The Daoist pursuit of immortality included physical exercises for correct breathing – a silk chart of exercises was found in a tomb of the 2nd century BC – as well as sexual techniques to build up the life force in the body. But did this amount to a religion?

One undoubtedly religious cult that fatally weakened the Eastern Han was that of the Way of Great Peace, which offered forgiveness of sins, social support and the promise of a new world for the saved. This highly organized sect prepared coordinated uprisings across eastern China in 184. The rebels were called Yellow Turbans because their headcloths were the colour of the new heaven that was to take over the world. Han's own armies could not defeat them, so local magnates did so with their private armies then went on to fight among themselves for the empire. From then till the formal end of the dynasty in 220, Han emperors were only puppets of warlords.

One religion that reached China by the 1st century AD, probably as a result of contact with central, western and southern Asia following

Han intervention in Xinjiang, was Buddhism. The few mentions of it in accounts of Eastern Han suggest a private minority cult. It would await the disorder that followed the fall of Han to transform the Chinese mental world.

Two changes that Qin and Han made to the written culture they inherited were the

imposition of a unified script and the invention of paper. As a great empire could only be governed through written documents, it was essential that they should all be in the same writing. Qin insisted that its Chinese script replace the multiplicity of scripts in the various pre-Qin states. The Han standard script was much closer to modern Chinese writing. Once the technique of turning a pulp of vegetable fibres into sheets of light, flexible writing material had been developed in Eastern Han times, paper proved to be much more convenient than the bundles of wooden or bamboo strips used previously. Paper made the physical process of writing quicker and easier. The writing brush's freedom of movement on paper made possible China's supreme visual art form, calligraphy. By the end of the Eastern Han China was becoming a paper culture.

Eastern Han tombs in Sichuan are often walled with bricks illustrating scenes of manorial life. This one from Deyang shows work in paddy fields walled with low ridges to keep the water in them and mulberry trees beside them.

FURTHER READING

General

Alcock, S. E., T. N. D'Altroy, K. D. Morrison and C. M. Sinopoli (eds), *Empires: Perspectives from Archaeology and History* (Cambridge, 2001).

Baring, E., *Ancient and Modern Imperialism* (London, 1910).

Hardt, M. and A. Negri, *Empire* (Cambridge, MA, 2001).

Howe, S., *Empire: A Very Short Introduction* (Oxford, 2002).

Said, E., *Culture and Imperialism* (London & New York, 1993).

Egypt

Baines, J. E. and J. Malek, *Cultural Atlas of Ancient Egypt* (Oxford, 2004).

Dodson, A. M. and D. Hilton, *The Complete Royal Families of Ancient Egypt* (London & New York, 2004).

Gardiner, A. H., *The Kadesh Inscriptions of Ramesses II* (Oxford, 1960).

Grimal, N., *A History of Ancient Egypt* (Oxford, 1992).

Häsel, M., *Domination and Resistance: Egyptian Military Activity in the Southern Levant, c. 1300–1185 BC* (Leiden, 1998).

Kemp, B. J., *Ancient Egypt: Anatomy of a Civilisation* (London, 1989).

Kitchen, K. A., *Pharaoh Triumphant: The Life and Times of Ramesses II, King of Egypt* (Warminster, 1983).

Kozloff, A. and B. M. Bryan, *Egypt's Dazzling Sun: Amenhotep III and his World* (Cleveland, 1992).

Leahy, M. A., *Libya and Egypt, c. 1300–750 BC* (London, 1990).

Manley, W. P., *The Penguin Historical Atlas of Ancient Egypt* (London, 1996).

Manley, W. P., *The Seventy Great Mysteries of Ancient Egypt* (London & New York, 2003).

Moran, W. L., *The Amarna Letters* (Baltimore & London, 1992).

Morkot, R. G., *The Black Pharaohs: Egypt's Nubian Rulers* (London, 2000).

Murnane, W., *The Road to Kadesh: A Historical Interpretation of the Battle Reliefs of King Sety I at Karnak* (rev. ed., Chicago, 1990).

Mysliwiec, K., *The Twilight of Ancient Egypt* (New York, 2000).

O'Connor, D., *Ancient Nubia: Egypt's Rival in Africa* (Philadelphia, 1993).

Redford, D. B., *Egypt, Canaan and Israel in Ancient Times* (Princeton, 1992).

Reeves, C. N., *The Complete Tutankhamun* (rev. ed., London & New York, 2006).

Romer, J., *Ancient Lives. The Story of the Pharaohs' Tombmakers* (London, 1984/2003).

Sandars, N., *The Sea Peoples: Warriors of the Eastern Mediterranean* (rev. ed., London & New York, 1985).

Shaw, I. M. E., *The Oxford History of Ancient Egypt* (Oxford, 2000).

Wilkinson, R. H., *The Complete Temples of Ancient Egypt* (London & New York, 2000).

Hittites

Akurgal, E., *The Art of the Hittites* (London, 1962).

Beal, R. H., *The Organisation of the Hittite Military* (Heidelberg, 1992).

Beckman, G. M., *Hittite Diplomatic Texts* (2nd ed., Atlanta, 1999).

Beckman, G. M., R. Beal, and G. McMahon (eds), *Hittites Studies in Honor of Harry A. Hoffner Jr* (Winona Lake, IN, 2003).

Bryce, T. R., *Life and Society in the Hittite World* (Oxford, 2002).

Bryce, T. R., *Letters of the Great Kings of the Ancient Near East* (London & New York, 2003).

Bryce, T. R., *The Kingdom of the Hittites* (new ed., Oxford, 2005).

Chavalas, M. W. (ed.), *The Ancient Near East* (Oxford, 2006).

Freu, J. and M. Mayozer, *Des origines à la fin de l'ancien royaume hittite: Les Hittites et leur histoire* (Paris, 2007).

Gurney, O. R., 'The Hittite Empire', in M. T. Larsen (ed.), *Power and Propaganda* (Copenhagen, 1979), 151–65.

Gurney, O. R., *The Hittites* (London, 1990).

Hoffner, H. A., *The Laws of the Hittites: A Critical Edition* (Leiden & New York, 1997).

Hoffner, H. A. and G. M. Beckman (eds), *Kaniššuwar: A Tribute to Hans Güterbock on his Seventy-Fifth Birthday* (Chicago, 1986).

Kitchen, K. A., *Pharaoh Triumphant: The Life and Times of Ramesses II* (Warminster, 1983).

Klengel, H., *Geschichte des Hethitischen Reiches* (Leiden, 1999).

Klock-Fontanille, I., *Les Hittites* (Paris, 1998).

Macqueen, J. G., *The Hittites and their Contemporaries in Asia Minor* (rev. ed., London & New York, 1986).

Macqueen, J. G., 'The History of Anatolia and of the Hittite Empire: An Overview', in J. M. Sasson (ed.), *Civilizations of the Ancient Near East* (vol. 2, New York, 1995), 1085–1105.

Singer, I., 'New Evidence on the End of the Hittite Empire', in E. D. Oren (ed.), *The Sea Peoples and their World: A Reassessment* (Philadelphia, 2000), 21–33.

Van den Hout, T., 'Khattushili III, King of the Hittites', in J. M. Sasson (ed.), *Civilizations of the Ancient Near East* (vol. 2, New York, 1995), 1107–20.

Yener, K. A. and H. A. Hoffner (eds), *Recent Developments in Hittite Archaeology and History, Papers in Memory of Hans G. Güterbock* (Winona Lake, IN, 2002).

Assyria and Babylonia

Bahrani, Z., *Rituals of War: The Body and Violence in Mesopotamia* (Cambridge, MA, 2008).

Boardman, J. (ed.), *The Assyrian and Babylonian Empires and other States of the Near East* (*Cambridge Ancient History,* 2nd ed.: vol. 3, pt 2) (Cambridge & New York, 1991).

Curtis, J. E. and J. E. Reade (eds), *Art and Empire: Treasures from Assyria in the British Museum* (New York, 1995).

Finkel, I. L. and M. J. Seymour, *Babylon: Myth and Reality* (London, 2008).

Joannès, F., *The Age of Empires: Mesopotamia in the First Millennium* (Edinburgh, 2004).

Kuhrt, A., *The Ancient Near East* (vol. 2, London & New York, 2005).

Larsen, M. T. (ed.), *Power and Propaganda* (Copenhagen, 1979).

Oates, J. *Babylon* (rev. ed., London & New York, 2008).

Oates, J. and D., *Nimrud: An Assyrian Imperial City Revealed* (London, 2001).

Parpola, S. and R. M. Whiting (eds), *Assyria 1995* (Helsinki, 1997).

Porter, B. N., *Images, Power, and Politics: Figurative Aspects of Esarhaddon's Babylonian Policy* (Philadephia, 1993).

Reade, J., *Assyrian Sculpture* (Cambridge, MA, 1999).

Saggs, H. W. F., *The Might that was Assyria* (London, 1984).

Van De Mieroop, M., *A History of the Ancient Near East, ca. 3000–323 BC* (2nd ed., Oxford, 2007).

Wiseman, D. J., *Nebuchadnezzar and Babylon* (Oxford & New York, 1985).

Persia

Allen, L., *The Persian Empire* (London, 2005).

Boardman, J., *Persia and the West. An Archaeological Investigation of the Genesis of Achaemenid Art* (London, 2000).

Briant, P., *From Cyrus to Alexander. A History of the Persian Empire* (Winona Lake, 2002).

Brosius, P., *The Persian Empire from Cyrus II to Artaxerxes I* (Lactor 16, Cambridge, 2000).

Cawkwell, G., *The Greek Wars: The Failure of Persia* (Oxford, 2005).

Cook, J. M., *The Persian Empire* (London, 1983).

Curtis, J. and N. Tallis (eds), *Forgotten Empire: The World of Ancient Persia* (London, 2005).

Dandamayev, M. A., *A Political History of the Achaemenid Empire* (Leiden, 1989).

Dandamayev, M. A. and V. G. Lukonin, *The Culture and Social Institutions of Ancient Iran* (Cambridge, 1989).

Drews, R., *The Greek Accounts of Eastern History* (Cambridge, MA, 1973).

Dusinberre, E. R. M., *Aspects of Empire in Achaemenid Sardis* (Cambridge, 2003).

Farrokh, K., *Shadows in the Desert: Ancient Persia at War* (Oxford, 2007).

Fried, L. S., *The Priest and the Great King: Temple–Palace Relations in the Persian Empire* (Winona Lake, IN, 2004).

Frye, R. N., *The Heritage of Persia* (London, 1962).

Gershevitch, I., *The Cambridge History of Iran, vol 2. The Median and Achaemenian Periods* (Cambridge, 1985).

Hall, E., *Inventing the Barbarian: Greek Self-Definition through Tragedy* (Oxford, 1989).

Harper, P. O., J. Aruz, and F. Tallon (eds), *The Royal City of Susa: Ancient Near Eastern Treasures in the Louvre* (New York, 1992).

Harrison, T., *Greeks and Barbarians* (Edinburgh, 2002).

Kuhrt, A., *The Persian Empire: A Corpus of Sources from the Achaemenid Period* (2 vols, London, 2007).

Mackey, S., *The Iranians: Persia, Islam and the Soul of a Nation* (New York, 1996).

Malkin, I., *Ancient Perceptions of Greek Ethnicity* (Cambridge, MA, 2001).

Matheson, S. A., *Persia: An Archaeological Guide* (London, 1972).

Miller, M., *Athens and Persia in the Fifth Century BC: A Study in Cultural Reciprocity* (Cambridge, 1997).

Olmstead, A. T., *History of the Persian Empire* (Chicago, 1948).

Roisman, J., *Brill's Companion to Alexander the Great* (Leiden, 2003).

Root, M. C., *The King and Kingship in Achaemenid Art: Essays on the Creation of an Iconography of Empire* (Leiden, 1979).

Sancisi-Weerdenburg, H., 'The Fifth Oriental Monarchy and Hellenocentrism', in H. Sancisi-Weerdenburg and A. Kuhrt (eds), *Achaemenid History, vol. 2. The Greek Sources* (Leiden, 1987), 117–31.

Tuplin, C. (ed.), *Persian Responses: Political and Cultural Interaction with(in) the Achaemenid Empire* (Swansea, 2007).

Wiesehöfer, J., *Ancient Persia from 550 BC to 650 AD* (London & New York, 1996).

Wilber, D. N., *Persepolis: The Archaeology of Parsa, Seat of the Persian Kings* (Princeton, 1969).

Athens

Boedeker, D. and K. A. Raaflaub (eds), *Democracy, Empire and the Arts in Fifth-Century Athens* (Cambridge, MA, 1998).

Camp, J., *The Athenian Agora* (rev. ed., London & New York, 1998).

Cargill, J., *The Second Athenian League* (Berkeley & Los Angeles, 1981).

Finley, M. I., 'The Fifth-Century Athenian Empire: A Balance Sheet', in P. D. A. Garnsey and C. R. Whittaker (eds), *Imperialism in the Ancient World* (Cambridge, 1978).

Hornblower, S., *The Greek World, 479–323 BC* (3rd ed., London, 2002).

Hurwit, J. M., *The Athenian Acropolis: History, Mythology and Archaeology from the Neolithic Era to the Present* (Cambridge, 1998).

Kagan, D., *The Peloponnesian War* (New York, 2003).

Low, P., *Interstate Relations in Classical Greece* (Cambridge, 2007).

Meiggs, R., *The Athenian Empire* (Oxford, 1972).

Neils, J., *The Parthenon: From Antiquity to the Present* (Cambridge, 2005).

Parker, R., *Athenian Religion: A History* (Oxford, 1996).

Samons, L. J., *Empire of the Owl: Athenian Imperial Finance* (Stuttgart, 2000).

Alexander and his Successors

Austin, M. M., *The Hellenistic World from Alexander to the Roman Conquest.* (Cambridge, 2006).

Bowman, A. K., *Egypt after the Pharaohs, 332 BC–AD 642: From Alexander to the Arab Conquest* (2nd ed., Berkeley, 1996).

Bugh, G. R., *The Cambridge Companion to the Hellenistic World* (Cambridge, 2006).

Cartledge, P., *Alexander the Great: The Hunt for a New Past* (Woodstock, 2004).

Chamoux, F., *Hellenistic Civilisation* (Oxford, 2003).

Erskine, A. (ed.), *A Companion to the Hellenistic World* (Oxford & Malden, MA, 2003).

Gehrke, H-J., *Geschichte des Hellenismus* (2nd ed., Munich, 1995).

Gruen. E. S., *The Hellenistic World and the Coming of Rome* (Berkeley, 1984).

Kuhrt, A. and S. Sherwin-White, *Hellenism in the East* (London, 1987).

Préaux, C., *Le monde hellénistique: La Grèce et l'Orient de la mort d'Alexandre*

à la conquête romaine de la Grèce (323–146 av. J.-C.) (Paris, 1978).

Sherwin-White, S. M. and A. Kuhrt, *From Samarkhand to Sardis: A New Approach to the Seleucid Empire* (London, 1993).

Shipley, G., *The Greek World after Alexander 323–30 BC* (London, 2000).

Walbank, F. W., *The Hellenistic World* (3rd ed., London, 1992).

Weber, G. (ed.), *Kulturgeschichte des Hellenismus: Von Alexander dem Großen bis Kleopatra* (Stuttgart, 2007).

Parthia and Sasania

Butcher, K., *Roman Syria and the Near East* (London, 2003).

Colledge, M., *The Parthians* (London,1967).

Colledge, M., *Parthian Art* (London, 1977).

Curtis, J. E. (ed.), *Mesopotamia and Iran in the Parthian and Sassanian Periods* (London, 2000).

Dąbrowa, E. (ed.), *Ancient Iran and the Mediterranean World: Proceedings of an International Conference in Honour of Professor Józef Wolski* (Krakow, 1998).

Dignas, B. and E. Winter, *Rome and Persia in Late Antiquity: Neighbours and Rivals* (Cambridge, 2007).

Dirven, L., 'The Palmyrenes of Dura-Europos: A Study of Religious Interaction in Roman Syria', in M. H. Dodgeon and S. N. C. Lieu (eds), *The Roman Eastern Frontier and the Persian Wars (AD 226–363)* (Leiden, 1991).

Edwell, P., *Between Rome and Persia: The Middle Euphrates, Mesopotamia and Palmyra under Roman Control* (London, 2007).

Errington, E. and V. S. Curtis, *From Persepolis to the Punjab: Exploring Ancient Iran* (London, 2007).

Hopkins, C., *The Discovery of Dura-Europos*, ed. B. Goldman (New Haven & London, 1979).

Isaac, B., *The Limits of Empire: The Roman Army in the East* (rev. ed., Oxford, 1992).

Kennedy, D. and D. Riley, *Rome's Desert Frontier from the Air* (London, 1990).

Lepper, F. A., *Trajan's Parthian War* (London, 1948).

Lerouge, C., *L'image des Parthes dans le monde gréco-romain* (Stuttgart, 2007).

Millar, F., *The Roman Near East, 31 BC–AD 337* (Cambridge, MA, 1993).

Sarkhosh Curtis, V. and S. Stewart (eds), *The Age of the Parthians* (London, 2007).

Sartre, M., *The Middle East under Rome* (Cambridge, MA, 2005).

Wiesehöfer, J. (ed.), *Das Partherreich und seine Zeugnisse* (Stuttgart, 1998).

Wiesehöfer, J, *Ancient Persia from 550 BC to AD 650* (London, 2001).

Wolski, J., *L'empire des Arsacides* (Lovanni, 1993).

Yarshater, E. (ed.), *The Cambridge History of Iran: The Seleucid, Parthian and Sasanid Periods* (vol. 3, pts 1–2 Cambridge, 1983).

Rome

Cameron, A., *The Later Roman Empire, AD 284–430* (Cambridge, MA, 1993).

Eck, W., *The Age of Augustus* (Oxford, 2003).

Goodman, M., *The Roman World, 44 BC–AD 180* (London, 1997).

Gruen, E. S., *The Hellenistic World and the Coming of Rome* (Berkeley, 1984).

Harris, W. V., *War and Imperialism in Republican Rome: 327–70 BC* (Oxford, 1979).

Heather, P. J., *The Fall of the Roman Empire: A New History* (London, 2006).

Jones, A. H. M., *The Greek City from Alexander to Justinian* (Oxford, 1940).

Millar, F., *The Emperor in the Roman World (31 BC–AD 337)* (New York, 1977).

Millar, F., *The Roman Near East: 31 BC–AD 337* (Cambridge, MA, 1993).

Potter, D. S., *The Roman Empire at Bay, AD 180–395* (London, 2004).

Potter, D. S., *Rome in the Ancient World* (London & New York, 2009).

Scott, S. and J. Webster (eds), *Roman Imperialism and Provincial Art* (Cambridge, 2003).

Sherwin-White, A. N., *Roman Citizenship* (2nd ed., Oxford, 1973).

Sommer, M., *Römische Geschichte II: Rom und sein Imperium in der Kaiserzeit* (Stuttgart, 2009).

Treggiari, S., *Roman Social History* (London, 2002).

Ward-Perkins, J. B., *The Fall of Rome and the End of Civilization* (Oxford, 2005).

Wells, C. M., *The Roman Empire* (2nd ed., London, 1992).

Woolf, G., *Becoming Roman: The Origins of Provincial Civilization in Gaul* (Cambridge, 1998).

India

Agrawal, D. P., *The Archaeology of India* (London, 1982).

Allchin, F. R. (ed.), *The Archaeology of Early Historic South Asia: The Emergence of Cities and States* (Cambridge, 1995).

Coningham, R. A. E., 'The Archaeology of Buddhism', in T. Insoll (ed.), *Archaeology and World Religion* (London, 2001), 61–95.

Coningham, R. A. E., 'South Asia: From Early Villages to Buddhism', in C. Scarre (ed.), *The Human Past* (London & New York, 2006), 518–551.

Coningham, R. A. E. and I. Ali (eds), *Charsadda: The British-Pakistani Excavations at the Bala Hisar* (Oxford, 2007).

Coningham, R. A. E. et al., 'The State of Theocracy: Defining an Early Medieval Hinterland in Sri Lanka', *Antiquity* 81: 1–21.

Coningham, R. A. E. and M. J. Manuel, 'Warfare in Ancient South Asia', in P. de Souza (ed.), *The Ancient World at War* (London & New York, 2008), 229–242.

Dani, A. H. and V. M. Masson (eds), *History of Civilisations of Central Asia, vol 1. The Dawn of Civilisation: Earliest Times to 700 BC* (Paris, 1992).

Harmatta, J., B. N. Puri and G. F. Etemadi, *History of Civilisations of Central Asia, vol 2. The Development of Sedentary and Nomadic Civilisations: 700 BC to 250 AD* (Paris, 1994).

Kulke, H. and D. Rothermund, *History of India* (London, 1992).

Marshall, J. H., *Taxila: An Illustrated Account of Archaeological Excavations* (Cambridge, 1951).

Morrison, K. D., 'Trade, Urbanism and Agricultural Expansion: Buddhist Monastic Institutions and the State in the Early Historic Western Deccan', *World Archaeology* 27: 203–221.

Rangarajan, L. N. (trans.), *Kautilya, The Arthasastra* (New Delhi, 1992).

Raychaudri, H., *Political History of Ancient India* (Calcutta, 1972).

Seneviratne, S., 'The Mauryan State', in H. J. M. Claessen and P. Skalnik (eds), *The Early State* (The Hague, 1978).

Thapar, R., *Asoka and the Decline of the Mauryas* (New Delhi, 1963).

Trautmann, T. R., *Kautilya and the Arthasastra: A Statistical Investigation of the Authorship and Evolution of the Text* (Leiden, 1971).

Wheeler, R. E. M., *Charsada: A Metropolis of the North-West Frontier:* (London, 1962).

China

Balazs, E., 'Political Philosophy and Social Crisis at the End of the Han Dynasty', in Arthur F. Wright (ed.), *Chinese Civilization and Bureaucracy: Variations on a Theme* (trans. H. M. Wright) (New Haven, 1964).

Bodde, D., *China's First Unifier: A study of the Ch'in Dynasty as seen in the Life of Li Ssu* (Leiden, 1938/1967).

de Bary, W. T. and I. Bloom (eds), *Sources of Chinese Tradition* (2nd ed., vol 1, New York, 1999), 225–374.

de Crespigny, R., *Northern Frontier: The Policies and Strategy of the Later Han Empire* (Canberra, 1984).

Di Cosmo, N., *Ancient China and its Enemies: The Rise of Nomadic Power in East Asian History* (Cambridge & New York, 2002).

Hulsewé, A. F. P., *Remnants of Ch'in Law: An Annotated Translation of the Ch'in Legal and Administrative Rules of the 3rd century BC, discovered in Yün-meng Prefecture, Hu-pei Province, in 1975* (Leiden, 1985).

Hulsewé, A. F. P., with an introduction by M. A. N. Loewe, *China in Central Asia, the Early Stage, 125 BC–AD 23: An Annotated Translation of Chapters 61 and 96 of the History of the Former Han Dynasty* (Leiden, 1979).

Lewis, M. E., *The Early Chinese Empires: Qin and Han* (Cambridge, MA, 2007).

Loewe, M., *A Biographical Dictionary of the Qin, Former Han and Xin Periods (221 BC–AD 24)* (Leiden, 2000).

Loewe, M., *Crisis and Conflict in Han China, 104 BC to AD 9* (London, 1974, reissued 2005).

Loewe, M., *Everyday Life in Early Imperial China during the Han Period, 202 BC–AD 220* (London & New York, 1968).

Loewe, M., *Records of Han Administration* (Cambridge, 1967).

Portal, J. (ed.), *The First Emperor: China's Terracotta Army* (London, 2007).

Twitchett, D. and M. Loewe (eds), *The Cambridge History of China, vol. 1, The Ch'in and Han Empires, 221 BC–AD 220* (Cambridge, 1986).

Wang Zhongshu, *Han Civilization*, trans. Chang Kwang-chih and others (New Haven & London, 1982).

Watson, B. (trans.), *Records of the Grand Historian: Qin Dynasty* by Sima Qian (Hong Kong & New York, 1993).

Watson, B. (trans.), *Records of the Grand Historian: Han Dynasty* by Sima Qian, 2 vol. (Hong Kong & New York, 1993).

Yang Hsienyi and G. Yang (trans.), *Selections from Records of the Historian* by Szuma Ch'ien (Beijing, 1979).

Contributors

Thomas Harrison is Rathbone Professor of Ancient History and Classical Archaeology, and Head of the School of Archaeology, Classics and Egyptology, at the University of Liverpool. His publications include *Divinity and History. The Religion of Herodotus* (2000), *The Emptiness of Asia: Aeschylus' Persians and the History of the Fifth Century* (2000) and as editor, *Greeks and Barbarians* (2002) and *The Edinburgh Companion to Ancient Greece and Rome* (2006) (with Ed Bispham and Brian A. Sparkes).

Alastair Blanshard is a senior lecturer in the department of Classics and Ancient History at the University of Sydney. His publications include *Hercules: A Heroic Life* (2005). In addition to myth, he has written on Athenian law, epigraphy, Greek sexuality, and the classical tradition. He is currently working on a project on the afterlife of Greco-Roman erotica in western culture.

Trevor Bryce is a Near Eastern historian who has published extensively in the Classical and Near Eastern fields. He is Honorary Research Consultant at the University of Queensland, Australia, and has been awarded an Australian Centenary Medal for Service to Australian Society and the Humanities in the Study of History. His publications include *The Kingdom of the Hittites* (2005) and *The Trojans and their Neighbours* (2006).

Robin Coningham is Pro-Vice-Chancellor and Professor of Early Mediaeval Archaeology at Durham University. He has conducted fieldwork throughout South Asia, directing major excavations at the cities of Anuradhapura in Sri Lanka and the Bala Hisar of Charsadda in Pakistan, and has led seven UNESCO missions to the region. His publications include research on Anuradhapura (1999 & 2006), Charsadda (2007), the archaeology of Buddhism (2001) and the origins of Indian Ocean trade (2002), as well as two chapters in *The Archaeology of Early Historic South Asia* (R. Allchin, ed., 1995). His current research includes a survey of the hinterland of Anuradhapura and a programme of survey and excavation within Iran's Central Plateau.

W. J. F. Jenner is a professorial research associate at the School of Oriental and African Studies, University of London. For 45 years he has been writing on Chinese history and culture. His books include *Memories of Loyang* (1981), *The Tyranny of History: The Roots of China's Crisis* (1992), and many translations.

Ted Kaizer is a senior lecturer in Roman Culture and History at Durham University. His main research interest is the social and religious history of the Near East in the Late Hellenistic and Roman periods. He is the author of *The Religious Life of Palmyra* (2002).

Lloyd Llewellyn-Jones is a lecturer in Ancient History at Edinburgh University, specializing in the history, culture and society of Greece and Achaemenid Iran, and of ancient Greek perceptions of Persia. He is the author of *Aphrodite's Tortoise: The Veiled Woman of Ancient Greece* (2002) and *Ctesias' History of Persia: Tales of the Orient* (2009) (with James Robson), as well as numerous articles. He has led study tours and filmed documentaries in Iran. Forthcoming work includes a study of the harem in the ancient Near East.

Bill Manley is Senior Curator for Egyptian Scripts at National Museums Scotland and an Honorary Research Fellow of the University of Liverpool. His books include *The Penguin Historical Atlas of Ancient Egypt* (1996), *How to Read Egyptian Hieroglyphs* (1998, with Mark Collier), and, as editor, *The Seventy Great Mysteries of Ancient Egypt* (2003). More recently he has collaborated on the publication of the coffins of the pharaohs, and been a member of an archaeological expedition to Mo'alla in Egypt.

Mark Manuel is a Postdoctoral Research Associate in the Department of Archaeology at Durham University. His PhD research focused on the social and political organization of the Indus Valley Tradition, and he is currently focusing on projects in Sri Lanka and Iran.

Michael Sommer is a lecturer in Ancient History at the University of Liverpool. He has published extensively on Phoenician history, economy and culture as well as the Roman empire. Most recent books include a volume on the battle in the Teutoburg Forest, a monograph on the Roman frontier in the east and a history of the city of Rome.

Marc Van De Mieroop is a professor of Ancient Near Eastern History and chair of the History Department at Columbia University. His publications include *Cuneiform Texts and the Writing of History* (1999), *A History of the Ancient Near East, ca. 3000–323 BC* (2007), and *The Eastern Mediterranean in the Age of Ramesses II* (2007).

SOURCES OF QUOTATIONS

p. 24 'Why do I … with me?' Tablet Cairo 41790, 1: 3. **p. 25** 'Avaris was … for slaves.' Tomb-inscription of Ahmose-Saibana, cols 13–14. **p. 26** 'Year 23, … to that town.' *Karnak Annals of Thutmose* III, sec 1, cols 84–86. **p. 26** 'At a slab … of his arms.' *Stela Armant* S.443, 11: 3–5. **p. 27** 'As for the gold … my daughter.' *Amarna Archive* Tablet EA 3, 11: 36–43. **p. 27** 'Look, Pihanate … my commissioner.' *Amarna Archive* Tablet EA 60, 11: 19–32. **p. 27** 'I have reached … back safely.' Thutmose, Papyrus Turin 1972, 11: 4–10. **p. 28** 'If any … no heirs.' Rock-inscription at Hagar el-Merwa. **p. 31** 'We will not … pleased to.' *Stela Boston* MFA 23.733, 1: 24. **p. 34** 'Tell Nimmuariya … all go well.' Tablet EA 17, 11: 1–10. **p. 34** 'To the king … my lord.' Tablet EA 60, 11: 1–9. **p. 52** 'Formerly Labarna … of the sea.' *The Proclamation of Telipinu, secs 1–3.* **p. 52** 'What is this … Land of Hatti!' *Mursili II Prayer to the Sun-Goddess, secs 6–7* (trans. Goetze). **p. 52** 'I marched … Hattusa with it.' *Annals of Hattusili I, sec. 10.* **p. 53** 'I would … into subjection.' *Mursili II's Comprehensive Annals for his fourth year, sec. 26,* col IV, 27–33. **p. 53** '"Why have you … Good!"' *Siege of Urshu text,* reverse 10–21 (trans. Gurney). **p. 53** 'Then he … given life.' *Ramesside Inscriptions* (trans. Kitchen). **p. 53** 'For Hatti it … sex with her.' *Treaty of Suppiluliuma of Hatti and Huqqana of Hayas, sec. 25* (trans. Beckman). **p. 53** 'When I assumed … yet done this.' *Letter from Hattusili III of Hattie to Adadnirari of Assyria, sec. 4.* **p. 62** 'Military expansion … sport of kings.' O. R. Gurney. **p. 92** 'As the Lord … land were left.' 2Kings 24: 10–14. **p. 92** 'With the support … equal to me.' Assurnasirpal. **p. 93** 'The king knows … die of thirst.' *The Correspondence of Esarhaddon* (trans. Reynolds). **p. 93** 'On the outside … I surrounded it.' *Nebuchadnezzar II* (trans. Langdon). **p. 93** 'My hands captured … to Assyria.' Assurbanipal (trans. Onasch). **pp. 106–107** Adapted from Marius Brosius *The Persian Empire from Cyrus II to Artaxerxes I* (2000), Lactor 16, Cambridge. **p. 130** 'I am not blaming … to submit.' Thucydides *The Peloponnesian War* 4.61. **p. 130** 'I have had plenty … superior strength.' Thucydides *The Peloponnesian War* 3.37. **p. 131** 'Our city … education to Greece.' Thucydides *The Peloponnesian War* 2.39–40. **p. 131** 'Even before … Pillars of Heracles.' Plutarch *Life of Alcibiades* 17. **p. 131** 'As for the allies … lower class.' Old Oligarch *Constitution of the Athenians* 14. **p. 131** 'During the archonship … in an oven.' Aristophanes *Acharnians* 65–69. **p. 137** 'If Athens … actually is.' Thucydides *The*

Peloponnesian War 1.10.2. **p. 162** 'What great … without effort.' Arrian *Anabasis* 26. **p. 162** 'From King … sails with us.' From R. S. Bagnall and P. Derow, *Historical Sources in Translation: The Hellenistic Period* (Malden, MA, 2004). **p. 162** 'The girdle-wearers … against Egypt.' *Oxyrhynchus Papyri* XXII 2332, 28–32. **p. 163** 'In the reign … Beloved of Ptah.' *Rosetta Stone*, from R. S. Bagnall and P. Derow, *Historical Sources in Translation: The Hellenistic Period* (Malden, MA, 2004). **p. 163** 'Then a mighty … to others.' *Book of Daniel* XI: 2–4. **p. 163** 'Your ancestors … come to me.' Arrian *The Campaigns of Alexander* II: 14. 4–7. **p. 184** 'On an island … lot to see.' Velleius Paterculus *History of Rome* 2.101.1–3 (trans. Loeb). **p. 184** 'They are really … against us.' Cassius Dio *Roman History* 40.14.4 (trans. Loeb). **p. 184** 'I, the Mazda- … following lands.' *Res Gestae Divi Saporis* lines 1–2 of Greek text (trans. Frye). **p. 185** 'At which time … deal of hisses.' *Thirteenth Sibylline Oracle* 155–169 (trans. Lieu). **p.185** 'Even from afar … furthest distance.' Heliodorus *An Ethiopian Story* 9.14 (trans. Reardon). **p. 185** 'A great battle … and Cappadocia.' *Res Gestae Divi Saporis* lines 24–26 of Greet text (trans. Lieu). **p. 202** 'Young Romulus … toga-bearing Romans.' Virgil *Aeneid* I.275–282. **p. 202** 'He was … capital offence.' Suetonius *Life of Caligula* 50. **p. 203** 'Welcome … than at Rome.' Tacitus *History* I.4. **p. 203** '[Trajan] used to … he had conquered.' Cassius Dio *Roman History* 68.29. **p. 203** '"The boar … its legal system.' *Bereshit Rabbah* 65.1. **p. 203** 'I extended … on any people.' Augustus *Res Gestae.* **p. 232** 'The welfare of … is also progress.' Kautilya *The Arthasastra* 6.2.1–3 / 7.1.20–22. **p. 232** 'The greatest … had 64 gates.' Arrian *Indica* (trans. Brunt). **p. 232** 'When he had been … and Alexander.' Asoka *13th Major Rock Edict.* **p. 233** ' With respect … and reaping.' Hiuan-Tsang *A Description of India in general by the Chinese Buddhist pilgrim Hiuan-Tsang.* **p. 233** 'Thus speaks … truthfulness and purity.' Asoka *2nd Pillar Edict.* **p. 260** 'Everywhere … with the seasons.' Sima Qian *Shi Ji*, Zhonghua shuju ed. (Beijing, 1959), p. 245. **p. 260** 'In handling … at the truth].' Shuihudi Qin mu zhu jian zhengli xiaozu (ed.) *Shuihudi zhu jian* (Beijing, 1978), pp. 245–6. **p. 260** 'The common … to the poor.' Sima Qian *Shi ji*, Zhonghua shuju ed., (Beijing, 1959), p. 3274. **p. 261** 'Dong Zhuo … a dog remained.' Sima Guang *Zi zhi tong jian*, Zhonghua shuju ed., (Beijing, 1956), p. 1912. **p. 261** 'Every family … to obey.' Yang Kuan *Yan tie lun jiaozhu, ding ben* (Beijing 1992), p. 543.

SOURCES OF ILLUSTRATIONS

a: above; b: below; c: centre; l: left; r: right

Maps drawn by Drazen Tomic,
© Thames & Hudson Ltd, London

1 Bridgeman Art Library/Getty Images; **2–3** Chris Bradley/Axiom Photographic Agency/Getty Images; **6** Dreamworks/Universal/Kobal Collection; **7** Peter Macdiarmid/Getty Images; **8 (Egyptian)** Egyptian Museum, Cairo; **8 (Hittite)** Dagli Orti/Museum of Anatolian Civilizations, Ankara/The Art Archive; **8 (Assyrian & Babylonian)** Bridgeman Art Library/Getty Images; **8 (Persian)** Dagli Orti/Musée du Louvre, Paris/The Art Archive; **8 (Athenian)** Musei e Gallerie Pontificie, Vatican; **9 (Alexandrian)** Acropolis Museum, Athens; **9 (Parthian & Sasanian)** British Museum, London; **9 (Roman)** Musée du Louvre, Paris; **9 (Indian)** Benoy K; Behl; **9 (Chinese)** AISA; **12** Casa Del Fauno, Pompeii; **13** Museo Capitolino, Rome; **14** Trustees of the British Museum; **15** Harish Tygi/EPA/Corbis; **16** AISA; **17** Walter Bibikow/Jon Arnold Images; **18–19** Mortuary Temple of Ramesses III, Thebes; **20** Egyptian Museum, Cairo; **22** Hay Kranen/Kunsthistorisches Museum, Vienna; **23** iStockphoto.com; **24** Alfredo Dagli Orti/Egyptian Museum, Cairo/The Art Archive; **25bc** D. O'Connor, *Ancient Nubia. Egypt's Rival in Africa*, University of Pennsylvania, 1993; **25br** Manfred Bietak, *Eine Stele des ältesten Königssohnes des Hyksos Chajan*, Germany, 1981; **26** R. Mond and O.H. Myers, *Temples of Armant, A Preliminary Survey*, London, 1940; **27** Dagli Orti/Musée du Louvre, Paris/The Art Archive; **28** Erich Lessing/Musée du Louvre, Paris/akg-images; **29** Andrew McConnell/Robert Harding World Imagery/Getty Images; **30a** from E. Naville, *The Temples of Deir el-Bahari*, London, 1894–1908; **30bl** Egyptian Museum, Cairo; **30br** Dagli Orti/The Art Archive; **32** Ashmolean Museum, University of Oxford; **32** Agyptisches Museum, Berlin; **33** Egyptian Museum, Cairo; **36** Dagli Orti/The Art Archive; **37** iStockphoto.com; **38a** Dagli Orti/The Art Archive; **38b** Dagli Orti/Egyptian Museum, Turin/The Art Archive; **41t** François Guérnet/akg-images; **41b** Georg Gerster/Panos Pictures; **43** Musée de L'Armée, Paris; **44–45** Gérard Degeorge/akg-images; **46** J. Powell/Museum of Anatolian Civilizations, Ankara; **48** Simon Klaus-Peter; **49, 50–51** Gérard Degeorge/Corbis; **52** Dagli Orti/Archaeological Museum, Aleppo/The Art Archive; **53** Erich Lessing/Musée du Louvre, Paris/akg-images; **54** Dagli Orti/National Museum, Damascus/The Art Archive; **56–57** Yann Arthus-Bertrand/Corbis; **58** Gérard Degeorge/akg-images; **60al, 60bl, 61ar** Metropolitan Museum of Art/Art Resource/Photo Scala, Florence; **61al, 61b** Trustees of the British Museum; **63** J. Powell; **64** Xavier Navarro/AISA; **65bl** C.M. Dixon/HIP/Photo Scala, Florence; **65br, 66al** Erich Lessing/akg-images; **66ac** Dagli Orti/Musée du Louvre, Paris/The Art Archive; **67** C.M. Dixon/HIP/Photo Scala, Florence; **69** J. Powell; **70–71** Dagli Orti/British Museum, London/The Art Archive; **72** Flammarion/Giraudon/British Museum, London/Bridgeman Art Library; **74** AISA; **75** Georg Gerster/Panos Pictures; **76** Trustees of the British Museum; **77** Werner Forman/Corbis; **78al** Peter Willi/National Museum, Damascus/Bridgeman Art Library; **78b** British Museum, London; **79** Dagli Orti/British Museum, London/The Art Archive; **80a, 80c, 80b** Bill Lyons/Alamy; **81, 83, 84** Trustees of the British Museum; **85** Erich Lessing/akg-images; **86–87** Vorderasiatisches Museum, Staatliche Museen zu Berlin; **88cla** Erich Lessing/Musée du Louvre, Paris/akg-images; **88b** The British Museum London/Werner Forman Archive; **89** London Art Archive/Alamy; **90** Dagli Orti/Archaeological Museum, Aleppo/The Art Archive; **92, 93** British Museum, London; **94** J.R. Freeman; **95** Georg Gerster/Panos Pictures; **96** Trustees of the British Museum; **97** Kunsthistorisches Museum, Vienna; **98–99** Gianni Dagli Orti/Corbis; **100** Dagli Orti/Musée du Louvre, Paris/The Art Archive; **102** Nick Taylor; **103** Legendary Pictures/Warner Bros/Kobal Collection; **104** Trustees of the British Museum; **105** Christophe Boisvieux/Corbis; **106** University of Chicago; **107** Alfredo Dagli Orti/Archaeological Museum, Naples/The Art Archive; **108** Roger Wood/Corbis; **109** Museo Archeologico Nazionale, Naples; **110cla** Dagli Orti/Archaeological Museum, Tehran/The Art Archive; **110b** Georg Gerster/Panos Pictures; **112** Dagli Orti/Archaeological Museum, Isernia/The Art Archive; **113** Corbis; **114l** British Museum, London; **114br** iStockphoto.com; **115a, 115b** British Museum, London; **118–119** Musée du Louvre, Paris; **120** Trustees of the British Museum; **121** iStockphoto.com; **122–123** British Museum, London; **124** courtesy Ministero Beni e Att. Culturali/Photo Scala, Florence; **126** Mimmo Jodice/Corbis; **128** British Museum, London; **129** Georg Gerster/Panos Pictures; **130** Royal Ontario Museum, Toronto; **131** John

Paul Getty Museum, Malibu, California; **132** Acropolis Museum, Athens; **133** Archaeological Museum, Piraeus; **134** British Museum, London; **135** Musée du Louvre, Paris; **136–137** Heidi Grassley © Thames & Hudson, Ltd., London; **138** Peter Connolly/akg-images; **139** London Art Archive/Alamy; **140** David H. Seymour/iStockphoto.com; **141** British Museum, London; **142** AISA/Bridgeman Art Libary; **143** Marie-Lan Nguyen/British Museum, London; **144** Peter Connolly/akg-images; **146** Gianni Dagli Orti/Corbis; **147** Roger Viollet/Getty Images; **148-149** Dagli Orti/Archaeological Museum, Istanbul/The Art Archive; **150** Musée du Louvre, Paris; **152** Dagli Orti/Archaeological Museum, Thasos/The Art Archive; **153** Dagli Orti/Pella Museum, Greece/The Art Archive; **154** Dagli Orti/The Art Archive; **155** Dagli Orti/Archaeological Museum, Istanbul/The Art Archive; **156–157** Casa Del Fauno, Pompeii; **158** Ariadne Van Zandbergen/Alamy; **159** Gianni Dagli Orti/Egyptian Museum, Cairo/The Art Archive; **161** Trustees of the British Museum; **162** Acropolis Museum, Athens; **163** British Museum, London; **164al** Gianni Dagli Orti/Musée Archéologique, Naples/The Art Archive; **164bl** British Museum, London; **165, 166** iStockphoto.com; **167** M. Borchi/De Agostini Editore/Photolibrary; **168** National Archaeological Museum, Athens; **169** Museo Pio-Clementino, Vatican Museums, Vatican City; **170** Thierry Ollivier/Musée Guimet, Paris/Getty Images; **171** © Franck Goddio/Hilti Foundation; Graphics Yann Bernard; **172** Kunsthistorisches Museum, Vienna; **173** British Library, London/The Art Archive; **174–175** J. Powell; **176** Dagli Orti/Archaeological Museum, Baghdad/The Art Archive; **178** Adam Woolfitt/Corbis; **179bl** Robert Harding Picture Library Ltd./Alamy; **179cr** Iraq Museum, Baghdad/akg-images; **180, 181** Ted Kaizer; **182** Eric Gaba/Musée du Louvre, Paris; **183** Images&Stories/Alamy; **185** The Art Archive; **186a** British Museum, London; **186b** Claire Venables; **188** Manuel Cohen/The Art Archive; **189** Oriental Institute/University of Chicago; **190** Bibliothèque Nationale, Paris; **191** Robert Harding Picture Library Ltd./Alamy; **192a** Musée du Louvre, Paris; **192bl** Foroughi Collection, Tehran; **192br** National Museum, Tehran/akg-images; **193** British Museum, London; **194** Ted Kaizer; **195** Michal Gawlikowski; **196–197** AISA; **198** Araldo de Luca/Corbis; **200** Archaeological Museum, Ankara; **201** Georg Gerster/Panos Pictures; **202** David Bjorgen/Museo Nazionale del Bardo, Tunisia; **203** The Art Archive; **204** Kunsthistorisches Museum, Vienna; **205** Dagli Orti/The Art Archive; **206ar** Dagli Orti/Museo della Civilta Romana, Rome/The Art Archive; **206cra** Araldo de Luca/Corbis; **208** Metropolitan Museum of Art/Art Resource/Photo Scala, Florence; **209bl, 209bc, 209br** AISA; **210–211t** Atlantide Phototravel/Corbis; **211br** Alessandro Argentieri/iStockphoto.com; **213** BPK, Bildagentur für Kunst, Kultur und Geschichte, Berlin/Photo Scala, Florence; **214** Sally Nicholls; **215** Pentocelo; **216** iStockphoto.com; **217bl** Dagli Orti/National Museum, Damascus/The Art Archive; **217br** Charles O. Cecil/Alamy; **218-219** Adam Woolfitt/Corbis; **220** iStockphoto.com; **221** Georg Gerster/Panos Pictures; **222** Erich Lessing/akg-images; **223** Kunsthalle Bremen; **225al, 225ar** iStockphoto.com; **226–227** J. Powell/Kabul Museum; **228** Musée Guimet, Paris; **230** Metropolitan Museum of Art/Art Resource/Photo Scala, Florence; **231** Nimatallah/akg-images; **233** Bridgeman Art Library; **234** Professor Robin Coningham; **235** AISA; **236** iStockphoto.com; **237** Lindsay Hebberd/Corbis; **238al** Martin Hürlimann/Archaeological Museum, Sarnath; **238bl** British Museum, London; **239** Bridgeman Art Library/Getty Images; **240** Kabul Museum; **241** Dagli Orti/Musée Guimet, Paris/The Art Archive; **242cl** British Museum, London; **242bl** J. Powell/Kabul Museum; **243cr** Photo Scala, Florence; **243b** Japan Travel Bureau/Photolibrary; **245** Giraudon/Bridgeman Art Library; **246–247** Japan Travel Bureau/Photolibrary; **248** De Agostini Picture Library/Getty Images; **250–251** Danny Lehman/Corbis; **252** Art Exhibitions China, Peking; **254** Gianni Dagli Orti/Galerie Ananda Louvre des Antiquaires, Paris/The Art Archive; **255** FOTOE; **256, 257a** Huber/SIME; **257bl** I. Shimada; **257br** Xia Juxian and Guo Yan; **258** Shaanxi Provincial Archaeological Institute; **259** Far Eastern Seminar Collection/Princeton University Art Museum; **261** Matthieu Paley/Corbis; **262, 263** Laurent Lecat/akg-images; **264** National Museum, Beijing; **265** Georg Gerster/Panos Pictures; **266** FOTOE; **267ar** Royal Ontario Museum, Toronto/Corbis; **267b, 268** FOTOE; **269al, 269ar, 269b** Asian Art & Archaeology, Inc./Corbis; **270** FOTOE; **272a** Genius of China Exhibition/The Art Archive; **273a** Art Exhibitions China, Peking; **272–273b** Asian Art & Archaeology, Inc./Corbis; **274** Wu Liang Tzu Tomb, Shantung; **275** FOTOE.

INDEX

Page numbers in *italics* refer to illustrations.

INDEX